D0039603

Rude Awakenings

No one walks around the Buddhist holy land. Not today. They go by bus between the holy sites. And with good reason. The Buddha's homeland is now one of the most desperately overcrowded and poverty-ridden places on the planet. It is also very dangerous. But wildlife ecologist Nick Scott and Buddhist monk Ajahn Sucitto decide to do just that: to walk for six months and for over one thousand miles, sleeping out at night and living on alms food, just as the Buddha would have done.

More Praise for *Rude Awakenings*

"Utterly delightful and filled with insight. With a moving earnestness and sincerity of heart, this book has much to teach about expectations and humility."
—Narayan Liebenson Grady, guiding teacher, Cambridge Insight Meditation Center, and author of *When Singing, Just Sing: Life As Meditation*

"A delightful, amusing, and sometimes harrowing journey across a surprising landscape of Buddhist history, with a pair of honest and endearing travel guides. Ajahn Sucitto and Nick Scott prove that enlightenment can be found anywhere, even on a dusty back road."
—Dinty W. Moore, author of *The Accidental Buddhist: Mindfulness, Enlightenment, and Sitting Still*

"This is the written crystallization of a unique journey to the Buddhist holy places of India, a trek of 1000 miles made on foot, by two religious seekers. As the reader accompanies them along the dusty trail of their juxtaposed accounts—of the glories and horrors of teeming pungent cities, somnolent villages, ancient sanctuaries and tiger-haunted forests—the reading too becomes something of a pilgrimage. And just as this pair of travelers were challenged, inspired and transformed by their journey, we too find ourselves similarly changed."
—Ajahn Amaro, abbot of Abhayagiri Monastery

Rude Awakenings

Two Englishmen on Foot
in Buddhism's Holy Land

Ajahn Sucitto and Nick Scott

Foreword by Stephen Batchelor

WISDOM PUBLICATIONS • BOSTON

Wisdom Publications
199 Elm Street
Somerville MA 02144 USA
www.wisdompubs.org

© 2006 English Sangha Trust & Nick Scott
Chithurst Monastery, Chithurst
Petersfield, West Sussex GU31 5EU, England

All rights reserved. No part of this book may be reproduced in any form or by any means, electronic or mechanical, including photography, recording, or by any information storage and retrieval system or technologies now known or later developed, without permission in writing from the publisher.

Library of Congress Cataloging-in-Publication Data
Sucitto, Ajahn, 1949–
    Rude awakenings : two Englishmen on foot in Buddhism's
holy land / Ajahn Sucitto and Nick Scott. Foreword by Stephen Batchelor.
    p. cm.
    Includes bibliographical references and index.
    ISBN 0-86171-485-7 (pbk. : alk. paper)
    1. Buddhist pilgrims and pilgrimages—India. 2. Sucitto,
Ajahn, 1949—Travel—India. 3. Scott, Nick, Dr.—Travel—India.
I. Scott, Nick, Dr. II. Title.
BQ6450.I4S83 2006
294.3'435'0954—dc22
                                              2005025142

ISBN 0-86171-485-7
10 09 08 07 06
5 4 3 2 1

Cover design by Patrick O'Brien.
Interior design by Gopa & Ted2, Inc. Set in Dante MT 11/15.5pt.

Wisdom Publications' books are printed on acid-free paper and meet the guidelines for permanence and durability set by the Council of Library Resources.

Printed in Canada.

The mindful exert themselves;
they are not attached to any home.
Like swans that abandon the lake,
they leave home after home behind.
Dhammapada

Dedicated to our teacher,
Luang Por Sumedho,
and to our parents:
Charlie, Win, Bert, and Dot.

Contents

Foreword

This is a book about a pilgrimage. A pilgrimage to those places in India where the Buddha, Siddhattha Gotama, lived, taught, sat, and walked some two and a half thousand years ago.

To be a pilgrim is to put yourself in those places on earth where the presence of a long-departed but revered person is allowed to resonate anew in the mind. This exercise involves a certain ambiguity. For one thing, when you stand in such a site, no trace of the revered person survives. In the case of the Buddha, even artifacts from his time are scant. The few shards of pottery, clay receptacles, and relics excavated from his period are all housed in museums. Moreover, even the ground upon which the pilgrim reverentially treads is now several feet above the ground on which the Buddha and his disciples would have walked.

The Buddha was deeply aware of how all things—himself and his teaching included—arise and pass away. More pertinently, he knew that no place or object could in any true sense be identified with his "self." So why, shortly before his death, did he encourage his followers to visit the places where he was born, attained enlightenment, "turned the wheel of Dharma," and passed away? "Any who die while making a pilgrimage to these shrines with a devout heart," he added, "will, at the breaking-up of the body after death, be reborn in a heavenly world" (Digha Nikaya 16:5.8).

I very much doubt that he thought these places were somehow imbued with special "vibrations" or "resonances" of his person that were mystically embedded in the earth and stones. I suspect it is because he understood how, for human beings, the memory of a person and what he or she stood for is strangely enhanced by association with the physical places where that person once moved. On numerous occasions I have found that being in the places described in this book "earths" my sense of belonging to the tradition founded all those centuries ago by the Buddha. This earthing, however, takes place primarily in my own mind.

Despite knowledge of a tradition's history and devotion for its founder, the pilgrim is thrust into an unpredictable encounter with those places in the present. Since Buddhism has long vanished from the land of its birth, one does not find many fellow pilgrims and only a few temples and shrines, most of which have been constructed or restored in recent decades. Mostly one finds archaeological sites excavated during the past hundred and fifty years, first by British and more recently by Indian archaeologists. The people who live in the vicinity today are almost entirely Hindus and Muslims, who have little if any awareness of the significance of these places for Buddhists. Consequently, to set out on a Buddhist pilgrimage today as an Englishman, particularly on foot (as the authors of this book have done), is to embark into the teeming chaos of modern India as an object of curiosity and incomprehension for the locals.

The present, however, is precisely where the practices taught by the Buddha take place. In the act of seeking out the sacred sites of Siddhattha Gotama, one is challenged repeatedly to put into practice what he taught. The foundations of a Gupta period temple might evoke a pious memory of a distant community and teaching, but it is the insistent pleading of beggars, the taunts of teenage boys, the unpredictable behaviour of a group of staring people who have suddenly swarmed around from nowhere that call upon the pilgrim to maintain mindful attention, to respond wisely and kindly, to be tolerant.

In *Rude Awakenings,* Ajahn Sucitto, a senior monk in the Thai Forest Tradition, and Nick Scott, his lay attendant and all-round sorter-out of problems, recount just such a pilgrimage. Their journey takes us from the place of the Buddha's birth in Lumbini to the site of his enlightenment in Bodh Gaya. But to say where they went says little about the core of their experience of pilgrimage. For theirs is a journey into the heart of the human condition, a condition displayed in all its beauty and horror, compassion and violence, simplicity and complexity in the impoverished parts of India and Nepal through which they lead us. And it is a journey into themselves, a test, at times severe, of their commitment to what the Buddha taught.

Stephen Batchelor
Aquitaine, May 30, 2005

Ajahn Sucitto and Nick at Harnham Buddhist Monastery in England just prior to their departure. It was this photograph that the authors handed out during the pilgrimage.

Preface

What follows is the narrative of a pilgrimage around the Buddhist holy places of India and Nepal made in the winter 1990–91. We made the pilgrimage on foot over six months, but recording it has taken more than ten years. While our journey took us to all the main pilgrimage sites, it was also a pilgrimage through the sacred and profane of two very different men's lives and the lessons learned from making this pilgrimage together.

We wrote this account to honour the people—many of them humble Indian and Nepali villagers—who supported us in the pilgrimage. We also wished to communicate some of the grittier realities of practising the Buddhist spiritual life on the road—with the understanding that this is where, in the time of the Buddha, it all began. Thus this pilgrimage is also a down-to-earth analogy for spiritual practise as we understand it. The living thing is both tougher and more wonderful.

Early in the writing we realised that both our voices needed to be heard. Alternating authors fit better the Buddhist understanding that realities depend on perspective. It also freed us to be really honest with our thoughts about each other. The completed account we called *Where Are You Going?* something we were asked over and again as we walked through India. We present here the account of the first three months, and although this is just half our journey, it retains all the difficulties and comedy of the pilgrimage plus a climax and a resolution.

Sources and references for works quoted in this book are contained in the chapter notes at the back. The narrative's Indian locale and Buddhist context required the use of some foreign and technical terms, and to make this easier for the reader, we have appended a glossary. Quotes attributed to the Buddha are set in italics. Modern place names follow the use by the Survey of India, and Buddhist terms use the Pali-language version from the Theravadan texts unless the Sanskrit version is well known.

We hope you enjoy this book, but more than that we hope that by reading it you may share in the insights our journey gave us into ourselves.

Ajahn Sucitto
Nick Scott
Chithurst Monastery, April 2005

The First Moon

THE MIDDLE LAND

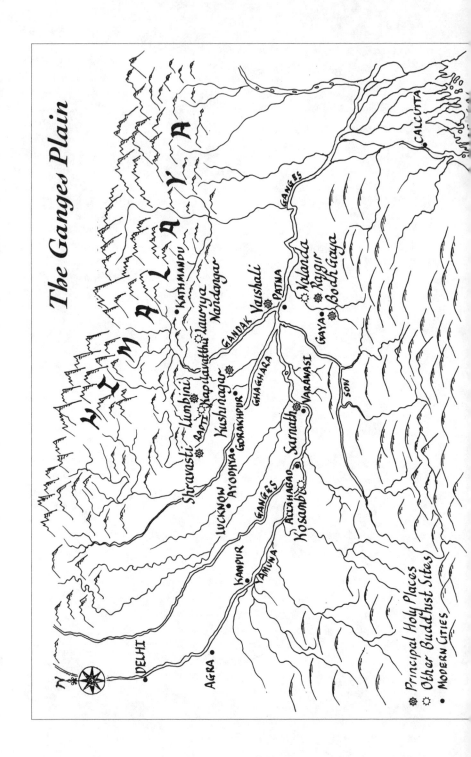

The Ganges Plain

I

Pilgrim's Way

AJAHN SUCITTO

"Chomp, chomp, chomp! Slurp!" Something devilish about that sound, a deliberately provocative prod to assail my meditation. When the eyes are closed and the mind turned inward, you feel that the world should leave your unguarded hearing alone. (It doesn't.) Let alone such lip smacking in the middle of the night on a rooftop in New Delhi when I am seeking to contemplate higher things.

"Chomp, chomp, chomp! Slurp, slurp!" It *must* be just beside my left shoulder. A slow turn and opening of the eyes reveals only the brown-black murk that is a slurry of night sky, smoke and dust; and a tree back beyond the roof whose branches extend overhead. In front of me beyond the parapet is the street, still half alive with a cycle-rickshaw driver rocking and aimlessly pirouetting his bike while sporadically conversing with someone squatting on the road; a few people on the pavement, children mostly, asleep in blankets; scraps of paper tumbling spasmodically when the dull air rolls in its sleep: New Delhi's Chelmsford Road, at night, half lit with yellow sodium lights, lacks the energy of a full-blown hell. No slobbering imps here. No, the sound again comes from behind and above: something dark moving, hanging upside down under the tree—flapping, beating leathery wings, then still and chomping. "Giant fruit bat," comments Nick-Who-Knows when I go over to where he is slumped.

Eating upside-down is anyway no more contrary than sitting and pacing on a roof in the moonlight. It depends what position you take. For us this full moon night of November 2 is the *uposatha* night. In the time of the Buddha, the Sangha would sit up on these moon nights meditating and giving talks until dawn. In the forest monasteries of Thailand and Britain, we still carry out this observance. Or attempt to. Having arrived in New Delhi only yesterday at two in the morning after a flight from Heathrow, we're jetlagged and in a time warp, but we might as well get used to it—disorientation is going to be a normal mindstate for the next six months at least. If we survive. Our aim is to walk around the Buddhist holy places of Uttar Pradesh and Bihar and then head for Kathmandu; avoid the main roads, wander across country living on alms food and whatever.... "It's a bit risky," said Nick a few months ago, "I've made out my will and given away any money that I had left in Britain."

"I can arrange a car for you!" Ravi, an Indian guest at my home monastery, had exclaimed. "Bihar is very dangerous! Bandits, murderers—no one travels on foot in Bihar!" Or sleeps out in the open. However, Bihar and the eastern section of Uttar Pradesh were the "Middle Country," the land where the Buddha was enlightened and wandered teaching for forty-five years. "Bihar" even comes from the old word *vihara,* meaning a dwelling place for a Buddhist monk. Remains of some of the old viharas were still visible. After the death of the Buddha, the Middle Country—then called Magadha—prospered as the centre of the empire of the Buddhist monarch Ashoka (268–231 B.C.E.). Some of the stupas that he erected over portions of the Master's ashes, as well as towering pillars engraved with the emperor's edicts on righteous conduct, still loom over the paddy fields of the Ganges plain. Even after his death and the dissolution of the empire, the wisdom of the Buddha continued to mould the culture: from the middle of the first millennium C.E., great Buddhist universities such as Nalanda, a light of learning unparalleled in the world in its time, arose in this region. It fell in 1200 to Turkic raiders. And now? With a 26 percent literacy rate, there is some justification for Ravi's comment that "Only the Buddha could have got enlightened in Bihar; the people are the stupidest in India. And if when you're driving at night, you come across somebody lying across the road, don't stop, drive over them! It's a ruse, you see ... sometimes it's a woman with a baby in her arms by the side of the road, you stop, and they come out of the bushes and jump on you ..." Well, really....

Anyway, there was never any question in our minds but that we would be walking. We were going on a pilgrimage, not a sightseeing tour; so the logic was to walk and be absorbed into India as much as absorbing it. A pilgrimage has to be about surrendering oneself, to allow a new centre of being to develop. To realize, rather than to travel, is a pilgrim's aim and momentum.

It's difficult to keep that clear. Yesterday night as we were arriving above India in the tightly controlled space of a DC10, the fake detachment of soaring above it all had given me a last chance to recollect the pilgrimage in visionary terms. Below was the arena for spiritual development—the turmoil to be at peace with, the determined journey to no apparent destination. Then began the slow wheeling down from that lofty space. Soon I knew the mind would be wanting things to go "my" way, squabbling over petty inconveniences, hungering after trivia; according to Indian religious thought it was inevitable—forgetting one's higher nature is an essential part of the spiritual journey.

Down we had plunged, from where Delhi seemed to be a cluster of gems twinkling on the dark breast of Mother India, into the pattern of lights on the airfield and the concrete maze of human structures eager to pull us in. India had absorbed so many on this Ganges plain: the Aryans had flowed down here in the second millennium C.E., with sacrifice and liturgy to benevolent gods—she had slowly replaced their deities with a divinity of shifting forms and a thousand names. Long after the Aryans, the Greeks had inched in, thought better of it, and returned to more manageable philosophies—she captured some of their generals and made them into Indian kings. Iranians and Afghans and Turks and Mongols had stormed down this plain to grab and plunder—she had swallowed and digested their cultures and languages. Emperors had marched up and down—Alexander, Ashoka, Kanishka, the Guptas, Harsha, Babur, Akbar, and, *in absentia*, Victoria—the remains of their visions were still crumbling into separatism and ethnic conflict. The land had borne millions of farmers, traders and administrators occupying one of a thousand subcastes and clans; a hundred thousand saints, pilgrims, and yogis following one of a thousand gods, gurus, prophets, or scriptures. Here Mother India murmured the human fugue in a hundred languages. No wonder Indian scriptures and epics assume that all the world is contained in this land.

There was a thud of wheels, a slow turning and then the clank of the stairs connecting to the hull. The midnight transit through customs offered a last moment to step back and cast a cool eye on circumstance. Then, with a friendly nod from a Sikh customs man, we were in and moving.

NICK

It was when we got outside the airport building that we really knew we were in India: we were immediately in a crowd being hassled by taxi drivers, beggars, and young men promoting different hotels; it was warm although it was midnight; and there was that distinctive urban Indian smell, somewhere between spices, incense, and stale urine. Following advice we had been given by a friend, we escaped our assailants, skirted the yellow ambassador taxis and the shiny airport coaches, looking for the cheap option, the ex-servicemen's bus into New Delhi.

There were four of them, battered oblong metal boxes standing side by side in the gloom some way off from the terminal. As we got close, we could tell which was going first by the two passengers and two crew sitting inside in the darkness. Looking closely into the others, as we passed, I could see they too had crews, but huddled asleep under blankets. We clambered aboard; inside there were two rows of simple metal seats with the minimum of padding between red plastic covers and the hardness of their bases, there was no door for the passenger doorway, half the cover for the oily engine was missing, and there was no glass in the side windows.

The bus must have been waiting for our plane because, once we and three others had boarded, the engine was coaxed into shuddering life, a few dim internal lights came on, and we pulled out for New Delhi. As we rattled along the nearly empty road, the conductor made his way down the aisle. Presumably an ex-serviceman, he now wore a simple uniform of khaki shirt and pyjama bottoms, flip-flops, and an old scarf wrapped round his head. He sold us two tickets printed crudely on thick paper.

The excitement of arriving and the nostalgia of being back in India made everything seem romantic. We shuddered along looking out on a country neither of us had seen for fifteen years; the empty streets bathed in the light of the moon giving our passage an extra sense of magic. Every so often the bus would shudder to a stop in the middle of nowhere to let strange characters get on or off: a fat man struggling down the steps with an impossible bundle and boxes tied up in string, or an old lady arising out of the shadows with a shopping bag. Each time a cry of "Chalo" (Let's go) from the conductor would set the bus off again like a spooked cow. Eventually it was our turn. The bus stopped and the conductor cried out, "Connaught Circus." We clambered down with our bags to the pavement and with another "Chalo" it was our turn to be strange characters exiting into the night.

AJAHN SUCITTO

It was a relief to get walking after the long flight. Striding along the spacious tree-lined pavement, skipping the potholes, dodging the debris, with only a shoulder bag bouncing on my back. Crows croaked down from the trees, rickshaw drivers swooped, begging for business: we threw them a few smiles and jogged along cheerfully. "Where are you going?" was their mantra, more a slogan than a query. "Where are you going!"

In the short term we were heading for the Sri Lankan Buddhist Pilgrims' Rest on Chelmsford Road. Is it odd to find a pilgrim's resthouse in the centre of a modern city? Not in India, where the sacred has always hidden itself in the mundane. Pilgrims have been moving through this world for centuries: they are the earthworms in the culture's soil that break down the deposits of religions, digest them, and render them into living forms. They keep its spirituality alive. It was the translation of the accounts of Fa Hsien and Hsuan Tsiang, two of the Chinese pilgrims who once fared through this land, that verified that the Buddha had been a real man who lived in India rather than in legend. For about five hundred years "India's greatest son" had been buried under Hinduism and Islam; even nowadays, the Buddha hardly figures in the folk culture of India. Here Buddhism is seen as an aspect of Hinduism, or as a religious teaching to a breakaway movement within the Untouchable caste. Having turned away from gods and rituals and castes, the Buddha is her greatest outcast. He had to be. Despite various conquests and changes of religion, the Buddha is the one whom India hasn't managed to break down and digest.

This is because Buddhism went international in the Ashokan age. Apart from the scores of Chinese, pilgrims have come from Tibet, Burma, Sri Lanka—even Britain—to trace the Master's footsteps or study his teachings in its country of origin. Even nowadays followers of the Buddha from many countries find a few weeks in their lives to turn things around by bussing between the holy places. A touch of the home country, a sense of support, and familiarity helps in all this sometimes hectic journeying. Hence rest houses, sponsored by governments and institutions.

We banged on the steel door at the entrance at 2:00 A.M. The watchman shuffled to the gate and let us in without a murmur; we signed the book, followed him across a courtyard illuminated in the centre of which was a Bodhi tree with a Buddha image sitting serenely underneath it. The padlocks were removed from the doors of a couple of rooms in the simple whitewashed block that extended along one side of the courtyard. In my cell, the light switch worked—the light bulb revealed a bare cement-floored room, with one bed, even water next door. Not bad at all.

I had brought a water-filtering gadget with me, with which I scrupulously filtered water from the tap. It was an act of bravado: I was eager to show the great Indian gut rot that I had come prepared. Then we had our Plans against being hypnotized by the spells of India: no sightseeing, no rushing around a hot, teeming city, just business—book a ticket on the train to Gorakhpur to get us to the Nepalese border so that we could begin the pilgrimage in southern Nepal at Lumbini, the birthplace of the Buddha. We both were travelling light and drab, unlikely to attract pickpockets: I just had the robes that I was standing up in, a shoulder bag containing my alms bowl with a few spare clothes and medicines for the pair of us in it, an old lightweight sleeping bag, a Buddha image, and various sacred objects given by people for me to use on the pilgrimage.

Nick and I had known each other for about ten years, so I wasn't expecting any major personality clashes. Admittedly we had different styles. I was more reticent, plodding, and tenacious by nature as befitted my birth sign of the Ox. Nick was definitely a Dragon—spontaneous, ebullient but erratic, but then, as he put it later, we made a "dangerous combination"—he would come up with crazy ideas, and I would resolve to stick to them, come what may.

NICK

The next morning I woke to that awful retching sound the Indians make as part of their predawn cleansing ritual. India might be pretty dirty, but the people themselves are into personal cleanliness in a big way. They soap and sluice themselves down with buckets of water a couple of times a day and clean parts that the rest of us never think of. First thing every morning they get to work on their throats and noses, snorting and retching a welcome to the day.

I lay in bed listening. He had got to the nose now and was snorting loudly. I reckoned it must be the janitor who had let us in the night before. In the background was the noise of the street getting under way, people shouting, traffic, the constant refrain of rickshaw bells and horn blasts. There are always two opposing possible views of India: the night before it had seemed magical; now after only four hours' sleep, I had the other view. Our arrival in the middle of the night seemed like a pleasant dream from which I had been rudely awakened.

Memories of the last time I had arrived in New Delhi from England came to me; it had been with a friend called Fred, and we had come overland. We had set off in the summer of 1972 when I was nineteen, catching a cheap student flight to Amsterdam having told everyone we were going round the world. In fact we had got cold feet in the last month and had decided to go only to Amsterdam and then come back with some excuse. After a week in Amsterdam we got up the courage to hitchhike to Greece and, once there, just kept on going. We somehow hitched the whole way to India, arriving in New Delhi on a local truck in time for Christmas. Now I remembered how unpleasant it had been then. It was my birthday, and we both had dysentery for the first time. We lay there in our hotel room, one on each bed, feeling miserable. Eventually Fred got into Hinduism and gurus, very much the thing then, and went back after a year. He became a disciple of Shri Chinmoy and so did the lady I had left behind, my girlfriend from my teenage years. I stayed away for three years and got home in time to see them married with other devotees singing sweet devotional songs.

This time I had come with a Buddhist monk from one of a group of four Theravadan Buddhist monasteries now established in England. Theravada Buddhism is a tradition known for the simplicity and austerity of its practice, so this would be a very different trip. Ajahn Sucitto was the second senior monk at the biggest monastery and known for his intellectual abilities. He edited the newsletter, wrote the books, understood the more difficult scriptures, and gave wonderful talks. He had a good sense of humour and I was very fond of him. However, eyebrows had been raised when I said who I was going with. Ajahn Sucitto was also known for his disinterest in the material world. He could be a liability with tools, had trouble doing things the rest of us found easy, and not so much leant as toppled toward the ascetic view of spiritual practice. It should be an interesting journey.

I could hear him up and pottering about next door. He had probably already done an hour's meditation. I reluctantly got up to join him with a feeling that it was going to be a difficult day. Then with a sinking heart I remembered that it was going to be even more difficult as that night was the full moon, and we would be spending it meditating! I had never been much good at all-night meditation vigils. I was too fond of my sleep.

When we first met to discuss this pilgrimage, Ajahn Sucitto had suggested that we should keep up the daily practice of his monastery. That meant doing daily morning and evening pujas and meditation, sitting up in meditation until midnight on the quarter phases of the moon (i.e., once a week), and sitting for most of the night on the full and new moons. This had all seemed reasonable, even inspiring, as an idea back in England, but now the reality was here. One day after arriving, still jet-lagged and woozy from the flight, we were going to try to sit up all night.

AJAHN SUCITTO

Before his enlightenment as "The Buddha," Prince Siddhattha is commonly believed to have seen four "signs" that caused him to take up the homeless life of a spiritual wanderer: an aged man, feeble and withered, a sick man in a pool of his own vomit and diarrhoea, and a corpse were the first three. Such states were the inevitable lot of all, his charioteer assured the naive prince. Then there was the fourth of these "heavenly messengers"—a holy man, sitting still and serene under a tree, wearing simple robes made from rags, one of those who had from time immemorial in India abandoned home, social position, and security to meditate on life's meaning. "This is one who searches for the deathless," said the charioteer, "Look how bright and clear are his features." From these sights, actual or conceived, Siddhattha Gotama got his cue to "go forth from home to homelessness."

In 1974 I had hitchhiked and bus-hopped overland from Amsterdam to India on an indefinite spiritual quest. India was going to be the place; holy men under every tree, serenity, yoga, ashrams; might even spend my days in some remote mountain cave...I got it right in a way, though I had imagined the signs wrongly. As it turned out, truth presented the same images as she had shown to the Buddha: images of sickness and degeneration. It was no picture show, but rather four months lived out through dazed wandering with amoebic dysentery while my assumptions about normal life steadily fell away. My life view had always been one in which I could do unpredictable things but unpredictable things would not be done to me. But in India human helplessness became apparent—there was no hiding it behind a technological smoke-screen—and even more undermining was the fact that here people were not running away from that impotence. In fact they had a strange strength within their powerlessness. They knew, or imagined, God.

For me, the last messenger appeared in Thailand, whence I fled once I had the strength and the wits to do so. A meditation class caught my attention in Chiang Mai. It presented the possibility of finding a calm inner space within which to check out my life. One class was just a taste; then early one morning sitting in a cafe, I saw the bhikkhus from a local monastery walking on alms round. They were in a line, barefoot in the dusty road, walking toward me. The rising sun glowed through their brown robes. Each bhikkhu had only a simple alms bowl with him, and their faces were serene and gentle. Their walking was calm and unhurried. The weight of years of self-importance lifted off my heart; something soared within me like a bird at dawn.

So, incredibly enough, I became a Buddhist monk. I ended up sitting in a little hut in the monastery for three years, on my own for most of the day, with nothing much else to do except channel the mind's outgoing energies inward. It was a struggle. Strangely enough, the pain and the frustration, as well as the physical and emotional collapse from being in India, helped to keep me there. To leave would have required conviction that things would be better somewhere else. At that time in my life conviction narrowed to one insight: any suffering is mind-wrought, and the way to the end of it has to come through getting to its root. Instead of figuring out different places to go, I realized I had to come to terms with restlessness. Instead of muttering about the lack of interesting things to do and the stifling heat and poor food and hideous mindstates, I realized that the crux of the matter, although hard to come to terms with, was my own aversion. Sometimes I would recognize that I was holding out against things, and then I would relax, let go. That left the Way It Is, the pilgrim's way.

On our first morning, we cautiously emerged from our rooms, paid our respects to the Buddha image sitting serenely under his Bodhi tree in the courtyard, passed through the gate of the Pilgrims' Rest, and made our way up Chelmsford Road to New Delhi railway station. "Making our way," because Chelmsford Road, as we timorously stepped into it, was in full flood. Buses, lorries, and cars were in the main stream, so we joined the other currents of cows, rickshaw drivers (horse and cycle), and pedestrians that wove around it. The currents surged and eddied around deserted road works, street vendors, and stalls great and small selling the inconceivable, the poignant, the quackish, and the banal. Fruit, bangles, charms, toiletries, unknown substances in bottles, and dishes with pictures of holy men beside them—we couldn't see too well through the crowds, and our attention was largely taken up with keeping in touch with the pavement and dodging the traffic.

To a foreigner such chaos, even without the prospect of imminent death or mutilation from a snorting bus or careening motorcycle, is unnerving. In India, however, chaos is sacred: shops and stalls bob in the flow protected by their shrines to saints, goddesses on the backs of tigers, and elephant-headed gods; the wild trucks are painted with images of Shiva. The senses are jangled by the clamour of bells, horns, klaxons, and screeching music; eye-grabbing forms of impossible figures crouched on the pavements and stalls; and nose-stabbing pungencies of horse dung, human urine, sandalwood, and diesel. But the locals are attuned and flow accordingly, are prepared to stop at a moment to inspect a stall, instinctively confident that the scooter behind them (with six people on it) will dart to the left, brake, and weave into another opening. Everything moves fast but no one is hurried: cows have priority and move languidly in any direction scavenging leaves, banana skins, or newspaper smeared with curry; buses bound for head-on collision swerve at the last moment into the hair's breadth spaces that appear momentarily in the human torrent. Detached perspectives are not available: the "personal space," a metre-wide buffer zone in which every Westerner dwells remote from contact in order to think and make the thousand minor decisions of the day, does not exist in this realm.

The railway station, one of the Great British imprints that India has made its own, was only a few hundred yards upstream. The British must have built railways in India as much for psychological reasons as to travel around, to plant order on top of the chaos that is made even more unnerving by India's ability to flow along in it. The grandest of them are like temples. However, since the Raj dissolved, railways, like every other cultural influence, have gloriously mutated to fit India. Now they bear the signs of their contradictory inheritance. Signs, timetables, and manuals say one thing, the actual system works another way. This contrariness is so accepted as to pass without comment; Westerners getting irate about the discrepancy are regarded with the bemused patience that one would reserve for the antics of the mentally retarded.

Our business-like trip to the railway station was an introduction to what becomes a major theme for the traveller in India. Following the main stream of people up the steps into the ticket hall, a tiny sign, dangling from the roof about fifteen feet up, modestly stated "No Entry" without a hope of carrying out this prohibition, or any indication of a reason why entry to the ticket hall should be forbidden. Never mind. A patient queue in the Foreigners' Ticket Reservation Office eventually rewarded us with an interview with a woman whose body, propped on one elbow on the desk, and laconic remarks suggested an utter indifference to the matter of our going anywhere. The shrug of one shoulder activated a few words: "All trains to Gorakhpur are cancelled." Nick's questions produced a few more shrugs. Perhaps we were supposed to rot into the soil here like all those before us. We moved to the back of the office to review the situation.

We decided that the trains must have been cancelled because of the rioting in Ayodhya—which lay in the direction of Gorakhpur. The Ayodhya business had been a bone of contention between Muslims and Hindus for about five hundred years, ever since the Mughal emperor Babur decided to build a mosque on a spot that devout Hindus believe to be the birthplace of Rama, the hero of the religious epic *Ramayana*. Simmering over the sacrilege committed to Rama's holy place for centuries, Ayodhya had erupted in the last couple of months, with Hindus threatening to tear down the mosque. Outbursts of impassioned fighting between them and the Muslim community had taken place in the city and in other parts of Uttar Pradesh (U.P.), and the government was concerned that it could break out into a holy civil war. An elderly official at the back of the office was sympathetic to our scanning of the train timetables. As we wanted to go to Gorakhpur, there *was* a train to Gorakhpur; a timetable was produced to back up this sympathetic reality, and the details of the train conveyed. Back at the reservation desk, we tried again. "The train is cancelled." This occasioned an exchange between the two ends of the office. This time literal truth prevailed. We withdrew again to the timetables. Nick's finger hit Lucknow, capital of U.P., more than halfway to Gorakhpur. "Maybe there's a train to Lucknow." "Is this train to Lucknow running?" he inquired of the man. "Certainly." "And could we get a train from Lucknow to Gorakhpur?" Suitably chastened by his recent defeat, our friend came up with a polite waggle of the head: "Who knows?" The only reality that inevitably pertains. So the woman booked us a ticket to Lucknow, where we hoped to connect with the "who knows?" express.

The Buddha image in the courtyard was still imperturbably sitting under his Bodhi tree when we made it back to the "Buddhist Pilgrims' Rest," frazzled after a few frustrating hours attempting to get things done in the city. The afternoon swam with heat and some excruciating pop song that had become this month's mantra. An overhead fan stirred it all and added its pulse. A few hours bathed in all that made some quiet open space an attractive proposition, hence the roof: as evening fell, we moved upward toward the sky and the cool moon. The stillness and serenity of meditation seemed like a plausible option, but that had also been cancelled. We started off with some chanting, gallantly enough, but went soggy in no time. Nick began to droop soon and spent a few hours in various crumpled positions before disappearing. My mind teetered around in the darkness, occasionally glimpsing the Buddha gleaming under his electric light in the courtyard below or prodded by the chomping and slurping of the upside-down demon. Although my lights dimmed by midnight, I managed to hang in the dullness until an acceptable cave-in sometime after two o'clock. So much for the Plan.

But we were doing well. Managing to book a seat on a train for the ensuing evening that was going in the right direction was a considerable achievement. To expect more was hubris. Nevertheless, Nick decided to use the next day for further business-like activity; I put it down to the mild delirium of sleep deprivation. However, benevolence did seem to be the mood of the day when Mr. Dyas, manager of the Pilgrims' Rest, being Sri Lankan and a Theravadan Buddhist, visited us in our rooms and offered to provide us with the daily meal. Buddhist daylight broke after the Indian night, and we took comfort in the familiar gestures and attitudes. I stayed behind to converse on religious matters befitting a pilgrim while Nick ventured off into the city.

NICK

On our second afternoon, I went shopping in New Delhi. Most important was a pair of binoculars. The pair I had brought with me had been badly knocked by the men who are paid to throw airline baggage about, and now they had a big dent in the side and two images of everything when I looked through them. I was upset at the prospect of no binoculars—seeing Indian wildlife was an important part of the trip for me— and it was with an increasing sense of gloom that I was passed from shop to shop and then to little men in the back streets mending cameras, without finding anyone who could repair them. Then I spotted a pair of Russian binoculars, old-fashioned and a bit on the heavy side, but better than the cheap plastic ones in the other shops. I had to bargain for them, acting only vaguely interested and starting to walk away twice, until the price was reduced to something I could afford. I left the shop clutching my new binoculars and feeling relieved.

The binoculars, and a small guidebook to the birds of India, were the only nonessential items I had allowed myself. Everything fitted into a small army-green daypack, light enough to carry in the heat of India, that I had deliberately got well worn and dusty looking so as not to be too attractive to thieves. I had cut things down to bare essentials—except, that is, for Ajahn Sucitto's water purifier. This weighed a good kilo with the spare filter, and although I felt it was not needed—surely we were never going to go through the laborious process of pumping every glass of water we were offered—he still wanted to bring it along. There being no room in his pack it was now in mine, and I hoped to be able to ditch it soon.

The other stop was the Khadi Emporium. In England I had decided to get my clothes for the pilgrimage in Delhi, remembering the wonderful Khadi Emporium in Connaught Circus in the centre of New Delhi. Much of New Delhi had changed since my visit sixteen years previously, but the Khadi Emporium was still as crazy as I remembered. Set out as an Indian imitation of a large Victorian department store, it was filled to overflowing with jostling crowds. *Khadi* is the movement inspired and begun by Gandhi to base the Indian economy on traditional Indian village crafts. Although most of Gandhi's ideas were ignored by the new republic, khadi manufacturing was encouraged, and stores built in cities and towns across India sell the village products. As with so much in India, they immediately fossilized, never developed any further, and remain to this day as they were set up. The products are wonderful, hand-spun, handwoven, hand-dyed material sold as bolts of cloth or made up into clothing (again in the villages) for sale very cheaply in the store.

The stores, however, are a nightmare. There were counters selling everything from white cotton shirts, very thin and long for summer, through hats, traditional sleeveless jackets, embroidered shawls, and saris to large, thick woollen blankets for wrapping oneself in on cold winter nights. All made of lovely earthy materials. The trouble was, none of it could be seen, as each counter was engulfed by people pushing and shoving, reminding me of an English jumble sale ten minutes after opening. I had to fight my way to a counter just to find out what it stocked, and then, when I thought I had the right one, try to get one of the harassed assistants to help me, only to be sent elsewhere. When I did eventually find what I wanted I couldn't simply buy it; instead, I was given a bill that had to be taken to a long queue for the cashier's cubicle. When I finally reached this—and luckily I had the right change as for some unfathomable reason such cashiers never have change—I got a "chittee." This had to be taken to the queue for the packaging counter, where eventually I could exchange my chittee for my purchases, which by now had been wrapped in brown paper and string.

So I struggled round the store, befuddled by lack of sleep and jetlag, confused by India, driven by desire for all this fabulous stuff, and involved in a tortuous internal debate over whether I should be buying the boring and impractical white clothing that I thought I ought, or the really neat brown speckled cloth I really wanted. We had discussed my attire before leaving. A monk had suggested that I should go as an *anagarika,* someone halfway to becoming a monk. I asked Ajahn Sucitto what he thought of the idea in a way that made it easy to guess that I hoped he would dismiss it. However, Ajahn Sucitto felt I should at least look like a religious pilgrim: "You could either shave your head or wear white." Both ideas sent shivers through my mind. The white cloth would take so much work to keep clean, to say nothing of how silly I felt I would look. For some reason at the time I thought it would be easier to shave my head, but I was having doubts. In my befuddled state, part of me felt I should be getting white clothing, while another thought the idea silly and best ignored. So I came away with far too much in every shade from white to brown. My heart sank as I looked at all this stuff back at the rest house. The feeling of excitement and greed had ebbed, and I was left wondering what to do with it all.

Eventually I decided to take some white, but mostly the coloured, clothing, and an off-white wrap near enough to white to wear when I might need to look like a pilgrim. The rest I would get rid of. As to shaving my head, I decide to leave that till Lumbini, the first of the holy places. That would be a more appropriate place to do it. It was also a good excuse to put it off.

AJAHN SUCITTO

Nick returned at tea time frazzled and crestfallen with bundles wrapped in brown paper under his arms. We glumly reviewed the results. It was far too much for a pilgrim to carry around India. Eventually Nick, trying to make something positive out of it, decided to take it as far as we were going on public transport and send the greater portion back to England as presents. Anyway we took our leave of the manager of the Pilgrim's Rest and paid our respects to the Buddha sitting serenely, illuminated by his half-smile in the Indian dusk. Above us all the bat chomped on.

After the babble and the light-bangled street market, we were in the half-lit gloomy cavern of the New Delhi railway station, where great one-eyed monsters hiss smoke. Somewhere in the catacombs, our names with the seat reservations were pinned on a notice board. I was in tow here; Nick-Who-Knows, bundles and all, strode around and located our train, our carriage, our seats. "Here we are, Bhante. Upper or middle berth?" We could swing two platforms folded up against the wall of the carriage down to form beds. But first, I just wanted to gaze at the creatures of steam and iron, now mythic forms in the West, that still flourish in India.

Our carriage, heading for Lucknow, was quite empty. It contained only one fellow passenger, a businessman in a suit whose belly seemed to be attempting to escape over the top of his trousers. He had come from Lucknow to Delhi by train and was trying to return: Ayodhya was upsetting all the schedules. Although he had a car, he might not have been able to return by roads owing to the Ayodhya riots. If that were the case, he would have had to leave his car unattended in Delhi—and therefore liable to looting—so eventually he left his car with an uncle and travelled by train. Unlike foreigners he would have had to book the express several weeks in advance, a fine act of gambling with virtual realities. Business is not easy in India: no wonder his belly was trying to escape.

By the time he concluded his remarks, we had left the Cyclops' cave. The night was taking over. We let down our sleeping platforms and I clambered onto the top one. The man in the suit opened a bag and took out an old whisky bottle filled with water and slugged it back vigorously; then he replaced the bottle in his bag, lay down on the berth opposite, and took out a chain and lock. With this he fastened his bag to his wrist, slid the bag under the berth and floated off into sleep.

Attempting to follow suit, I put my bag under my head and lay back: back to the posture where the chaos of dreams is the norm, and wakefulness and functioning thought are considered a nuisance. Lying down, we enter another reality; not to enter it would be torment. Yet most of us accept only the waking reality, which grants us a semblance of control: until we delve inward, sleep—or drugs and alcohol—are the only things we trust to take us back to the mystery. But India makes you aware of the pain of trying to walk clenched in your private and inert space. Here you have to let go. No matter how much the patterns of thought might recoil or fume, here the natural law of unpredictable change pertains. For me that was the attraction of the place.

In a matter of minutes, night's mystery waved a wand over the man in the suit. After the free fall, he had landed, to take on the form of a giant wild pig. His snoring assumed a vigour and confidence far beyond any of his waking acts—it was heroic snoring, lusty, unabashed as warriors feasting after a battle. The belly had broken free at last: it shook and resounded. The throat rasped, the nose snorted; the lips, not to be left out, added their flapping. Surely an epic was being enacted in his other world. Reassessing how much sleep I would get this night, I felt myself let go and slip a little farther into India—and then feel tenderly disposed toward our travelling companion, strangely glad for his escape from his suit and chained bag.

Clackety clack! Clackety clack! Grunt, snoorrrrrre!

2

Over the Border

AJAHN SUCITTO

Sitting upright, emerging from the dark to take in a cold and unfamiliar world ... the lights of the carriage, which have been on all night to illuminate the nocturnal comings and goings of phantom fellow voyagers, grow dim as daylight blooms. Cries of tea—*Chai garam! Chai garam!*— are echoing the desire in my mind. It is my birthday, forty-one today, and I need to start suckling.

However, as my lifestyle does not permit me using money, and furthermore I have made a vow not to ask for anything, I have no way of procuring tea. Nick is awake but gazing dully out of the window oblivious to such needs: "Rotten night. I was cold and there was so much racket." He then swings back into his bunk and huddles under a blanket in a doze. Tea passes, stridently advertised; giant pots and cups on a tray, within a few tantalizing feet of my desire, spawn a few spluttering emotions and then they cease.

The carriage had filled up in the night, and the travellers were eager to enter the day. The man in the suit got his belly back in order and his bag out from beneath his seat. In the dim light there was a scramble of bodies as a final spasm in the carriage, accompanied by a clatter and scramble and flurry of bags, delivered us in Lucknow.

23

The damp grey morning was littered with people—a few in a rush, others randomly strewn around, barefooted, squatting on their heels with heads wrapped in cloth. Staring. A few blanketed forms were still asleep on the platform. Seven in the morning is a threshold that must be crossed gently, especially on a raw and empty stomach with a thick head, but arrival meant galloping behind Nick, who was in organizational mode. Of course every notice board said no train to Gorakhpur. Getting out was not going to be easy.

Nick left me in the tea room at Lucknow station while he foraged for biscuits. He returned having found the station master's office. "Ye-ee-s; he reckons there's a local train to Gorakhpur at eleven something this evening. The whole city is under curfew because of the Ayodhya riots; none of the through trains from Delhi are running, so as to prevent organized fundamentalists from pouring into the area. So what would you like to do, Bhante? There's nothing worth seeing or doing in Lucknow, might as well stay here for the day." Interesting way with options, Nick.

I straggled along behind Nick as he went through the ticket queue for the left-luggage office and checked out the waiting rooms and the cafeteria. We in turn were subject to scrutiny by various stares: Nick is all red—red hair and beard and red freckles (Indians think he has some kind of skin disease)—me, head newly shaven, bald and white as a baby and swathed in ochre-brown robes. Thus the stare, whose chief function is to keep our curious presence at an objective distance. Its glassy quality emphasises that contact is not what is sought. In fact, if you speak to someone sustaining a stare, they become disconcerted, as if you had somehow defiled a sacred ritual.

The duty to keep the stare going was passed from person to person as we cantered up and down the platform, the staircase, this office, and that notice board, arriving where we started with a few fragments of information. All this getting nowhere proved to be quite a business—it was soon eleven o'clock and time for a meal. In the cafeteria we snared a waiter who moved around with such a highly developed stare that he managed to ignore everyone. The catching of eyes and the raising of a timorous index finger do not register as signals. Thank goodness for ears: the raised voice and imperious tone is the language of contact here. After forty minutes of attention-hunting followed by negotiations (most of the items on the menu were "unavailable"), our patience was rewarded with two white plates, each a centimetre thick and containing a brown puddle: curried eggs. "Happy birthday, Bhante."

Then more waiting: our white (or freckled) skin got us into the waiting room (first class) with its two rows of beds. The blend of the monotony of the overhead fans, a night of little sleep, the midday heat, and a stomach preoccupied with digesting curried eggs and bananas, all helped to set consciousness sliding over the borders of time.

British India was conjured up by the Edwardian writing above the door, the ponderous decor, the predominance of heavy wood on the door and window frames, and the discreet reservation of facilities for "ladies" (not women). Steam hissed and whistles blew. In this happy realm, the Siege of Lucknow has ended, the Indian Mutiny has been quelled, and a new imperial order has replaced the East India Company's backstage rule by proxy, bribery, and personal connections. This new age ushered in grand buildings and even cities: the British influence still lingers. The weighty architecture, the infrastructure of the railways with their 1940s tea rooms and menus—even the form of English that is used—have an Edwardian flavour. Being India, this subculture will be preserved for millennia: the revamped Morris Oxford car that is the dominant model on the streets will probably be going strong through the twenty-first century. There will still be tiffin (lunch) and Wills cigarettes and bread and butter with the crusts cut off when Britain has become Eurodivision 7.

It is familiar but bizarre, like reading those children's classics written before the First World War where Agnes and Bertram have nannies and father wears a suit to the evening meal. With these kind of perceptions, absurdly implanted on a raw and pungent Asian backdrop, it's difficult

to feel real. In this strangeness we instinctively made attempts to preserve our personal world, finding our corner of the waiting room and
commenting on the scene, using words rather than stares as a way of
keeping it outside ourselves.

For Nick the indeterminate state was brief: he lay down and was
asleep in minutes. I dutifully sat on the bed to spend a little time in meditation. A young married Indian couple, with their two children,
reclined on top of the two beds opposite, she wearing a shiny green sari,
occasionally stroking the children's hair or playing with them. The little boy and his sister, dressed in white, kept throwing shy soft-eyed
glances at me from behind their hands. In my pilgrim mode, I remembered one of the training rules: "A bhikkhu should not lie down under
the same roof as a woman," and I plumped for adherence to duty. Like
some bhikkhus, I have for months on end (some do for years) taken up
the "sitter's practice"—an austerity wherein one refrains altogether
from lying down—and so it was not difficult to drift between half-awake
and half-asleep for a few hours sitting in lotus posture propped against
a wall, waiting for things to begin.

I was living at Amaravati monastery in Hertfordshire when this voy-
age was conceived. My teacher, Ajahn Sumedho, who is the abbot, was
himself in India that winter. So I was minding the shop and teaching the
monks and nuns at Amaravati during the two months of the winter. In
the aloneness of meditation you can probe the clarified pool of the
mind, feeling subtle currents, touching into the stuff at the bottom of
consciousness. Time and again as I touched into that, there was something like a weariness with home and human ease. Something set me to
gazing into the bitter wind over the bleak hills and wondering, "Maybe
I should just walk off into the snow. Make it a pilgrimage, a going forth
as an act of faith ... visit the holy places of Britain ... wherever *they* are..."

A few weeks after his return at the end of February, Ajahn Sumedho
stopped me briefly as I was passing by where he sits to receive visitors.
"Nick Scott was talking to me about going on a pilgrimage to the

Buddhist holy places of India; he'd like to take a monk along." Assuming he was asking for some suggestions, my mind whirred to come up with some names of who would be suitable. "... So I was wondering whether you'd like to go." A further quarter of a second was taken up with weighing this up in my mind and formulating a reply: "Uh—yes ... when do I go? Tomorrow?" "Not sure, you'd have to contact him ... I think it's in a few months' time." Then someone else came by.

I held that incident like a kid does his last bite of chocolate, just to savor the delight of the possibility before rude reality should dawn and tell me that the whole thing was a mistake and a miscommunication. Sister Jotaka, the monastery's perfect secretary, was more precise and practical: "Yes Bhante, Nick made the offer last year, and he'll be going later in the year. He will be covering all the costs. So I reminded Ajahn Sumedho to choose someone. You had better phone up Nick." I gave it a month, just to enjoy the fact that Ajahn Sumedho had chosen me, even though it had probably all fallen through. Then a tentative phone call: "Er, Nick, I er ... Ajahn Sumedho said...," and Nick, enjoying his part, played it as if he hardly remembered—"Ohh, yee-es, I did say that..."— and gradually let his plan emerge until the fantasy descended into the conceptual womb. There it fattened for months—sucking in well-wishes, suggestions, gifts of pilgrimage equipment, traveller's tales, books of Hindi grammar, maps from the time of British India—and grew plump with wonder.

By August our embryonic pilgrimage had developed a ponderous head and lively heart. Sitting under the apple trees in the monastery's orchard, Nick and I mused over plans and aspirations: information about climate and disease and the sites of Ashokan columns mingled with our individual ideals. Nick's idea of a good walk is rambling hills, mountains, forests, and glades where you can sit and enjoy the wonders of nature, not a flat plain with paddy fields stretching as far as the eye can see, a giant farm five hundred miles wide full of people working the land. "It's not going to be easy, the Ganges plain is unpleasant—hot and

27

flat and really boring and people everywhere." But I was still starry-eyed: I'd heard glowing reports from monks in Thailand who had walked around the Middle Country, meeting sadhus and receiving alms from villagers. And the idea of following the Buddha in faith was made even more attractive by the possibility that it might be difficult. What is a pilgrim's duty if it's not to endure? Yes, there was a fundamentalist glow in my heart.

Every now and then the pain in my back or knees, or the banging of my head against the wall, or the clicking of my neck as the head fell forward, would drag me back to Lucknow. The body seems to revert to a fetus-like state when its instinct to sleep is checked: the head becomes too massive to balance on top of the crumpled body. Sometimes I'd come to with the top of my skull wedged against the wall, so that my face pointed to the ceiling with the jaw dropped open: the fans droned on oblivious to such attention. The young Indian family continued their archetypal activities—murmuring, feeding, grooming, and cuddling the children—and were at ease with mine. Mother India's benevolent aspect allows many kinds of religious observance, or *dharma*—in fact family life is dharma. However, you practice dharma for its own sake; humans and gods cheer or curse, but the Great Mother looks on impassively.

All good fundamentalists base their reality upon legend, and I am no different. My dharma as a Buddhist pilgrim is patient endurance, a quality much venerated in Buddhist legend. The stories say that immeasurable eons ago, in the time of Dipankara Buddha, the young nobleman Sumedha left home and took up the ascetic life. Moved by the demeanour of the Buddha of that age, he avowed to undertake birth after birth of spiritual endeavour in order to develop the Perfections that would result in him becoming a Buddha in the future. And that meant not just the arduous business of liberation, but doing it utterly alone, with neither supportive company nor a suitable teaching.

Furthermore, it meant developing the understanding and the compassion to show others the way. How else to ripen that vast empathy of a Buddha except through living life from every angle? And so the Great Being went through the life experience hundreds of times: for one lifetime he was a hare, another time a monkey, on another occasion a minister, a farmer, a prince. Many were the occasions when the Buddha-to-be gave away his own life for the welfare of others, or practiced forgiveness toward those who hacked his body apart. In birth after birth he renounced wealth and possessions. Having abandoned his own life so many times that it meant nothing to him, in his penultimate birth as Prince Vessantara he was presented with the test of giving up that which he held even more dear—the sight and company of his wife and children.

This was the last test—to give up the sweet taste of human warmth. When the Great Being passed the test and his family was subsequently restored to him, the gods rejoiced. The next birth was to be the last, and it took place where the Ganges plain terminates in forest and marshes a few miles south of the Himalayas. And it took place in history around the fifth century B.C.E., when Maha Maya, a queen of that region, dreamt that a white elephant entered her womb. Nine months later, she was making her way to her father's house, it being the custom to bear the first child under the parental roof, when labour pains forced her to stop and give birth in a grove of sal trees. That's where Nick and I were headed—Lumbini.

The waiting afternoon dozed under the fans. Lucknow was darkening by the time the stiffness and pain in my body finally held me awake and we got moving again. We made our way over to the queues for the ticket office, allowing four hours to get the tickets, retrieve the bags, and find the train somewhere. Chaos as usual—but something unusual was going on—rhythmic shouts beat through the random hubbub. In the main hall of the station a throng of men was agitating, stirred by roars of "Jai Ram! Jai Ram!" I could glimpse unkempt black hair wrapped in grubby headbands, red cloths thrown over shoulders; from the wildness of their eyes you could tell it was something religious. Tamer folk moved around them; Nick and I kept a watchful distance, murmuring quietly about Ayodhya; police in khaki with riot sticks stood by measuring the tension. Fear waited ready to burst out of the darkness like a tiger: "Jai Ram! Jai Ram!!"

The kar sevaks were performing their dharma: rallying to move on to Ayodhya to destroy the mosque defiling the holy birthplace of Lord Ram. Like the other great Hindu hero, Arjuna, Lord Ram's dharma encompassed exile and renunciation but is chiefly remembered as the duty of righteous war. Tough stuff, religious duty—and dangerous when interpreted outside of the context of the struggle of the spirit. What may represent fine points of conflict in the heart can get acted out in some horrendous forms on the manifest world. The gleaming eyes of Rama's righteous volunteers made one grateful for the gentler archetypes presented by the Buddha's dharma. Renunciation is painful enough; but for the world in general, deluded renunciates are less dangerous than deluded heroes.

As we moved through the crowds to the ticket office, we could see the mass of Lucknow, dark as a thundercloud. Curfew. A few lights around the station were glowing to indicate a place of security; around it ever-hopeful stalls selling charms and sweets—ragged beggars—rickshaw drivers hovering, a few army jeeps. Time ticking away charged with passion and history.

I don't remember how we got out; journeys on second-class Indian rail blur together in the mind. Arms and legs thrust through all the windows and doors of the carriage as the train pulled up in the station. Bags are definitely a liability in the press for a seat, but don't put them down for a moment in this press; this is the ideal time for thieves to strike. One tide of passengers trying to leave swelled against the incoming torrent; it's a matter of holding your bag tight and pushing and squirming. No quarter is expected, but there are no hostile feelings whatsoever. This is just the way that one gets on a train. Our relative height and team strategy gave us an advantage on these trips: Nick would forge ahead through the maelstrom, sometimes scaling the carriage walls and swinging ape-like from one stanchion to the next along the carriage to our seat. I would wait on the platform, guarding the bags with doglike fidelity; when a triumphant red head appeared at a window, I would pass the bags through and make my own way along, or actually just let go into the incoming tide.

The local train to Gorakhpur, being the only one, was crowded, which by Indian standards means that not just the interior of the carriage, the aisles, the luggage racks, and the lavatory were crammed with human bodies, but the exterior too. The roof bore a battalion of people, patiently squatting, knees under their chins, darker than the night sky. In the mesh of sound, the amalgam of thousands of human voices merged into a sea swell with hissing steam and the slamming doors; the guards' whistles shrieked and "Jai Ram!" hovered in the memory, waiting to swoop. Wasn't there something about Muslims or Hindus getting butchered on trains at the time of Partition? I could see the headlines now: "Religious fanatics riot on train—Buddhist monk bludgeoned to death."

"Sometimes the roof's the most comfortable place to be," said Nick. "Of course it's not allowed, but this is India; when a whole mass of people just get up there, there's nothing anybody can do. Last time I was in India, going somewhere or another, the train was completely packed, so I got up there—course the roof was packed too. The guard was really upset, trying to get me off the roof. "You must come down, sir, this is not allowed." So, I said, "What about all these other people?!" Eventually I wrote a little note saying that I accepted complete responsibility for my foolish actions. Once I had given him that everything was all right. 'Course people do get killed from time to time—overhead power lines, low bridges."

Getting out is never easy, even when you know where you want to go. Our standard seemed to be to get squeezed out in spasms: a night smothering in the gloom and stench of stale urine, then Gorakhpur just after dawn; an hour or two in limbo looking for transport to the border; then a sudden scramble onto an old biscuit tin of a bus with Nick shoving a grease-sodden newspaper bag of vegetable mush and *puris,* small fried breads, into my hands. At the border there was more waiting. But a pilgrim's duty is to be patient, fanatically patient. And so one enters the waiting realm, a place around which irritation and the frustrated possibility of action continually flicker but do not burn. If you can willingly surrender yourself to that fire and go beyond hope, the gods salute you: men in uniforms whose sole purpose seems to be to ask obtuse and pointless questions about the purpose of your visit and have you hang around in fly-blown offices filling in forms will gradually metamorphose. The supreme dharma of patience melts official formalities, and glasses of sweet tea are produced. With smiles, intimate recollections and archaic courtesies, after hours, one has passed the test. The passport is stamped and returned: you can move on.

NICK

Really there didn't seem to be much difference between Nepal and India, at least when it came to the border town of Sonauli. Both sides had a dusty street lined with shops selling food and not doing much business. Both sides had the same slightly shifty-looking characters who tried to get you to change money, and on both I could see through gaps in the row of buildings to a flat land of rice paddies with no obvious border where the two countries met. The crossing consisted simply of two raised barriers each with an empty sentry box and each with a queue of waiting Indian lorries. The immigration official on the Nepalese side at least looked Nepalese, a man from the mountains, shorter, squatter, with a slight Mongolian look, and a friendly open face. Everyone else on the Nepalese side looked Indian, and they passed unheeded back and forth across the border. It all made the actual border post seem a bit surreal, like something set up for a Hollywood movie.

I read a sign in the Nepalese office with some apprehension. It said that all foreign visitors with tourist visas must have proof when they leave of having exchanged at least $10 for every day they had been in the country. Although that was not much more than the amount of money I imagined spending, Ajahn Sucitto had no money, so I would have to exchange money for both of us. When the official turned up I asked him about it. "My companion is a Buddhist monk and cannot handle money, so how can he exchange $10 into rupees for each day?"

He was not fazed. "This is not a problem, we will simply ignore this rule when you return."

Visas were stamped in our passports, I paid the fee, and we entered Nepal.

Being with a Buddhist monk adds some additional twists to travelling. The Buddha deliberately set things up so that monks would be dependent on laypeople. As well as not being allowed to handle money they are not allowed to grow food or to store it until the next day, and they are not allowed to eat things that have not been offered to them. He was clearly delineating a dependence. Based on the tradition of wandering *samanas*, religious ascetics, which exists in India to this day, the laypeople support the monks' spiritual life, and the monks ennoble the laypeople's material one. This relationship is one of the keys to why the Buddhist order of monks has survived 2,500 years. It has prevented the monastic communities from becoming cut off from, and irrelevant to, society. And dependence on the laity has acted as a check on monastics' activities—if the laity do not approve, the monks will not get fed.

It is a relationship I have grown to respect, for I have gained much from my association with monasteries and monks. They have provided both teachings and a peaceful refuge to help me deal with my life, and it brings joy to my heart to be able to repay this. When their tradition began, life was much simpler; monks just needed food and the occasional piece of cloth. With our modern, complicated life, the things a Buddhist monk cannot do for himself have multiplied. Travelling revealed this to me very clearly. It was like having a helpless child with me sometimes, except the child did not mind being left on his own to look after the luggage for hours while I foraged. However, once we were wandering on foot across the Middle Country, he would return to the kind of life all his rules were originally designed for. It should be like returning a duck to water.

Buddhist monks have a lot of rules, hundreds of them. Ajahn Sucitto comes from a tradition that emphasizes trying to keep them all. Many of the rules just define the best way to do things; the restraint they create makes it easier to live a spiritual life. There are also five moral precepts that all Buddhists are encouraged to keep: to refrain from killing, from lying, from stealing, from intoxicants, and from sexual behaviour that harms others. These I try to keep. But for this trip I had undertaken instead to keep the eight precepts traditionally taken by lay Buddhists on pilgrimage. With these the sexual precept is celibacy, as for the monks, and I would be keeping three of the monks' training rules: not going to shows or entertainments, not using luxurious sleeping places, and not eating after midday. I could not imagine wanting to break any of them while travelling in India, except, that is, for the last one.

No eating after noon was a rule the Buddha introduced for his monks partially out of compassion for the laypeople. He did not want the monks going to collect food at all times of the day. It also simplified the monks' daily life. It does feel pleasant to have evenings free from the business of eating, free for practicing meditation. However, it also gave the final twist to the daily travel problems: not only did I have to sort out train tickets and shop for both of our various needs, I also had to make sure we ate by midday and that we both got enough to last until the next day.

From the border we decided to walk to Lumbini. It was twenty-eight kilometres (seventeen miles) away, and walking seemed the right way to arrive at our first holy site. It would also be a practice run for the one thousand miles to come. Walking along the short road from the border to Bhairawa, the nearest town, we began to notice some differences about Nepal. We passed large billboards advertising alcohol: the local Singha beer, Western brands such as Johnny Walker whisky. India has prohibitions on the sale of alcohol; the signs here would be for Indians coming over the border to buy it. The other noticeable thing was the Western goods: there were also billboards for Marlboro cigarettes, we were passed by a couple of Japanese-made cars, and when we reached Bhairawa local youths were wearing American-style baseball caps and T-shirts emblazoned with the insignia of American universities. India had strict import laws, Nepal evidently did not.

It was in Bhairawa that I rid myself of the excess clothing bought in Delhi. Just walking the two miles from the border had underlined the foolishness of buying so much. Now the wise action was to simply give the stuff away, but I could not bring myself to do it. Instead I sent them by post to Kathmandu, where we hope to be at the end of our journey. It was colder there and the extra clothes would be of use, and from there I could take them home to England. So Ajahn Sucitto waited patiently while I, at the post office's insistence, had the bag sown up in cloth by a tailor, sealed with wax, stamped, and eventually accepted. It was a lot of bother but the grasping mind was temporarily at peace.

Back outside the heat had gone out of the day, and it felt good to be walking. As we strode along we left behind the discomfort of trying to make our way in India by public transport. We both felt good, and the squat, painted concrete posts every kilometre, showing the distance to Lumbini, went by steadily. Lumbini 26 km, the first one read. We had to get to Lumbini in time for the meal next morning, so we would have to walk on into the evening before sleeping out somewhere. Still that didn't seem to be a problem, as the walking was so enjoyable. The road was lined with trees spaced every hundred yards or so, and between the trees on our right we could see the Himalayas. Beyond the foothills the distant peaks rose snow-covered and crystal clear from the recent monsoon. So beautiful and startling that to begin with I had to keep glancing at them as if they might disappear. The flat plain of paddy fields lay between us and the start of the foothills some twenty miles to the north, while to the south the plain stretched to the horizon.

It was a good road with a new paved surface put there as part of the Nepalese government's development of Lumbini to attract more visitors. They had even renamed Bhairawa as Siddhartha Nagar after the Buddha; it was on the reverse side of all the kilometre posts—not that anyone in the actual town was using the new name. There was little motorized traffic on the road: beaten-up buses with bars across the windows instead of glass would come by every hour or so full with local people; an occasional small lorry would pass with the open back also full of people; there were one or two cars and one swish tourist bus with tinted glass and air conditioning. That one bus was what the road was for. It was certainly not for the bullock carts. We passed a good dozen, in groups of three or four, trundling the other way, piled high with hay, with two bullocks pulling each and a design that cannot have changed much in a thousand years. The carts swayed as the bullocks ambled, and the wooden wheels, rimmed with bits of iron, rumbled on the road. The drivers, perched up on the straw, long stick in hand, would occasionally call to the bullocks or switch the stick at them. Also on the road were locals, some on foot but most pedalling old-fashioned bicycles on which they sat sedately upright. I took photos of bullock carts against the mountain backdrop, of the flocks of bicycles, of Ajahn Sucitto passing one of the kilometre signs, and just of the scenery. At last the pilgrimage had begun.

I first thought of the idea two years before. I had been on quite a few walks with Buddhist monks. As well as enjoying their company I had also come to appreciate doing something other than for my own pleasure. The feeling of offering to others is beautiful in itself. It also neatly sidesteps that mindstate usually encountered on holidays where you are constantly checking whether you are enjoying yourself. This insight had combined with a desire I had to do something as a thank you and an act of homage to the Buddha and his teachings, which had helped me so much. I did not do anything about it initially, because I realized that while a walking pilgrimage around the Indian holy sites might be a "great idea," the reality of trying to actually do it was likely to be far from pleasant. What finally compelled me to do something was the increasing mess I was making of my life at the time.

I was responsible for a large and very ambitious site at the Gateshead Garden Festival, which was to run for six months over the summer we left. Another "great idea," this was based on the habitat-creation work of my proper job: making a series of wetland nature reserves for birds on the Northumberland coast. I had found the sponsorship, and my employers, a small charity, were keen. But it had to be created within eighteen months, and I had to keep doing my old job at the same time. The site eventually proved a great success: we won many awards, including "best garden," and I got to be on all manner of television programs. However, there was an inverse relationship between my success and my personal happiness. The more praise I got, the more I became aware of the mess in my personal life. Trying to complete the site within a ludicrously tight time frame while doing my old job had meant little time for my assistant, who became totally fed up with me; no time for friends and family, from whom I now felt cut off; and no wisdom in my love life: I was involved with two women who did not want to share me when I did not even have time for one. I reached a state of despair. So the idea of going away somewhere totally different started to appeal. The fact that it would be difficult did not matter any more: I deserved a bit of hardship.

From the first I had planned to invite a bhikkhu to come with me—but which one? I had thought of inviting Ajahn Amaro, or Ajahn Sucitto whom I had walked with before. But choosing my favourite bhikkhu did not feel right: instead I should go to the abbot and let him decide. The trouble was he might choose anyone! My mind sank at the thought of various possibilities. I would be with this monk day in, day out for six months! When I did get up the courage to speak to him, Ajahn

Sumedho approved of the plan, and then, when I asked him with a hesitating heart if he would like to choose who would go with me, he said, "Yes, then I can choose a monk who doesn't think of himself, like Sucitto or Amaro." The next I heard was very much later when, out of the blue, Ajahn Sucitto phoned and this hesitant voice explained that Ajahn Sumedho had said that Nick Scott had offered to take a bhikkhu on a six-month walking pilgrimage around the Indian holy sites and would he like to go.

He seemed the ideal monk for the journey. He was good at language and interested in learning Hindi. He knew the scriptures and could interpret what we would see. His integrity as a bhikkhu was impeccable, and his application to meditation practice could be awesome. His ascetic personality would be a good counter to my tendency to always take the easy option, fudge rules and regulations, and indulge in sensual pleasures. It would be tough, but as I said, I felt I deserved it tough. And perhaps I would also be good for him. His disinterest in the material world could make him surprisingly incapable of dealing with it at times. I recalled several years before when he came to visit the small monastery near my home. He was taken by a layman to buy a pair of wellingtons at the local farm store but returned empty-handed. There had been too many pairs to choose from, and mindful of how upset people got when he just picked anything, he had opted for nothing. The abbot had to go back with him, and when I came round to visit, it was the much more practical abbot who showed us the pair they had just got, pointing out how they would be just the thing. Ajahn Sucitto just looked on with a bemused and slightly dismissive air. So we balanced each other, but the balancing would also mean we would be pulling in opposite directions. So it was good that we also already liked one another.

Ajahn Sucitto was now walking ahead of me, and the last kilometre post read Lumbini 18 km. We still had a way to go, but the sun was setting and it was time to do the evening puja. We left the road and sat on the grass bank facing the fields, just out of sight of those passing on the road. He set up a little shrine, and there we placed the Buddha *rupas*, or statues, we were each carrying. The incense was lit, we bowed three times, and began the evening chanting in praise of the Buddha, Dhamma, and Sangha while facing the paddy fields in the land of the Buddha. We sat in meditation for half an hour, sitting quietly with the sounds of people passing behind us: the trudge of feet, occasional conversation, and the tinkle of bicycle bells. We finished with a short chant and three bows and then rose to continue walking. It was now dusk, and although the light was fading we could still make out the distant peaks, the snow now a slight rosy pink from the setting sun.

We had met before the trip to discuss how we would do it. I was full of where-to-go and how-to-get-there; Ajahn Sucitto was more concerned with the spirit of the thing. He suggested we keep up the daily pujas and meditation and the full-moon vigils. I suggested we take light-weight sleeping bags, bivvy bags, and foam sleeping mats. He spoke of devotion and his wish to do it for others. I was concerned about water bottles, getting inoculations, and maps.

I went in search of the walking maps. Stanfords, the big map shop in London, could supply maps for the high Himalayas but not the plains of India. Although the government of India supposedly produced such maps, they were in fact unavailable. It was an early reminder of the frustration of trying to accomplish anything in India. Eventually I discovered the India Office: a remnant of British rule, it had become an outpost of the British Library in Vauxhall, containing the accumulated records of the British Raj. I was told that the British offered them all back but the new states of India and Pakistan were unable to agree on who was to hold them, so they are kept in London. They had wonderfully detailed maps of the area where we proposed to go, but they dated only up until Independence, and they could only let me copy maps that predated 1940 because of copyright rules. The librarian did explain that I could, in theory, get permission from the Indian government, who owned the copyright, but he did not hold out much hope of achieving this in less than a year.

When we next met, while I had the maps, bivvy bags, and other practical things, Ajahn Sucitto had a drawstring bag larger and heavier than a grapefruit sewn for him by one of the nuns. In it was a Buddha rupa, over two hundred years old, given to him by a lay supporter for the journey, and things that members of the community had asked him to take round the Buddhist holy sites. There were medallions, bits of coloured thread, a small shell from the shrine of one of the nuns, lots of other oddments—and the ashes of a recently deceased nun. He was going to wear this monster on a strap round his neck. I was flabbergasted, but Ajahn Sucitto was pleased. He also had a much smaller bag with a small Buddha rupa in it for me to wear.

The last kilometre post had read Lumbini 12 km, and we were getting tired. It had been good walking in the evening. The light from the sun had been replaced by that of the moon, which had risen behind us. The road had been quiet, with just the occasional bicycle swishing by. Now it was time to stop and sleep. We found a spot just off the road that seemed suitable—it was hard to be certain in the moonlight. We unpacked and unrolled our bivvy bags, a dull muddy green chosen to keep us hidden, filled them with our sleeping bags and mats, and then sat in meditation to let the day drain from us. This did not take long in my case. As I slid into my sleeping bag, I could just make out Ajahn Sucitto still sitting upright in the shade of a tree some twenty yards away.

3
Leaving Home

AJAHN SUCITTO

The first glowing afternoon on the road to Lumbini, moving across the flat farmland, was rich with the joy of leaving it all behind. The uniformity of the plain—paddy fields, a few trees, the repeated elements of bullock carts sauntering along, the occasional cyclist meandering by— blended perfectly with the simple repetition of letting one step flow after another. Nothing ahead any different from what was behind; no end and no beginning. Just the faring on and the rhythm of walking; out in the open at last.

Above the landscape spread around us, tiny dwellings with their cooking smells, pinpoints of light and family murmurings, the moon soared, lifting my heart with it. This was what I went forth for; I could have walked all night.

However, in the spirit of moderation, we stopped to rest in some drab patch of dried mud with a stunted tree as compensation. It was harder than walking: the body in its waterproof bag complained about the hard ground—now the hips, now the shoulders, jogged me awake to look enviously at the stars. I slept light and got up before dawn.

Early morning is a time I like to ease into slowly; on the road, out in the open, one can sit wrapped in the last vestiges of night and get centred. This is an asset when what comes on my first morning in Nepal is a sign bent on moving the mind. A ragged man came shuffling along in the half light, paused about a dozen paces in front of me, turned and squatted, pulled up his dhoti, and proceeded to empty his bowels. A dawn attack on the bastions of propriety! This area of life is the one above all that the West cannot accept into consciousness, and which Mother India therefore thrusts before our cringing gaze. Despite our "openness" about sexual matters—and our yielding recognition of death—the daily business of the body is still socially unacceptable. In India, back at Mother's bosom, we learn toilet training anew. Every morning in the country, people make their way out into the treeless fields with their little cans of water to defecate and then wash the anus with water and the left hand. Food goes in by means of the right hand and out to the ministrations of the left: there's symmetry in that. One can grow to like the cool matter-of-factness of something that is, actually, a matter of fact.

Having finished, he stood up, turned, and peered toward where I was in the half-light. Shuffled forward and finally recognizing what I was, he grunted, turned, and went on his way. Human contact, early morning.

Later that morning we came to the temples at Lumbini. There were two living Buddhist shrines. Round the bend in the road and across the river Til, the eye of a Tibetan gompa met ours in welcome. Behind it stood the Nepalese vihara, with its resident bhikkhu, Venerable Vimalananda Mahathera. It was getting to the crucial hour of eleven o'clock by the time we strode in; but the Mahathera darted out from the temple garden and promptly invited us to have the meal with him. Two other Theravadan bhikkhus were there, but there was no time or need for introductions as we were briskly tucked in around the humble table next to the kitchen. The aged cook, with Mongoloid features, and a younger Nepali with characteristic Indian features bustled round grinning and loading rice, pulses, chilis, and vegetables on our plates; Venerable Vimalananda hopped between his own meal and our plates to ascertain that all was well. Nothing much was said—the fellow bhikkhus knew the niceties of identity could be sorted out later.

After the meal and formal pleasantries, Bhante towed us swiftly around the temple and its grounds. Obviously he had been here many years; the birth of the Buddha in this grove, or in fact any aspect of the Buddha's life and teachings, did not merit a mention. He must have said it all so many times; and Lumbini had become a domestic reality—a temple to maintain, funds to be raised, helpers and assistants to be monitored, bureaucratic officialdom to be wrangled with. I sympathized: it takes a lot of insight to make the place you stay in a source of wonder and inspiration. Bhante's erratic conversation (in pretty good English) roved around the shortage of young supportive bhikkhus (the handful in Nepal liked to stay in Kathmandu where the living was easier), his wish to build a temple in his hometown of Tansen, and the shortcomings of the Lumbini Development Project.

This project had been started in 1967 after U Thant, secretary general of the U.N. (and, being Burmese, a Buddhist) visited the site. Funds had been solicited from Buddhist countries, a metalled road built from Bhairawa, and some other relatively minor constructions completed. A huge board by the gate indicated where new monasteries would be established, where a conference centre would stand, and the site of the new pilgrims' accommodation, which would house the thousands of devotees. Bhante's temple, which had been here since 1956 and which occupied a small but central position, would, according to the plan, be torn down. Bhante seemed pretty dismissive of the whole thing. "Planning, that's all they do is planning, for twenty, thirty years—nothing gets done!" Then he would dart off to pick up some litter and enter a brief dialogue in Nepali with one of the locals. We didn't have a lot of time together: he had to go and talk to some visitors. But he remembered Sister Rocana. "She got sick in Bodh Gaya, Bhante. They put her on a train to Delhi, but she died there. I think her heart gave out." "Oh-h." There was a pause before he had to go. He rattled out a few instructions to the young man who had helped serve the meal and made gestures that we should settle in.

Sister Rocana was one of the nuns from Amaravati. She was the eldest, aged 59, when she decided to accompany a party of pilgrims to the Buddhist holy places three years previous. The pilgrims, including two of our bhikkhus, travelled between the holy places by means of a hired bus, spending a day or two at each site. Sister Rocana was quite a character; she had been a herbalist and homeopath and in general was someone to whom benevolent action came easier than contemplation. Her energetic output could be difficult for everyone to live with, including herself: in the year prior to the pilgrimage she had had some very bad asthmatic attacks that made her feel death was on the way. Sister Rocana was also concerned about her twin sister: an amateur astrologer, she had calculated that her sister's astrological outlook was entering a critical stage. (It was of course the same as her own.) Therefore she undertook the pilgrimage: to pay homage to the Buddha and to share the goodness of her aspiration with her sister who remained in England. Recollecting her last words before she left, the other nuns understood that she was giving final instructions should she not come back. "After all, it's terribly auspicious to die on a pilgrimage." And sure enough, she burned out within a month: got too excited, wouldn't rest, got a fever, insisted on going to Bodh Gaya, and went unconscious there. Two of the other pilgrims took her on a train to Delhi, where her heart gave out. She was cremated there, and the bones, still in chunks because the furnace wasn't very powerful, came back to England. So Rocana's sister nuns had the contemplative duty to break the bones up and grind them so that they could be scattered as ashes according to her wishes. A few fragments were kept as relics, and they were in the bag of sacred objects that I had around my neck.

One of the things I was doing on this pilgrimage was bringing the whole family along. A lot of what I was wearing and the handy things that I had been given were to me reminders of the benevolence within which I live. The small items some of the monastics had given me to take around the holy places were to offer on their behalf. I felt like I was bringing it all back home, back to the domain of the Buddha. Undertaking the pilgrimage on behalf of others, as well as having the devotional theme of making offerings to the shrines, enriched the aspiration behind the pilgrimage and elevated its perspectives. I held my dead father in my heart, as well as my aged mother; my Sangha family were there too.

The lodging didn't come up to the artist's renderings of the future pilgrims' accommodation at Lumbini. Accommodation was a two-storey block of rooms—about a dozen in all, wooden floored, with scraps of mosquito screens on glassless windows, a couple of wooden-plank beds, and sporadic electricity. Mosquitoes would have to be blind and geriatric not to be able to find their way through the gaps in the screen. The room was small and crude, but Bhante's assistant was keen and responsive, his favourite phrase, "No problem." Finding some bedding, he flicked a brush over the floor and even gave us a lock for when we left the room.

I think I was trying too hard to be inspired; Nick had a much lighter time of it in Lumbini. When the afternoon cooled a little we wandered around the ruins behind the temple: Queen Maha Maya's temple—from which strings of Tibetan prayer flags radiated out to the trees in the immediate vicinity—the "tank," that is, a manmade rectangular pond for bathing, the Ashokan pillar with the inscription from 250 C.E., and some votive stupas from later periods. That was about it. We walked around it in ten minutes and then did it again more carefully to rake out whatever inspirational gems we could. Queen Maha Maya's temple was a small Hindu temple presided over by a Brahmin priest wearing a dhoti and ochre and white body paint. The shrine inside the temple centres on a stone tablet from the Gupta period (say fourth century C.E.) that depicted Maha Maya, the Buddha's mother, standing and holding on to a branch of a tree while her baby emerges from her side and devout heavenly beings look on. The innards of the temple are lit by oil lamps and smell greasy: plenty of soot everywhere, daubings of red paint, an emphasis on giving money and getting good luck. On the wide walkway at the front of the temple, a Tibetan monk performed a puja for some Tibetan visitors; the little flames of butter lamps trembled with the slightest breeze. I envied them their devotion.

The old ruins, the gompa and the vihara, lay in the centre of a grove that ran north-south for a kilometre or more. Right by the ruins were some little hillocks, grassed-over spoilage heaps from twentieth-century excavations. To the south there was a new monument to world peace, just outside the Lumbini Development Project complex. Nothing much was happening there except a rather languid strike. Inside the buildings it was dusty; a young assistant showed us the impressive plans and drawings. The paper was curling and developing brown patches.

The way north was more uplifting: beyond the central area I could see a flame flickering at the head of a long, wide tree-lined avenue. It was the Flame of Eternal Peace, kept continually alight in its stone dish. It seemed more quiet and reflective up there away from the tour-party zone. The avenue of trees lined a canal that proceeded north to the end of the site, passing by the recently completed shell of the Cultural Centre. The project, like many developments in poor countries, must have sprung up with enthusiasm but wilted as funds waned and leadership got dissipated.

Our stay in Lumbini spread over six days. I spent most of my time meditating and looking for a sense of wonder. The great Buddhist emperor Ashoka made a pilgrimage here and left an inscription, a very matter-of-fact one compared to the edicts that occupy his other pillars. It just says that he visited the place and, "because the Lord was born here, the village of Lumbini is exempted from tax and is required to pay only one eighth of the produce." Good news for somebody twenty-two centuries ago, but such an announcement hardly sends a shiver of religious awe through the marrow. The unadorned glossy pillar was impressive, I assure myself. They mined the stone from the Varanasi region and hauled it all the way up here in a block. It must stand about seven metres high. Fa Hsien hadn't been able to get here; the jungle was too overgrown in 400 C.E. By the time of the next famous pilgrim, Hsuan Tsiang, Lumbini was a legend—the thick forest of the Terai had swallowed the roads. Local Buddhist activity continued into the tenth century. Then Lumbini more or less disappeared. A few local people worshipped the shrine to Maha Maya, who had gradually mutated into Mahadevi, a minor Hindu deity, but the traces of the Enlightened One disappeared. A Dr. Führer dragged Lumbini out of oblivion in 1895 when he dug around a funny stump of stone and found it to be the top of an Ashokan column. Impressive folk, archaeologists.

But you can only stand trying to be impressed for so long with the tourists drifting by with their Nikons and shoulder bags. Even more jarring were the parties of Indians just out for the day to picnic in the grounds. The confused world washes through any place you stay. Maybe the Buddha got it right—the story says that on being born he took seven strides here; having done that, he never came back.

NICK

According to the old map we were using, the region around Lumbini was still covered in sal forest up until the 1940s. That had obviously long ceased to be the case. The forest had been felled and the land cultivated by people who had migrated north from India, forced by overcrowding to work the poor soils of this region. Some photos that Venerable Vimalananda had of the holy site from twenty years previously showed it in a very barren landscape. That also changed, this time due to the Nepalese government's grandiose scheme to create a tourist and pilgrimage site around the archaeological remains. Nepal did not want to be left out of the benefits India was getting from all the visitors to the rest of the Buddhist holy places. Scenic canals had been dug and flooded encircling the site, trees planted for shade along the proposed walkways, and ten square kilometres set aside for tree planting to recreate a semblance of the forest that was once there. Although the plan for all manner of buildings seemed overambitious for one of the poorest states in the world (only a couple had been started after fifteen years), the earth works and planting had created a wildlife haven. In addition to the wildlife habitat the project intended to create, there were now large areas of shallow open water caused by beginning the earthworks for all these buildings and then running out of money.

I spent a lot of my time at Lumbini roaming through this wildlife experience. The shallow pools lifted with water birds and wading birds. Most of the waders were species I was familiar with from the coastal wetlands I managed in England. There was also a pair of tall and elegant sarus cranes strutting about, with crimson heads atop their tall grey bodies. The most exciting birds though were the harriers. I never tired of watching these marshland birds hunting. Flapping slowly, they would fly low, looking to catch some small bird or animal unawares. There were three different species, hen, marsh, and pallid harrier. One would come by, slowly quartering the pools and surrounding vegetation, and a few minutes later another would appear and start to do the same thing. In England I would have been excited by the opportunity of seeing just one species just once; here they put on a nearly continuous show. There was a great spot by one of the canals where I watched a Pallas' fish eagle. That got me really excited. It sat in a tree opposite, watching the water as I watched it through my binoculars, a big and majestic bird with a hooked beak and intense beady eyes.

Venerable Vimalananda was a kind old monk. After we were shown our rooms, we met him in the temple. It was a big, simple hall, dark and musty with old photos on the walls of things that had been and gone: his teacher and other old monks in faded black and white, aerial shots of Lumbini before the development project, important people who had visited, and pictures of Nepal. He sat on a straight-backed chair beside the shrine which he must have used for years to receive visitors. He wanted us to draw up two other chairs, but first my companion had to pay his respects.

When Buddhist monks meet, whoever is junior is supposed to bow to the more senior. Ajahn Sucitto was trained in the Thai forest tradition in which surrendering to the rules and the form is central to the practice. So we had to pay our respects properly. Venerable Vimalananda made an attempt to stop us; it wasn't necessary as far as he was concerned, and most other visiting monks would have made do with a simple slight bow with their hands held together in *anjali*. We, however, got down on the concrete floor, kneeling, hands in anjali, and first Ajahn Sucitto and then myself bowed three times, heads coming down to the ground. Then, and only because Venerable Vimalananda insisted, did we get up, Ajahn Sucitto still keeping his hands in anjali each time he spoke. Despite Venerable Vimalananda's tutting and attempts to stop us, he also seemed charmed by the gestures of respect. It felt good to me, too, as I followed the monastic example. Venerable Vimalananda had spent a selfless life serving his religion: maintaining this temple and the rest house for pilgrims while collecting donations for two projects in his hometown of Tansen up in the Nepalese mountains. It was good to honour that. I could not help thinking, though, that it would be nice if he could now put it all down. He was getting old, and I wished he could now experience some of the peace that the monastic life was really set up for.

When the half moon came round at Lumbini, we sat up till midnight. The night started with the waning moon absent from the sky so that I could see by the stars that we were in a land to the south of home. Thereafter, though, I was hardly conscious. I took a walk to try to wake up and was startled by a cow in the dark. It seemed to be charging me, and I had to jump sideways, but then I realized that it, too, was startled and was just trying to get out of the way. I remember little else beside being slumped against a tree, trying to look like I wasn't sleeping.

As for the head shaving, I thought about it but still could not bring myself to do it. I looked at the razor Ajahn Sucitto gave me, then decided to leave it until Kushinagar—I reckoned that when we went back across the border my passport photo with hair and beard would look so unlike me. If nothing else I was realising how powerful an act shaving the head is. The hair has so much of our identity in it, and in my case there was the beard too, which I would find even harder to part with.

I did spend some time in the holy site itself, but only in the early mornings and evenings when the visitors had receded. Then, after our evening and morning pujas, the site was pleasantly peaceful. The small Tibetan prayer flags, once colorful but now partly washed out, were strung like bunting between the two bodhi trees and the temple. They swayed gently above the tank; both them and the night sky reflected in the still water. After our chanting I would go and sit under one of the trees and just let the ease of the place wash over me; in the mornings watching light come slowly into the sky and in the evenings watching it fade from the mind until I retired to bed leaving Ajahn Sucitto to sit on.

AJAHN SUCITTO

Rather than trying to evoke something from the distant past, I found it better to sit at night under the great tree by the tank and watch the flow of stuff arising and ceasing in the mind. It's a paradox: the apparently motionless meditator actually experiences total flux. Thoughts unwind and subtler moods intertwine with physical sensations and reactions to those sensations, often in a confusing and hypnotic flow. Then sometimes the meditation can click into place, and the mind seem bright: strongly defined, yet amorphous; responsive, yet still. So like a gambler at a casino, you hope for the lucky break. We would make our way out to Maya's tank each dawn and evening, set my Buddha image up on the brickwork by the giant tree that overlooked the tank, offer incense, chant, and sit for an hour or so. At least, I would sit there; Nick wandered off. My wanderings were more internal. I'd start off thinking of the Buddha's mother: she was probably married off when she was young for dynastic reasons, then became pregnant and gave birth in a forest. The legends weave poetic fancies around it, but it must have been tough—at any rate, she died a week later. Then my thoughts wandered to my own mother, who was quite frail and poorly when I left Britain: did she know what she was letting herself in for when she had me? It was still difficult for her to acknowledge that I was a Buddhist monk—a bit like one of the family going nuts or becoming a junkie. And what good could what I was doing with my life do for her? Things weren't clicking.

Meanwhile, modern Nepal was too involved with getting on its feet to be supporting inner tranquillity. Money needs to be made, and that means servicing tour parties. Business was hardly booming in the snack bar by the lodging where the afternoon's heat confined me, but the radios certainly were. I tried a couple of times to get whoever was lodging in the room beneath us to turn the racket down so that I could sit peacefully in my room in the hot afternoon. Inner mutterings about "this being a holy place" and "why don't people meditate" and "serious pilgrims (like me)" got me pacing up and down the room. Then I stopped and sat down with my squalling and took it into my heart.

"When you go to practise in the place of the Buddha, you must not find fault with anyone; if you find fault, it is because you have not made peace with the world. If you have not made peace with the world, it is because you have not made peace in your heart." Master Hua, a Chinese Buddhist master who was visiting Amaravati a month before the pilgrimage began, had come out with that comment when addressing the assembled Sangha. It appeared as a general exhortation directed to nobody in particular, but it stuck in my mind like an arrow in a target, and now the recognition shivered in my mind. And as the radio jangled and blared and the wave of irritation collapsed, I remembered Bernie.

Twenty years ago, Bernie in the room next to mine at Warwick University was devotedly applying himself to his study of economics, while

I was heavily committed to loud music. Pounding on the wall—did I let up? No way! Pleas and threats would bring about a momentary respite, but not for long. I loved music—I *knew* that it was bothering him, but so what?

Now was the time to listen and ask for forgiveness. To hold Bernie in my mind and empathise with him for a while was a lot more useful than getting irritated that not everybody around was meeting my special requirements. I interfered with Bernie's dharma; now on pilgrimage it was proper to make my dharma one of noncontention. That fitted. So there was a birth of sorts at Lumbini, not the inspirational mode that legends are made of, but something earthier. It struck me that wherever we went on the pilgrimage, the life of this journey was not going to be in the ruins and the temples, it was going to be conceived and nurtured wherever my mind flailed or fumed.

However, in the manifest world, there was the matter of going places to be carried out. So after three nights at the birthplace we set off. We left at dawn, walked north along the canal and came to the dirt road going west. About twenty-five kilometres along that road was Tilaurakot, which the Nepalese hold to be the ruins of Kapilavatthu, renowned as the city where Queen Maya's son grew to manhood.

I wanted to dedicate this time to my father, reciting a mantra and recollecting this bittersweet family business as I walked. But just as the recollections focused so that I could open the old buried feelings, something would pull me out over and over: a bus careening around the potholes and showering us with dust as we stepped back; then a jolting bullock cart with the driver clucking and whooping at his beasts; sometimes it was Nick drawing my attention to an aspect of the landscape. Having had a lovely time at Lumbini watching the birds, he couldn't help but explode with glee at some bird perching on a telephone line. "Look, Bhante, a red-vented bulbul!" "Uh-huh." I had a sinking realisation what this trip was going to be all about: leave it all behind, all the positions, the expectations, and the choices—these six months would be a crash course in keeping the focus very open.

We stopped in the shade of a tree: a ploughman came over and squatted beside us. I started some tentative Hindi phrases, he shared a handful of roasted grains with us: there was sharing and smiling and parting. Around ten o'clock we came to a roadside village. I arranged my alms bowl under my robe, put all thought of food out of my mind, and wandered through the winding network of backyards and paths with chickens and great slow-moving buffaloes and half-naked children. A little throng clustered questioningly behind us as we made our way slowly through the earthen dwellings and eventually came into a clearing with a small shrine. The throng produced one or two better-dressed men, and my feeble Hindi sparked off a sputtering conversation.

The man in the clean white dhoti asked us about food and beckoned us across the clearing to his house, a large properly built dwelling. Two *charpoys* (string beds) were brought out for us to sit on; hidden womenfolk were told to produce a meal. After the meal, I glimpsed one of them peering shyly through a crack in the window shutter at us; she instinctively pulled the hood of her sari across her face and disappeared. This male–female business is such a strange act. You're either running after, hanging on, or pushing away; there just doesn't seem to be a peaceful abiding place.

There was one more woman to come on this journey around the Buddha's home ground. Taulihawa, three kilometres before Tilaurokot, was where Bhante had advised us to seek out the Bajracariya family as one of the few Buddhist families in this predominantly Hindu area. Mr. Bajracariya was an ardent supporter, who would be delighted to receive us, we were told. But it was dark by the time we arrived at the town, and with no address it looked unlikely that we would locate this philanthropic gent. As it turned out, it would have been more difficult to avoid him: a throng accumulated around us, following us eagerly through a few winding streets, before a youth who spoke some English (almost incessantly) insisted that we follow him. We didn't even get a chance to explain about Bajracariya. And so our little entourage proceeded to a fine house with a garden and an illuminated Buddhist shrine next to it: the Bajracariya home. The door was open and a Bajracariya male easily ushered us in as if were expected. The visitors' book was produced and we signed in: we were the latest in a intermittent procession of Western pilgrims over at least fifteen years.

Theirs was a wealthy home. Residents and neighbours in the front room were watching the news in Hindi and English on the TV; another lounge that we were invited into had a couch and armchairs. It reminded me that after a day on the hot and dusty road, I felt and smelt like a buffalo. Then along came Mataji, obviously Bajracariya's mother, nearly as wide as she was tall, vigorous in manner and thick-armed, shiny grey hair pulled back to a knot. Nothing bashful about this stage of the female life: we could hear her bellowing out the orders to servants in the unapproachable recesses of the kitchen. We were allowed to abstain from the evening meal, but the matter of our receiving breakfast and tomorrow's midday meal was underlined—even before the duties of bathing and resting. Household dharma was no trivial matter. Conversation was minimal—the young male Bajracariya (Bajracariya the Great was absent) did not have much English, and my Hindi was worn out by this hour—but firm application of dharma by Mataji rendered a lot of conversation obsolete.

NICK

The day after the midnight sitting we set out to walking to Kapila-vatthu. Up until that walk I had not yet resolved what I was going to do about food on the pilgrimage. Ajahn Sucitto wanted to live on alms-food as bhikkhus always had in India. All very well for a penniless bhikkhu, but I had money and a job to return to in England. How could I accept food from poor Indians who did not earn my weekly paycheck in a year, or, for the poorest peasants, in a lifetime? I had done what I could not to feel like a rich tourist, deliberately bringing enough money to allow us to complete the journey but not enough to ever live in luxury. The rest of my savings, about the same amount again, I had given away. But I could still afford to buy food. I had imagined in England that Ajahn Sucitto would go on alms round while I bought food to supplement it. Once we started walking, however, it became obvious that this would not work. Away from the towns there was little or no cooked food for sale, just tea shops. So I put my reservations aside, and then, when we stopped at ten at that first village, went with him on the alms round. I was so nervous as I got my plastic bowl out and pulled on my white wrap. Why? Fear of the unknown, of looking silly, of being rejected? Whatever, I was really agitated as I followed Ajahn Sucitto, walking slowly, into the village.

As we walked through the village people stared but no one responded and I slowly calmed down. When it eventually became obvious that no one was going to put anything in our bowls I felt relieved, even though this meant we might not eat that day. As we sat in the square surrounded by a small gathering of inquisitive faces, I began to open up and enjoy being there. The man who eventually asked if we had eaten turned out to be the village headman, and we were taken to sit down outside his house. That first meal, the simple beauty of the offering and the joy they all got from having us there, dissolved all my reservations—to say nothing of the food, which was simple yet wholesome and delicious: rice, chappatis, dhal, vegetables, sweetmeats, and lots of curd.

During our meal, villagers came in with the last of the rice crop, women, and the young and old, with bundles of cut paddy on their heads. Oxen were being used to thrash the rice. Walking round in a circle tied to a central pole and driven by the occasional whack of a stick from a boy, they tramped piles of the stuff. With the end of the midday break, men started leaving with oxen to continue ploughing the fields. On the road we saw them at work, making their way slowly up and down the small fields behind their oxen, some just guiding the plough, others standing on it to make it dig deeper.

After the meal we asked for the rope beds to be put in the shade, and we made attempts at communication. Our host sat on a chair and other villagers stood or sat around watching these amazing apparitions that had come in off the road. We showed them photographs: Ajahn Sucitto's monastery, the community of nuns and monks, my mum and dad and their cottage in Northumberland. And we gave the headman one of the little photos of ourselves we had brought with us. Someone in England had suggested this. I had a hundred small prints made of the two of us standing outside the little monastery in Northumberland. The background of buildings, all of grey lichened stone, contrasted so much with where we now were. This gift was a great success and it was passed around with pride by the headman. Their lives and possessions are so simple that I could see we were leaving something behind that would reside in a special place for a long time. Such a contrast to our lives full of possessions. Were I to be given something similar, it would soon be lost amongst the clutter on my mantle.

The children followed us out of the village for a few hundred yards down the road to Kapilavatthu: a gaggle of small bodies left watching the two amazing strangers recede.

The main impression from the visit to Taulihawa was the food. We were fed like turkeys being fattened for Christmas, with large helpings of everything. It was all delicious and very rich, and the plump Mrs. B hovered in the hope of forcing more down us. It was a relief for once not to be able to eat in the afternoon. After breakfast I already felt stuffed and the main meal was yet to come. Exercise was on hand, however. The young man who met us when we arrived came to take us to the Kapila-vatthu site.

By the time we had gone the two miles to the site we had heard all about the young man's hometown, his job in a photography shop, how he would like to visit our countries, about Nepal, about recent world news, and about his family; most of all we had heard all about his family name. It was Sakya "the same as the Buddha, he was my kinsman." Once there the conversation changed, the monologue mostly revolved around the site. He pointed out the excavated walls of the old town, the red brick foundations of entrance gates, and some excavated buildings, "And this was King Suddhodana's palace, and this was a stupa, and how much did it cost to fly from England to Delhi?" No wonder, I thought, the Buddha left to take up the life of a wandering ascetic if all his kinsmen were like this.

There was not much to the site—it was never a big or important place, just a minor kingdom in the forested land beneath the foothills, but it seemed as if it could be a pleasant spot—given the chance. It was dotted with mature trees, with strange pterodactyl-like birds occasionally launching themselves from one tree to another. They followed long concave paths, down, gliding, and then up into another tree, while making strange cackling noises. I later realized the creatures were grey hornbills. On our way back to Taulihawa I quietly suggested we return in the afternoon but not to tell our guide.

AJAHN SUCITTO

In remembering his "going forth," the Buddha referred to a protracted process of negotiating with the family. Reading between the lines, the fact that his arranged marriage had only produced one child after thirteen years says quite a bit about where his interests really lay. Maybe having produced an heir, he felt he had fulfilled the obligations to the household and kingdom and was free to follow his true inclination. However, the legend created later has it that Prince Siddhattha, having seen an old man, a sick man, a corpse, and a holy man, decided that the household life could not avoid eventual grief for everyone concerned. Would his son's inheritance too be a transitory carnival climaxing in old age, sickness, and death? He resolved to seek another dharma: gazing tenderly on his sleeping wife and child, Siddhattha set off secretly one night on his horse "Kanthaka." He rode as far as the border of the Sakyan country, and then proceeded on foot in search of the deathless.

Whatever the truth of the matter, I'm sure that the locals still remember to their shame that he left without breakfast. Mataji certainly wasn't letting us get away so easily. I still remember the layers of freshly fried parotha that we packed inside us to her satisfaction before we caught a bus back to Lumbini. Dear woman. After Nick had lined the family up and taken a photograph, I managed to give her a small Buddha image before we left. A way of thanking my own mother. She looked neither happy nor sad, kneeling before me with hands in anjali.

At Lumbini I spent more time picking up the litter around the temple and trying to talk to Bhante about Dhamma. I made some offerings to the Buddha in the vihara's main shrine; it seemed more alive in there. And finally, the night before we left Lumbini, I dropped Sister Rocana's bones into Queen Maha Maya's tank. Maya: "the illusory play of life." The stars bobbed in recognition on the surface of the dark water for a few moments then returned to stillness.

Under the tree again the thoughts drifted around this matter of human relationships, now raw, now convivial, now aspiring, now irritating or generous or mean. You can never figure it out. I asked my mother to understand and know that I loved her—why are people too busy to say these things? Behind the thoughts a sad and questioning mood wafted up images of mothers and caring and loyalties, and sometimes behind the play, a measureless watching. I turned to that for some answer.

> But you should know this Ananda, the most marvellous quality of Transcendent Ones is that mindfully they know a thought when it arises, mindfully they know it as it persists, and mindfully they know it as it passes away.

Silently before dawn, before the human realm got going, we went back on the long and open road.

The Second Moon

LUMBINI TO VAISHALI

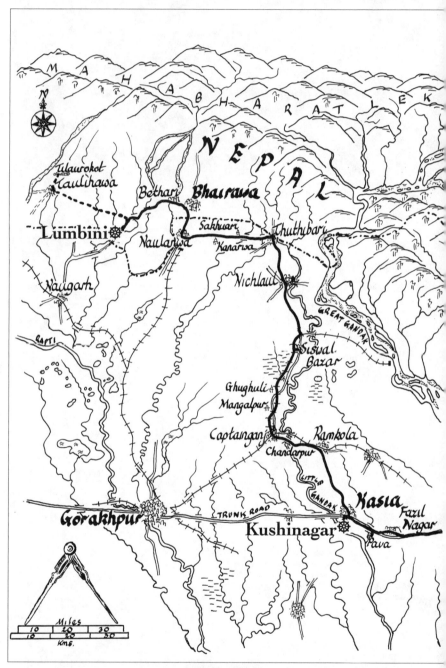

River Gandak, Part 1

4

The Observer

AJAHN SUCITTO

In the months before we left Britain, people asked us to keep a diary and to take a camera. To bring the impressions back home. Neither of us were keen. Nick didn't want to be looking at everything in photographic terms, and I didn't want to spend hours each day writing things down. Why not let it come and go without a trace? Personal history is a dead weight.

But as the months went by, and so many people became part of the pilgrimage, the perspectives broadened. A fellow bhikkhu sent a small lightweight alms bowl from Thailand; another gave me a homemade lantern that squashed down to a disk but popped up to contain a candle when needed. There was the water filter. A director of the Cambodia Trust loaned me a pocket-size wooden Buddha image; it was two hundred years old and came from Laos. Part of his aspiration to help Cambodia then came along with me. Sick bhikkhus who couldn't walk far themselves came along to the holy places—one via a set of mala beads that he made from box wood and another in the pouch he made to fit on my waistband. Another bhikkhu applied himself to fixing new rubber to the worn soles of my sandals. It went on. I wanted to bring them something back. So when one of the nuns gave me a diary that she had made and wrapped in ochre silk, I couldn't refuse to use it. And Nick relented: "If you keep a diary, I'll take the photos."

He carried the undertaking with enthusiasm. It was a tiny camera that fitted into one hand so he could take photographs in an unobtrusive way, and was getting some delightful shots of village life, Nepali children carrying bundles of wood twice their size, oxen munching at fodder, people threshing grain. Later, I wrote in the diary:

> Nov. 12th. Leaving Lumbini—walk north then east—crescent moon; quite cold. People lying asleep on tables in shop/tea stall. Dogs howl and muezzin call as dawn approached. Hot by nine o'clock; snow-capped mountains distant on left. Bhairawa by 10; post office. Cross border after midday—v. hot, rest in grove by road.
>
> Evening market; inquire after route at militia HQ. (khaki uniforms); friendly; not much English; new road (not on map) goes to Tuthibari, due East. Nick sees map on wall—they give it to him. After we leave, officer runs after us with my sitting cloth. Walk on in darkness; sleep in mango grove off the road. Starlings burst out of the trees chattering when I lit candle. Cold night; damp dawn.

Observation was easy up to a point. However it left the feeling that I wasn't doing enough. Nick was always *doing* things—he was the organizer, poring over maps several times a day and extracting every scrap of information from them about the nature of the land, the possibility of finding unmarked ways along old drainage channels, muttering into his beard and then breaking into cryptic ejaculations of discovery. He shopped for candles and torch batteries while I sat by the road, maybe softly intoning a mantra, adjusting the straps on my sandals, and putting plasters on the blisters. Having money, he could give it away. I just sat or stood around. I could use some time to learn Hindi from the little grammar and dictionary I had brought along, but Nick being the one who dealt with a lot of things, he often took the lead in conversations anyway, brushing aside my slow and painstaking Hindi sentences with a couple of Hindi words, vigorous gestures, and simple English thrown in. Amazingly enough, the mixture worked. My side of the action seemed a bit feeble. So there I was trying to be a great pilgrim. For me that means at least trying to acknowledge and undo blind compulsions. Frequently I'd prime the effort with a period of quiet devotional chanting as I walked, or use the mala beads and recollect inwardly the presence and the teaching of all the buddhas.

That end of the world wherein one is not born, does not grow old or die...is impossible to be known, seen, or reached by travelling. But friend, I do not declare that one can make an end of suffering without reaching the end of the world. Friend, I do proclaim that in this very fathom-length body, with its perceptions and consciousness, is the world, the world's arising, the world's ceasing, and the path leading to the world's cessation.

One's inner world can change if it is observed impartially. And in training the mind this clear observing entails careful preparatory activities— determinations, intentions, a setting up and attuning of attention from the moment of waking. In my case a few minutes would be needed after waking cocooned in the bivvy bag to get the mind to remember which direction in the darkness the torch was (generally to the left of where my head lay). Get the torch first, then sit up wrapped in the dew-dripping bag, light a candle, and make some arrangement with the robes to stay warm. Breathe deeply, take a few swallows of water. The stars were out— and at a distance a lump that moved and grunted occasionally signified that my fellow pilgrim was also going through his early morning rituals.

We generally got moving soon after waking, to work the stiffness and cold out of our bodies. Just after dawn, we'd stop by the side of the road and set our Buddha images on top of my alms bowl, light incense, bow to that shrine, and chant recollections on the Buddha, Dhamma, and

Sangha, aspirations for the welfare of all beings, reflections of gratitude and caring for all those who had helped or hindered us. This would be followed by a half an hour or so of silent meditation. The preliminaries over, the day would begin, generally with a man on a bicycle stopping to question us or a bullock cart squeaking by. Subsequent days presented the same scenario.

Trudging along the roads of India, you quickly get a feeling for the perspective of the renunciant traditions: the world is endless, it is a wearisome procession of illusory events that are repeated until one sees through them. Through non-involvement in this web of *samsara,* the heart is liberated from this mundane plane of sorrow and attains the sublime, *nirvana.* The landscape supported that mood. The flat Ganges plain, paddy field after paddy field, is almost hypnotic in its monotony: after a few days the mountains to the left faded away, and with no boundaries to move against, we could almost have been walking on the spot. Everyone was dressed the same: men in white dhotis with long shirts or jackets, women in plain saris; the men rode the same kind of black bike, which travels at the same dreamlike speed and jangles the same bell; the women are walking a flowing walk, a huge pitcher of water or a vast bundle of rice straw balanced on the head. Trucks clatter by, blasting their horns; and almost all the trucks are the same model, coloured red and travelling at thirty miles per hour. Villages put on the same scenario of tea stalls, tiny kiosks with the vendor squatting over his cigarettes, betel nut, and pan-leaf concoctions, sweets, and oddments. People are squatting, knees against their chests, talking, mending things, weaving baskets, fixing shoes, or threshing grain. The expressions are generally impassive, the tempo slow. Buffalos plod along forever, as dull as the mind in the afternoon heat.

Flowing into consciousness were not only the banshee howl of trucks and the shriller jangle of bicycle bells—but also the rhythmic stabs that denoted blisters, dull ringing in the head, memories and moods whispering of tea. I'd try to concentrate to find some degree of contemplative balance, but the real art was to let go: to drop all the forms, and the mind's spaciousness as well, in order to attend to the world. Its unpredictable turns regularly threw me into a mood, but that was what I was here to learn about. So when we interacted with people (which would be pretty continuously between eight in the morning and five in the evening), I would try to turn my responses around.

A lot of contact was the repeated questions: *"Kaha ja ra hai?"* "Where are you going?" "Where are you coming from?" "What is your name?" The questions were not real questions, they were excited verbal reactions using the only English phrases that the men (it was always men or boys) knew, just to make some contact. A cluster of children would break into "What is name what is name what is namewhatisnamewhatisname!!!" I smiled, tried to show interest, or at least look benign. A lot of times when one answered questions, it was apparent that their level of English did not extend to understanding answers. Then there were also the invitations to "stop at my house"—a kind gesture I thought. We should respond courteously, pausing to explain that we were pilgrims, disciples of the Lord Buddha, and we were wishing to get to Kushinagar in a few days. Entering into these dialogues was pointless in one sense, yet it was a religious activity to treat each person as unique. A couple of times I managed to get in a few remarks to catch the attention, ask a few polite questions in return—and feel things calm and open delightfully.

But then there were Nick's reactions to these encounters: brusque or cutting remarks that sealed off the interaction before I could respond, or overrode what I was saying. The situation then transformed into "them and us," with us getting up and leaving—more on the run than on pilgrimage.

But, Nick and I were together, so I had to learn to work with him, and with what being with him brought up, rather than come on self-righteously. When you're hot and dusty, and it's the twentieth person of the day asking the same pointless question, and the trucks are streaming by blasting their horns, it's not easy to treat each human as someone who matters. And Nick, was a do-er. Apart from the map reading and shopping, he loved to be helpful. The pad of self-inflating foam that was supposed to be a soft centimetre between me and the planet at night regularly deflated to leave me dumped on a rock. I accepted it with gloomy resignation, but Nick was going to fix it. Into the drainage ditch he went to ascertain the location of the leak and circle the spot with indelible marker. The next town had a bicycle repair shop, and he spent half an hour or so explaining, pointing out, and getting a patch stuck on. It didn't work. The next day he would try again in another drainage ditch, stopping in another town. But there was always another hole, or the patch came off. And on and on: this is samsara.

NICK

For the first few days we were walking across a land that must have been forest until recently. The road we were on looked very new, and it crossed, in a straight line, the rolling and slightly higher ground. There were fewer villages, bigger fields, and square remnants of woodland. It was typical of much of the Terai land that runs along the base of the Himalayan foothills. Here the silt deposited by the rivers coming out of the mountains is banked up, and the water table can be much farther down. On this higher ground the soils are poorer, and they suffer from drought for much of the year. This is why until this century and the introduction of mechanical pumps there were still great tracts of forest lapping the base of the Himalayas. They would have been dominated by the sal tree, the big straight trees with few low branches that make good timber and were once the most common species in northern India. The Terai sal forests have mostly gone from India and are going from Nepal. Lumbini would have been in such a forest both at the time of the Buddha and when it was rediscovered last century. The forest has since gone, cleared first by logging, which in Nepal's case was usually illegal, with the logs going into India, and then cultivation by people migrating north from India.

After that we entered lower country, turning south to follow a river, where people would have lived for much longer. This area had once been swampland, also common at the base of the Himalayas, and the reason for the Terai's old reputation for malaria. Here people were growing sugar cane, which needs the water, and we passed between high walls of leafy green stems. There were also areas of open water, dotted with lily pads and filled with water birds: grebes, moorhens, coots, and water hens all darting out of sight into the emergent vegetation, and occasionally the flash of bronze wings as jacanas took to flight.

That night a mongoose bolted past us, a black shadow in the gloom as we stumbled about in the half-light of dusk looking for somewhere to sleep. Although they can be a problem for the villagers, taking poultry if they can, they are tolerated for all the snakes, rats, mice, and scorpions they also eat. We, like the mongoose, rested up in bolt-holes near to human habitation. There was no other choice. This land was so crowded with people and they were so interested in us that we had to leave it till it was nearly dark to find somewhere to stop. Nowhere was far from people, and even if a small plantation looked remote, once we settled down we would hear the sounds of habitation near by.

At least by night everyone would be inside and we would be left in peace. Having found somewhere, we would unroll our sleeping things, set up our small shrine for the evening puja, and then sit on into the evening in meditation, invariably with me succumbing first to the call of my sleeping bag. The only night I can recall being conscious after Ajahn Sucitto had lain down was the first night I had dysentery. I spent much of that night stumbling off into the bushes and returning to my bed only to have to do it again half an hour later.

It was during our daily alms rounds that we got to see inside the villages. Indian village life is lived mostly outdoors, and we would pass by and through it all. One day we passed an old lady with crinkled, leathery features puffing at a hookah in the shade of one of the huts, and then rounding a corner found ourselves walking toward a beautiful young woman combing out her freshly washed, long black hair, shining in the sun. Everywhere people were working with the rice. It was mostly in by now, and much of it had been built into storage "huts" made of rice still on the stem and built up in a circle, heads to the centre, to the height of the real huts, and then capped with a roof of sloping straw. They were also threshing it, usually by beating sheaves onto tables or, if a village was beside the road, lying it out on the tarmac for the traffic to drive over. The threshed grains then had to be winnowed. I took one photo of an old man using a hand-turned fan to create enough draft to separate the chaff from grains thrown in front of it by a boy.

AJAHN SUCITTO

On the second day out from Lumbini, while walking through a village, we passed a small shrine, and people came out to talk to me, inviting us to visit it. It was a humble square brick-and-plaster structure about the size of a small garden shed with an overhanging roof and a covered walkway all around it; each face of the central block had an open entrance through which one person at a time could make offerings. I knelt at the shrine and bowed: it was a shrine to Hanuman, the monkey god and loyal helper of Lord Ram in his epic battle against the demons. Hanuman is that in us which selflessly and tirelessly serves goodness without asking for renown; a worthy and easy god to pay respect to, with none of the disturbing ambiguities of the loftier divines. Rather like Nick's good side. I knelt before the shrine for a few minutes, turning things over, with the handful of people standing back in a suitably hushed manner. A sadhu gave me a faint greeting—he was talking to an elderly woman who seemed to be asking him for some personal advice (her face was streaked with tears)—and then he moved off, leaving me to interact with the dozen or so people who had gathered. "No, we have not eaten today. We can eat anything, but we cannot eat after noon. It is forbidden. Religious duty." I could deal with about twenty percent of the remarks that came back.

They eventually offered cooked rice and dhal, and then sat in a semi-circle about a metre away, watching and softly passing comments among themselves on various things that they had observed about us. After the meal, I did some chanting as a blessing; this produced a ripple of excitement. The tearful old lady bowed and touched my feet; she seemed so sad that I sprinkled some water over her head and chanted a few auspicious verses. The ripple turned into a wave—a young man came forward, wanting a blessing, and offered a twenty-rupee bill. I explained that money was forbidden to bhikkhus. Checked, visibly frustrated, and a little abashed at having his offering refused, he tried to give the money again. The tension was resolved by a nearby tea stall. "Give tea, that is good!" I suggested. He returned with glasses of hot tea and some sweets. Things seemed to be flowing along very well, but we had to get to Tuthibari by the evening. Heaven knows why.

Later, I wrote in the diary: "Tuthibari—one-horse town. Trucks cross over to Nepal. Tea; candlelight—town has blackout. Walked on, slept in grove near some houses; mongoose; dogs barking."

NICK

It was about the third day that it began to dawn on me just how difficult this pilgrimage was going to be. The first few days after Lumbini had been hard but I was carried through by the wave of initial enthusiasm: even getting up at three-thirty (a compromise on Ajahn Sucitto's initial proposal of three o'clock!) to leave at four on the first day, and an awful trudge through the heat just before noon, with the border town shimmering like some mirage ahead, never getting any nearer. But then the hard pace we were trying to set, combined with the heat, the amount of people, the dysentery, and the endless flat roads began to get to me. This was not my idea of walking! Walking was striding out over the hills in a cool breeze with beautiful views, well away from people and surrounded by wildlife. Walking was pleasant. Instead we were passing through a landscape of endless flat fields all much the same, constantly pestered by people so that it was unpleasant to linger, there was hardly any wildlife, and we were walking in the heat. I've never been much good in heat; I have the kind of big and bulky body that is good in the mountains or on polar expeditions, but even in Kew Garden's palm house I have to sit down after ten minutes. In India, I enjoyed walking for the first hour in the cool of the early morning. Once the sun was in the sky, the heat was bearable till eight. Then it started getting really unpleasant and I would begin to wilt.

What made it worse was that Ajahn Sucitto was so much more able to cope with it than I. He was not so affected by the heat, he was much more patient with all the inane questions, and he could walk so fast on those flat roads. The strange walk he has, feet slightly turned out like some kind of duck, seemed to be an adaptation for walking fast on the flat.

I remember particularly walking beside the railway; I had noticed on our map that a small branch line followed the road we were on and thought it might be better away from the vehicles and all the people on the road. However, there were also far fewer trees, and so the pools of shade that I had crossed back and forth to walk under on the road had gone. The single railway line ran ahead through a landscape washed out by the brightness of the light, and as the heat increased, I would begin to drop farther and farther behind with my mind starting to whinge like some eight-year-old. In mid-afternoon it would eventually get so bad that, pissed off and way behind Ajahn Sucitto, I would come to a halt under a tree and just collapse. I was seething so much that I was not up to asking if we could stop, and anyway Ajahn Sucitto would usually be out of sight. Eventually I would calm down and trudge on to find him waiting patiently for me. During this period I decided not to shave my head. I had enough to deal with just trying to do the pilgrimage.

Somewhere along this stretch dawned the realisation of our difference in expectations. We were exchanging experiences of past walks; he told me about the walk from Devon to Chithurst on which he had done his back in by carrying all his belongings in two of the shoulder bags monks use in Thailand instead of a backpack, and how two of them had shared a tent so small that they had to sit up all night when it rained. He did that walk in a pair of rubber wellington boots, without socks and from which the heels fell off en route. Then there was the walk on which he had worn a pair of boots two sizes too small and had feet so badly blistered that the other monks had asked him to stop because *they* couldn't stand it. "Jesus," I thought, "no wonder he is not finding this one hard!"

Walking beside the railway line, the one thing which would always wake me out of my reverie were the steam trains. I remember particularly the first one: just after we joined the line it came snorting round the bend, and I had Ajahn Sucitto stand near the line to take a photo with it bearing down on him, smoke and steam pouring out and with the passengers hanging out of the windows grinning and waving. Ajahn Sucitto was so close that he was showered in cinders as the engine passed. The trains would come past every two hours in alternating directions, first one coming down the single line then one going up. The last time I was in India steam trains were still pulling some of the main line services, the Bombay Mail, the Hadrapur Express, or whatever. Now those trains have been replaced by big oily diesel engines. But India was reluctant to see them go entirely, as they use Indian-produced coal instead of imported oil. So on the thousands of branch lines all over India they were still thundering along belching smoke—which is even more impressive and polluting because the coal is brown lignite full of sulphur and tar.

As we walked by the railway line we would pass its various features, still as they were when left by the British. Unlike along the roads, milestones instead of kilometre posts lined the tracks. Level crossings were each manned by an Indian who lived in an adjacent railway hut, old-fashioned signals had big wooden hands and worn steel cables leading to the signal box, and stations were stone with wooden and slate canopies, like the abandoned stations on British branch lines. There were water towers for the steam trains and small collections of government houses for the railway workers. The reason India has kept all this running while we have closed most of our branch lines was apparent on each train and waiting at each station: the enormous number of people too poor to afford a car.

We reached the station for Siswal Bazaar in the early evening of the third day just after we joined the railway. This was the first place since Nepal we had been able to stop that had shops, and I went into town leaving Ajahn Sucitto on the platform. It was getting dark and all the street stalls lining the road from the station were lit with kerosene lamps. They were selling different food snacks, and I had to make my way through the enticing smells of frying pancakes, toasting peanuts, and the stalls selling eggs that could be had fried or boiled to order. Snack bars such as these appear in the little towns only in the evenings. Seeing them while not eating after noon was difficult; while my body tried to walk resolutely past, my mind would stop to linger at each one.

The town was not far off and was a lovely old place of meandering narrow lanes lined with small shops. Each consisted of one open-fronted room raised two feet above the dirty street with the owner sitting or squatting in it, usually with other family members. Most would be the size of a typical sitting room, and each was full of a great assortment of things. Big bars of rough soap, large open tea chests full of grains, rice, or raw sugar, rope, plastic shoes, cheaply made notebooks, and lots of other items that poor Indian country people might want. Some of the shops specialized in something, often brightly coloured cloth stored in bolts stacked to the ceiling, but many appeared to have much the same general wares. There were obviously subtle differences, though, because I was passed from shop to shop, each owner taking me to the next, before I found batteries of the right size for Ajahn Sucitto's torch.

From the railway line we went down to a village on alms round and ended up sitting beside a small Hindu shrine. Ajahn Sucitto often opted to sit beside these or under a bodhi tree, as they were religious places, an appropriate place he felt for us to be. They were also public places where anyone could approach us. This time, however, it turned out to be a private shrine, and so I was sitting there thinking we would never be offered food in such an out-of-the-way shrine (we had only got jaggery the day before because we had stood at the wrong place, by the road talking to some youths), when the man whose land it was came and invited us to his house. He was an older Brahmin of about sixty with grown-up children, and he spoke English well. We sat on his veranda and, as we waited, he told us about his family history, which was tinged with sadness.

Their family once held the post of local agent under the British Raj. This combined being the local magistrate with the collecting of taxes from the surrounding area and, as it was such a position of influence, their family prospered. With independence, things changed, and our host lost his inheritance. Indian agents like his father were not looked on kindly by the new rulers; his father's position was lost, and most of his lands were taken away. All he got when his father died was two acres and the buildings that now surrounded us: barns, a big house, offices where his father had presided, and the temple. It was now a sleepy backwater, the buildings gently falling apart with two small fields sandwiched between them. He explained that he could not afford to maintain the buildings, having spent all the money he inherited on his children's education.

His great sadness was that his eldest son was now at home with him again. The son had failed to find a job, and now his son's wife had left him to return to her own family. What was he to do? How could his son find a job, and without one how could he ever get another wife with just the income from the little land they had? The son was brought out to meet us as if we could do something. All we could do was empathise.

We spent a couple of hours there talking to the two of them, and our visit did seem to alleviate the air of despondency. We talked about our journey, things began to feel better, and they brought us some food. Probably remembering how British visitors were treated when he was young, the father offered us tea in proper English teacups along with a plate of biscuits. When these quickly disappeared, he sent his son for some toasted bread rolls. The effort was well intentioned but provided inadequate sustenance for walkers. It felt inevitable that we were not going to get enough; it was in keeping with the mood of the place.

That was the second day we had too little to eat. It was well past noon by the time we left and too late to do anything about it. At least we left with heartfelt thanks from both the father and son for our visit. We returned to the railway and walked on. Looking back, I can see it was not surprising that I found it all so difficult, with the dysentery, the lack of food, and the heat. At the time, though, I was blaming it on my surroundings, my companion, and, most of all, the Indians we met as we walked along. I was short tempered, and it felt like they were all deliberately making things difficult for me.

It was only a few miles from there to Captainganj, where our branch line met another, and where we would have to leave it. The railway line, which had until then been running due south, began to turn, and as we came round the bend we could see Captainganj station with a steam train pulling out on the other line. From here we had to head west and south to reach Kushinagar the next day. We left the railway line before the station and cut across some fields looking for a small river I had spotted on the map. This led slightly more directly to where we wanted to go than did the main road, and I thought it would make more pleasant walking. We reached the road first, and as we walked along it looking for the river we stopped an educated-looking man. I guessed that he might know some English and would be able to direct us.

Asking directions in India is not as straightforward as at home: here it was more like an elaborate game of chess. Mine was the usual simple Western opening gambit. "Excuse me, can you direct us to the river?"

"I am asking you first why it is you are wanting the river?"

With this move my opponent had opened up the board and given himself several possible lines of attack. Still keeping to my simple gambit, I replied, "We want to walk beside the river to Kushinagar."

"Then you must go by bus."

This was a well-used Indian ploy that I was familiar with and I had my reply ready. "We are on a walking pilgrimage and cannot take the bus."

"Then you must go by road. This road is going to Kushinagar."

"But we want to walk by the river; it will be quieter there, fewer people, no noisy lorries." My slight tone of desperation gave away the fact that I was beginning to lose the encounter. But I had not realized it yet.

His reply was masterful, "There are crocodiles in the river. You cannot go this way, it is dangerous. You will surely be eaten."

It was check, and although I still thought I might be able to get out of it, my king was more vulnerable than I had anticipated. Ajahn Sucitto asked if there were also crocodiles in the Great Gandak, which we planned to cross and walk beside later. "Certainly, and also *dacoits;* it is most dangerous to walk in India. You are better taking the trunk road."

With that it was check mate; I could see there was no way I was going to get my king out of that. Although I long ago learned to take all such warnings for what they really were, clever ploys to frustrate me, Ajahn Sucitto was more concerned by the news. As if the crocodiles were likely to eat us—we weren't going to walk in the water! In fact the idea of seeing some crocodiles appealed to me. I could see though that Ajahn Sucitto thought otherwise. I am afraid I am not gallant in defeat. I did not shake hands with my opponent; my abrupt thanks and goodbye gave away my true feelings.

As we walked off, I had one last go at it, but Ajahn Sucitto was for taking the trunk road, lorries belching fumes, lots of people, and all. He pointed out that I was still feeling the effects of the dysentery, and wandering beside a crocodile-infested river was not a good thing to do when ill. My king had fallen over by itself and now lay on its side in defeat. I walked on depressed; not only were we going to have to walk the last leg on the trunk road, but it seemed that my plans to try and cross the Great Gandak by a small passenger ferry shown only on my 1940s maps and then to follow the river south to the next holy site were also thwarted. The trunk road went there too.

AJAHN SUCITTO

"Siswal Bazaar—railway line—sleep in Muslim cemetery. Fifteenth Captainganj. Nick ill on road to Rumkula."

Nick's difficulties increased by the day. Whenever I paused and looked around, he would be way behind, struggling antlike across the broad palm of the earth. When he eventually lumbered up, head down and dazed, we would sit silently in a ditch and drink water, leaning on our bags. On the road, after a few minutes a group of people would gather; by the railway, there were fewer people but no shade. No rest in samsara.

On one occasion, after a rest of about fifteen minutes in a grove in the heat of the day, a few boys found me lying down and brought their fathers and mothers, relatives—I looked up to find about thirty people squatting around me. The men were a little gruff, the women quiet but obviously concerned. I could make out "Where is your house?" as one of the phrases they were repeating. I realized that to them my actions were abnormal and hence disturbing: houses and villages were where people were supposed to be; everybody belongs to some place. Strangers —especially white strangers—should be somebody's guest, they must belong to somewhere in the human system. At least not here in the dirt under the trees. Too many perceptions didn't match up in their minds: white, but robed and shaven-headed; in an unimportant grove in a nowhere region with hardly any possessions. It was too much to explain. We moved on.

But through all of it we gradually sank into the earth: the earth that swallowed excrement and suffered the plough, the mother that produced rice and sugar cane and teemed with humans. The bare earth gave us a few minutes' fleeting rest from the pain of blisters and the ache in the back; the dry earth caked our feet and grimed our bodies with dust; its cold hardness woke us up before each dawn. We were becoming part of that unquestioning mud, initiated into the soil.

On the last day before we came to Kushinagar, we left the metalled road and walked along a path to a village for alms. A dark-skinned farmer invited us into his mud and rice-stalk hut. We sat on the earth floor while he said a few words to his wife who was grinding flour back in the gloom. She turned wordlessly to slapping some dough into flat bread. "Chappati," we say, but Indians normally refer to them as *roti*. He poured water over our hands, then served rice, roti, and dhal onto giant leaves. We ate with our hands and washed again before giving the blessing after the meal. He followed us outside and as we left, looked up, and extended his outstretched arms to the sky. To me it was the same opening gesture to the sky, the fertile Lord of sun and moon and rain, that the wide earth of these plains makes.

That evening we would arrive where the Buddha lay on his right side between two sal trees and calmly passed away. After innumerable births and eighty years in this life, he had completed his wanderings. As for us, we had passed from the Buddha's birthplace to the site of his last breath in five days, but there seemed to be plenty of mileage left in samsara within and all round. It was impossible to pin it down as either right or wrong, pleasant or unpleasant, hostile, indifferent, or benevolent; but whatever it was, it went on as far as I could see—and in it there was nothing you could hold to. Nowhere to rest. Except in watching.

5

Looking for Purity

AJAHN SUCITTO

Dazed and in darkness, we came to the town of Kasia. At the time of the Buddha this was Kusinara, such a dump then that Venerable Ananda had begged the Buddha not to die in it. But at the end of a long day's walking, dying is of less importance than getting off the numbing road. Here was a good enough place to stop; getting up again was purely hypothetical. Slumped in a chai shop, my vacant stare rested on the old movie posters that revealed in their tears even older movie posters underneath. The effect was like a collage with the supposed present wrapped in, and patched up by, the supposed past. Events in India are just like that—never completely forgotten, just washed over by the next; never merely of the present either, but moulded by the apparent past, which juts through it like resistant bedrock.

Kushinagar—a settlement that had sprung up around the excavated ruins of the site of the Buddha's final decease—was a couple of kilometres east along the main trunk road to Gorakhpur. By the clock it was some time after seven when we hobbled past the welcoming Buddha image at the crossroads, but in the darkness of India, time is set free—it can be just like midday, with noisy markets under streamers of lights, and cobblers fixing shoes by paraffin lanterns, or it could be purgatorial night. People live in their own time zone, lying asleep on tables in the midst of revving buses and jangling music or hammering fine metalwork under flickering neon tubes. At the Burmese Vihara it was night; the metal gates required a little hammering to bring forth some life, which came in the form of a bhikkhu complete with torch and keys. On seeing a fellow bhikkhu, a mood of homecoming and companionship arose within me. He, however, was on automatic pilot and briskly conducted us to a narrow courtyard closed around by a single-storey block of rooms. There he opened one of the rooms, and while we were still putting our bags down and easing our blisters out of our sandals, dashed off and returned with the bedding—some mosquito nets and a blanket. The bathing facilities were nearby; a switch in the courtyard connected to a bare light bulb. Could we see the abbot in the morning perhaps? ... to pay our respects? "OK, OK. No problem." Then he was off. I guessed that he'd had a busy day.

We had aimed to arrive at Kushinagar in time for the new moon uposatha day. Apart from being the days that we used for the all-night meditation sittings, the *uposatha* days are the occasion when bhikkhus meet to refresh and redetermine their training rules. Any misdemeanors are mentioned to another bhikkhu, and one reflects on how they occurred and how to prevent them from happening again. All the bhikkhus in the monastery meet, and after they have done this, one of them recites the Patimokkha by heart in the Pali language of the scriptures. Recited rapidly by an experienced bhikkhu, this takes forty-five minutes or more. The Patimokkha is the core of the Vinaya discipline— a sequence of greater and lesser rules setting out the "gone forth" principles of harmlessness, celibacy, and renunciation, as well as procedures for dealing with controversial or uncertain incidents. The word *Patimokkha* means "a bond," that is, that which connects the fraternity and holds it together. Without the Patimokkha, the Buddha said, the holy life and the teaching would not last long. His rebukes to bhikkhus and bhikkhunis who shamelessly transgressed the training rules were ferocious; and there's even an account of the Buddha refusing to recite the *Patimokkha* because he could sense that one of the assembly was not pure in conduct—a senior disciple eventually took the offender by the arm and threw him out.

In monasteries of my tradition, the sense of occasion of the uposatha is heightened by shaving the head on the day before, so that each uposatha day is like a renewal of the going forth. So after setting down my bag, I went to the bathing area with a fervour for purity. In a kind of courtyard with a large cement-walled tank in the centre, I sloshed cold water over my grimy body using one of the plastic scoops that sat on the rim of the tank, soaped up, rubbed, scrubbed, sloshed, until my skin turned from brown to white, soaped up and sloshed again. While Nick recovered enough to borrow our communal bar of soap, I started on the laundry with a bar of blue soap and a lot of slapping and pounding on the cement floor. We didn't have a change of clothes, so nearly everything had been used and had to be washed in a shift system to allow one to wear something. The skin-changing, pounding, and slapping became like a purification ritual on arriving at a holy place.

At first, our meeting with the Burmese abbot, Ñanissara Mahathera, didn't flow; our minds were in very different spaces. I realized later that the vihara was mainly set up as a pilgrim's rest house, a place for coach parties of visitors from Buddhist countries to spend a night, have a look at the ruins, perform a devotional puja, and move on. So people would normally come to see him for a few minutes in their rushed itinerary to ask about where to go next. Then again, people did not normally arrive on foot, with the intention of continuing their pilgrimage in that way. So his most immediate conversation—about where to go next—was fine if one had a bus and could shoot off to Sanchi or Sankasya for the next day; but when the nearest of those would entail a four days' walk, it was not much to the point. It took a while to get across, over breakfast in his residence, that we were not in a hurry to go anywhere or see anything, that we were interested in what he was doing and how things were working out for him.

Eventually the conversation changed when we asked him if he was engaged in any teaching. He became quite animated about the spread of Buddhism in Uttar Pradesh; apparently thousands of people were turning up to take the refuges, and he was going to Agra today for a large gathering. Not only were there popular meetings with talks, but people were becoming bhikkhus—he himself had given ordination to many.

Things started to link up in my mind. The Indian Buddhist revival ... Untouchables ... mass conversions ... Ambedkar.... The books state that on October 14, 1956, the then abbot of the Burmese Vihara and seniormost bhikkhu in India, U Chandramani Mahathera, gave the five precepts to Dr. Bhimrao Ambedkar at Nagpur in Maharashtra State, thereby acknowledging his conversion to Buddhism. Even the books can't say how many of Ambedkar's followers converted with him— somewhere between 200,000 and half a million; statistics are wonderfully pliable, and who counts Untouchables? There may have been about sixty million of them at the turn of the century: people who were neither completely in nor entirely out of the system of four *varna* (called "castes," but maybe more like classes) that has acted as the social and ethical base of the culture since the Aryans invaded over three thousand years ago. These "Untouchables" were not included in the varna but were bound to its structure by the duty of performing menial tasks—such as handling corpses and excrement—on behalf of the others who held them in contempt and treated them as the lowest of the low. Physical contact with them, eating with them, or drinking from the same well was held to defile a high-caste Hindu. Gandhi renamed the Untouchables *Harijan* (Children of God) in an attempt to raise their dignity while preserving the structure of the varna and their position within it. However the Untouchables regard this title as the hypocrisy of a system trying to whitewash itself and nowadays refer to themselves as *Dalits*: Slaves.

Some say now that these Slaves had been the pre-Aryan inhabitants of India—but the mainstream of the culture and its interpretations has held to the social structure and ethos of the Aryans as expressed in the Vedas. The religious expressions and the forms of the divine have changed, but the dharma persists. And in Vedic thought, the dharma is the duty of one's class. "It is better to do one's own duty badly than another's well" state the Laws of Manu (second to third century C.E.), a sentiment given religious sanctity by the *Bhagavad Gita,* the cornerstone of Hinduism. So for the Untouchables at the time of Ambedkar and Gandhi, liberation from the Hindus was at least as important as liberation from the British. Toward that goal, Ambedkar directed most of his adult life. Although born an Untouchable, he had through force of character and intelligence acquired degrees in economics, philosophy, and politics in London and New York, and was subsequently called to the Bar. Despite his clashes with Gandhi over the caste system, his intellectual brilliance and political skills caused him to be appointed to chair the drafting committee for the Constitution of the newly created Indian Republic. It was due to him that this Constitution abolished Untouchability and declared: "The State shall not discriminate against any citizen on grounds only of religion, race, caste, sex, place of birth, or any of them."

Thus speaks the Law, but with a poor, illiterate, and dominated 35 percent of the population still forming what are now called "scheduled castes" as against an upper echelon of 5 percent, these high-minded statements and even legislation have not brought about equality, far less fraternity. Dr. Ambedkar himself must have realized that political power is fragile and finally ineffectual, so he also sought religious authority. His own personal convictions and the need to provide his people with a religion and culture that supported them, brought about his conversion to the way of the Buddha, whom Nehru himself had called "India's greatest son." And a multitude joined, and continue to join, him. The conversion lifted the Slaves out of the context of Hindu culture, gave them a new identity, and blessed them with dignity. The Buddhist population of India therefore grew from fifty thousand at the turn of the century to a present total of six million—say eight million if you like, it depends on who's counting.

A few days previous we had witnessed, in fact participated in, a minor incident in the struggle. On the road just before Siswal Bazaar we had encountered a very dark-skinned bhikkhu wearing a yellow robe; he was walking on the road toward us, and Nick and I greeted him with some enthusiasm, but no success as far as verbal communication: he had no English and no Hindi. The natural solution was tea in the chai shop on the other side of the road. We settled into a corner and ordered three teas, two without milk (for us). Then a well-dressed man parked his bike outside and stooped to enter the gloomy shack: pale-skinned, of upright bearing; someone of unquestionable and unforced confidence—obviously a Brahmin. His English as he courteously addressed us was rich and flowing, if a little out-of-date and overmeticulous in its consonants. He didn't sit down—standing seemed to suit his slightly theatrical delivery—but rounded on us (bright eyes underneath raised eyebrows) to introduce us to Buddhism, which he understood completely (as well as the Vedas, the Gita, and Christianity). "I am a *disciple* of the Lord Buddha, I *worship* the Lord Buddha every day—and it is scoundrels like *this*"—stabbing a magisterial finger at the Indian bhikkhu—"who are corrupting the Lord Buddha's teaching! They are just troublemakers who..." and so on.

Nick waggled his hand and started interjecting a few phrases about caste and Buddhism: "...and he is a Buddhist monk—that means he is practising a religion, he's not stirring up trouble!" Nick's dismissive laugh momentarily checked the flow: while the Brahmin recoiled and stiffened, I said something quietly about form and essence, but it was much too prosaic. Nick and the Brahmin joined in a rhetorical tussle, the Schedule bhikkhu cringed in the corner, and I decided to drink my tea. At least Nick and I got something to drink—the chai wallah wasn't going to serve an Untouchable tea in his shop, not with the Brahmin present. You don't turn three thousand years of assumptions and positions around over the table in a chai shop.

So we moved on. The Indian bhikkhu, embarrassed but relieved to get out of the shop, waggled his head and walked off in his direction with stooped shoulders—for another three thousand years probably. We hadn't gone far when the Brahmin came by on his bike, dismounted, chatted politely to us, and invited us to come and stay at his house. But it felt easier to keep moving along our own road: somewhere in that direction was the Buddha and some clear reflection.

He who shows no anger toward those who are angry, peaceful toward those who are violent, not grasping among those who are bent on grasping, is one I call a brahmin...The clear, calm, stainless, moonlike quality where the shackles of constant becomings are cut and thrown away; this is what brahmin *means...*

No one is born a brahmin; no one is born a nonbrahmin. A brahmin is a brahmin because of what he does.

After breakfast with the abbot, Nick and I sought out the shrine commemorating the Buddha's parinirvana; it was in the park immediately adjacent to the vihara. I didn't expect to see neat, green parks in India, so the gardens that the shrine presided over were a pleasant surprise. It was still early morning and there were not many people about. Birds were decorating the silence with trills and calls. Broad-leaved creepers gracefully adorned the trees; the vegetation was soft and yielding to the eye. The sensory world for once was on its best behaviour, gracing the simple shrine where, millennia ago, the Buddha took leave of it. With the hardships of the way sloughed off, a tingling eagerness carried us up some steps and into the simple tomb-shaped building that served as the temple of the shrine. Reclining along the length of the interior so that there was a passage of about two metres around it, was an image of the Buddha in the last moments of his life. The statue was about three times life-size. His head was pointing to the north and he lay on his right side, with his gently smiling face supported by his right hand. His left arm lay along his left thigh with the fingers of the hand resting against the side of his knee. The feet were placed one exactly on top of the other. A yellow robe was draped over his body, and the light from the huge windows that filled the north and south ends of the hall flowed over him. Images of attendant disciples, one weeping, one more composed, formed part of the sculpture's setting. We knelt and joined them, paying our respects to the Enlightened One.

It is recorded that even at this last moment of his life, the Buddha was solicitous of his disciples' welfare, asking them several times whether they had any queries about the teachings that he had given, or if they were too bashful, to ask one of their fellows to inquire on their behalf. All were silent. "Then I tell you, bhikkhus: all conditioned processes are transient, practise with diligence!" Closing his eyes to focus completely on his ebbing life force, the Buddha carefully guided his consciousness to final nirvana.

We paid our respects. I offered some incense and chanted some verses. The polished stone floor was cool. It was a still and peaceful place to sit for a while and listen to the silence.

Standing immediately behind the temple, like an attendant bhikkhu watching over its reclining form, was the Nirvana Stupa, a simple dome taller than it was round with a stubby square turret on top. A stupa's great dome echoes the totality and all-embracing nature of the awakened mind; its elevation toward the sky moves the mind upward to the vast and eternal. It is the eternal still point around which the world of events turns. Contemplating such themes, the pilgrim circumambulates the stupa in a clockwise direction, so that the "fortunate" right side is kept toward the stupa.

Stupas are a devotional expression that predates the urge to represent the Buddha in terms of a human image. This stupa also acted as a commentary on Buddhist activity in India, having accumulated and then lost forms as devotion waxed and waned. The invisible core of the stupa was Ashokan, dating back to some two hundred years after the Final Decease. Then Buddhism was widespread, popular, and supported by the emperor: stupa worship emerged as its primary devotional expression. This mood continued through the classic age of the Gupta emperors, and in the middle of the fifth century c.e. the monk Haribala (under whose directions the image of the reclining Buddha had been made) arranged for the construction of a new stupa to encase the old one. That was high tide. Then the tide turned Hindu and Muslim, and Buddhism petered out. It was the British with their sense of history who bored down through the earth to reveal the remnants that the flood of devotion had left. The cluster of long-deserted monasteries was exhumed and fingered by archaeologists, and then by pilgrims. Courtesy of Burmese devotees, the ruined stupa got reborn in 1927 ... and then came people more idly curious to add their touches: a few names were carved haphazardly in the stone. The stupa continued to reflect human impulses without comment.

It evoked and received our homage. Over the past few days' walk I had been setting my mind to a mantra that fitted to my footsteps: *"Namo Buddhaya, Namo Dhammaya, Namo Sanghaya"* (Homage to the Buddha, Homage to the Dhamma, Homage to the Sangha). Reciting this, we slowly circumambulate the stupa, following the dome's towering curvature. Then, on the second circumambulation, a very dark-skinned bhikkhu wearing a bright yellow robe strolled into view brandishing an alms bowl. He cut across my path with a broad grin: "Paisa, paisa." It wasn't food but money he was after. I waved him off with some irritation, but he was there as persistent as before on the third circuit, and I stopped to say, "No money, bhikkhus don't use money!" quoting one of the rules in the Patimokkha that prohibits a bhikkhu from accepting or using money. His response had a Zen-like edge to it: he pulled out a coin from his pocket, held it above the bowl with a grin, and let it drop in. Then he rattled it around.

"And wearing the Buddha's robe!..." The mantra's stillness collapsed under a wave of anger. It was even more upsetting to notice how my mind was echoing the brahminical sentiments that I had found so distasteful outside Siswal. We moved past him dismissively, descended the temple steps—which were flanked with signs prohibiting and warning about beggars—and drifted back past the ruins of Buddhism to the vihara.

Back at the vihara my impressions continue to flounder: the meal time with the Indian bhikkhus (the Burmese ate somewhere else) was like a works canteen, devoid of the contemplative silence and composure that is the acknowledged standard. There were only a few bhikkhus hanging around the shady dining room, and they were not bothered about refinement. The lodgings bhikkhu skidded in late and slid behind the table wolfing down food and coming out with highspeed incomprehensible sentences through mouthfuls of rice and dhal. When he finished eating I asked him about the Patimokkha recitation: he'd never even heard of it. There was an old Indian bhikkhu there too, sour-faced and monosyllabic, who spent most of the day sitting in a chair. The holy life didn't seem to be bringing him much joy.

One ray of light was the Nepalese nun. Small and slight with large spectacles propped on her tiny nose and long ears, swathed in the pink robe of a ten-precept Burmese nun, she knocked on our door late in that first afternoon while we lay down still recuperating from the walking. She bore a large thermos of tea. The next morning she was at the door again, tea and biscuits this time; and in the afternoon, when Nick was away rambling around the sites, there she was at the end of my walking meditation path, with her giant flask, her quietness, her matter-of-fact adoption of the pair of us. In other respects my Sangha refuge was going to have to be an internal affair.

NICK

When we first arrived I just sat in our room and relished the feeling of not having to go anywhere. The morning after, I managed to move into the gardens of the main temple, just next door. I spent the rest of that day sitting under the first tree I came to. Not to have to walk during the heat of the day, not to have to talk to people, just to be able sit alone amidst Nature. The gardens were a little green and leafy oasis, and I spent most of my time there.

The gardens were laid out amidst the ruins exposed by the archaeologists. Walkways that followed the foundations of old temples or monasteries and beside the bases of small stupas also passed under and through flowering trees and shrubs. Ground that had not been lowered to expose Gupta-age brickwork was laid out as lawns, their green complementing the orange red of the bricks. It was all well kept and a delight to stroll through in the evening or morning when the visitors were not there. Then it would be full of bird life, and I would sit under a tree with my binoculars trying to catch the smaller, more elusive, species flitting about the shrubs, to be suddenly surprised by a large flock of parakeets that would fly in from the fields chattering loudly and pile into one of the trees.

During the day the grounds would be full of people, not just the foreign pilgrims and tourists but also lots of middle-class Indians. India doesn't have much in the way of public space or parks, so the gardens had become somewhere to go for a day out. At the weekend there were Indian office workers and their women folk in their best saris strolling about or eating picnics on the lawns. On weekdays the office workers were replaced by parties of schoolchildren from the better schools, with uniforms resembling those of English public schools. The bird life withdrew then, but not the Hanuman monkeys. They were an integral part of the park, living, sleeping, and playing there and only occasionally making forages into the surrounding fields. They would sit, the troop of them spread through several of the small trees, oblivious of the visitors, with their long tails hanging down from the branches, curled slightly at the end. They also came across the walls and roofs of the vihara, grey and long-limbed, with their tails now held high, their black faces on the lookout for bits of food to make off with.

I imagined that the gardens at Kushinagar must have been laid out by the British. The trees looked about the right age, and I knew they had done the excavating. When the British first came to India, there were accounts of the great Buddhist shrines but no knowledge of where they were. Among the new rulers were people who were fascinated with all the physical remains of India's past. Unlike the Indians, the Victorian British were a people interested in material history: the British Museum is crowded today with the physical relics of other cultures.

The start of archaeology in India was led by one man, Sir Alexander Cunningham. He had come to India as a second lieutenant in 1833 at the age of twenty-one and went on to become an administrator, a surveyor, and an engineer. He distinguished himself at all these occupations, but what he is known for today is the uncovering of India's past. As he travelled about northern India on his other work, he would visit the thousands of forts, temples, and other ancient remains that dotted the landscape. He surveyed many of them, learned to decipher the ancient scripts, and built up a knowledge of the architecture of the different ages of India. When he retired from the army in 1861 he was made the first director general of the Indian Archaeological Survey.

Despite being a very committed Christian with a poor opinion of Hinduism and Islam, he developed a respect for the Buddhist teachings and their contribution to India's history. When he took charge of the Archaeological Survey he set about looking for the ancient Buddhist sites and was personally responsible for finding many of them. It was someone else who first suggested that the name of the town of Kasia might be derived from Kusinara, but it was Cunningham who came here in his first year as director general to inspect the sites, and it was his assistant A.C.L. Carlleyle who carried out the first excavation in 1876. This exposed the main stupa and uncovered the giant reclining nirvana statue of the Buddha buried in the debris of an oblong shrine.

There have been many excavations at the site since the first one, and they have uncovered layers of devotional building around the main stupa. Now the pilgrims have returned, coming from countries still Buddhist, and they have begun building anew. The first were the Burmese. The bhikkhu Venerable Chandramani made Kushinagar his home in 1903. He managed to get possession of the old temple ruins and made it a living shrine. Later he constructed the pilgrims' vihara where we were now staying, as well as a school for local children, and a college. This was all supported by the waves of pilgrims from Burma who could travel here easily during the time of the British, as Burma was then part of British India. The Burmese have been followed by the Sri Lankans, Chinese, Vietnamese, and Japanese, who have all built temples or rest houses in the vicinity of the shrine. It was the Indian government though that rebuilt the temple to house the giant reclining Buddha as part of the Jayanti celebration of 2,500 years since the Buddha's death. That was in 1956, so perhaps it was then that the gardens were laid out and not during British rule.

We entered the temple before it closed for the night at the beginning of another all-night sitting on the new moon. Once again I started the vigil full of determination, sitting under one of the trees looking up at the dark bulk of the stupa with the stars beyond it, then doing walking meditation when drowsiness began to set in. We must have been around seven when we started, and it was ten when I decided to sit for a while on one of the stone benches, just for a little rest. No harm in it, and I wouldn't fall asleep as the stone was so hard and cold.

I came to after midnight, very stiff and cold, sprawled sideways on the bench just in time to take Ajahn Sucitto a midnight drink of tea, which I had got earlier from a tea stall in the thermos left by the Nepalese nun. After that, I continued once more regularly walking round the stupa, trying to keep awake, and then finishing with Ajahn Sucitto—but with that familiar feeling of having failed again.

AJAHN SUCITTO

That night there was no moon at all. We began the meditation vigil at the Parinirvana Stupa some time after sunset, when everything was quiet. The stars lit up the stupa. Its hard surface was like all the ideas we have about transcending existence.

We lit incense, chanted and sat together for a while. The fatigue from the walk unrolled heavy waves of lethargy: before midnight my mind was shutting down in dullness, and I alternated walking with sitting meditation to stay awake. It was a long night and chilly: Nick produced a welcome flask of hot tea at twelve; the tea and the gratitude felt good. Later walking dully around the towering shrine in the thin starlight, scraps of Rilke's poem about the Buddha flickered in the blankness:

...Illuminated in your infinite peace,
a billion stars go spinning through the night,
blazing high above your head.
But in you is the presence that
will be, when all the stars are dead.

By three-thirty, I couldn't even pronounce "transcending existence." We climbed awkwardly over the railings to get back into the vihara. I felt grateful for the flowers though, giving their sweetness to the night when no one was around to appreciate them. Something very pure in that.

With the more mellow frame of mind that a vigil leaves one in, I could appreciate the vihara for what it was. It was much easier to meditate there than on the road. There were pictorial signs posted up reminding people to be quiet, particularly in the vihara's main shrine room. And the place *was* quiet, with long covered walkways around the courtyard which were excellent for walking meditation. I spent most of the next two days either in the courtyard or up on the flat roof. Up there it was completely deserted except for an occasional Hanuman monkey; the washing could dry in the sun while I meditated in the shade of a small shrine. Everywhere one was reminded of the devotion that supported the place. Engraved marble plaques set in the wall informed the reader that so-and-so of Rangoon with a dozen other names had donated this block, or that an association in Mandalay had sponsored the toilets; each smooth-faced Buddha image bore a little sign at its base to point out that someone from Burma, Thailand, or Malaysia had offered this to the temple in memory of a dear relative. The blades of the fans that rotated overhead were inscribed in red or blue with names in Burmese script. Wave after wave of pilgrims had deposited their aspiration here; on that was based the richness of privacy and silence.

Accordingly, the vihara was set up to accommodate parties of lay pilgrims. It was *the* original Buddhist pilgrims' resthouse; nowadays in Kushinagar it had been joined by many other viharas, and superseded in terms of size and elegance by lodges that were not viharas at all.

Although the abbot was away or busy most of the time during our stay, we did get a chance to talk to his brother, also a bhikkhu who added some details of the situation. Apparently there was very little training for the new bhikkhus—the Burmese were busy with other duties and it was difficult to get people to stay anyway. Many left and went their own way soon after ordination and wouldn't commit themselves to training. They made their living begging from Buddhist pilgrims. He didn't look pleased. Then again he had his own sadness: having protested against and been forced to flee from the military regime in Burma, he couldn't go back. India had accepted him; like us, the difficulty lay in accepting it in return.

NICK

The day after the all-night sitting I visited some of the modern shrines. I went alone as Ajahn Sucitto wasn't interested in looking around, he wanted to meditate. His zeal for the practise can be inspiring, but I was now realizing that it could also be intimidating when you were with him all the time. As I set off I consoled my sense of inadequacy with the thought that most other bhikkhus I had travelled with would have wanted to join me. Ajahn Sucitto was pretty unique. At least at the holy sites I could give myself a day off. On the road I was shackled to his ardent application.

Next door to the Burmese Vihara was a Chinese temple; all bright colours and oriental dragons, with a big golden Buddha, and musty inside from lack of use. A notice informed me that the temple was now the responsibility of a Vietnamese monk. Although it looked little visited and in need of some new paint, the grounds were well tended, the flowering shrubs had been recently watered, and the gravel paths raked. I left a donation in the collection box, a small attempt to make up for all the Chinese and Vietnamese Buddhists who could no longer come on pilgrimage.

Opposite the gardens was a modern Indian government tourist lodge, an oblong block of concrete painted pink with verandas and rows of big windows. This was where the Thai pilgrims were staying. They came from a culture that had outgrown the basic provision of the Burmese Vihara and expected en-suite bathrooms and air conditioning. In the Burmese Vihara the income they used to bring in was missed. There had been excitement about a Thai party coming that caused us to be moved into poorer accommodation. But when they arrived they decided to stay in the tourist lodge instead.

Further down the road there was a collection of slightly ramshackle buildings which turned out to be a temple supervised by an elderly Indian bhikkhu, who insisted on showing me around his dusty archaeological collection while also telling me his life history. He was a nice old chap, with impeccable Indian English that gave away his Brahmin birth, and I left a small donation to his fund to build a proper museum.

Next to this, and in complete contrast to the disorder I had just left, was a beautiful Japanese temple built using local bricks to resemble, from the outside, a big stupa. It was set about with manicured lawns and recent tree plantings and was enclosed in a wall to keep the Indian chaos out. Notices inside in several languages telling visitors how to behave were hardly necessary: the effect of the breathtakingly beautiful temple quietened even the most boisterous Indian family. The large hall under the stupa dome had been left mostly empty with that appreciation of space that the Japanese are so good at. Across the polished marble floor was a shrine with an enormous elegant gold Buddha, and around the circular wall were Japanese brushwork depictions of Buddhist *arahants* on tall wall hangings. The concave ceiling reflected the slightest sound, like a big cave, creating a well of silence that the echoing sounds disappeared into. I stood for a long time appreciating the emptiness, beauty, and silence. When I left I put a donation in their collection box too, not because they needed it but just out of appreciation.

I returned to the vihara to find my companion doing walking meditation, pacing up and down the cloister next to our room. He did agree to join me for a trip the next day to visit the cremation stupa, but only when I pointed out that this was a valid pilgrimage site.

Next day on the way to the stupa we stopped at the well from which Ananda fetched water for the Buddha's last drink. This had been fenced off and planted about with a few trees and shrubs and was overseen by an Indian *chaukidar,* or caretaker. When we entered, the chaukidar produced some flowers, picked from the shrubs, for us to lay before the small shrine. He hovered behind us as we paid our respects and when we had finished he asked for money. The flowers were not his, and he was paid already to look after them, so I declined.

The cremation stupa was big; a hill of old eroded red bricks with none of the original ornamentation left and surrounded by rice paddies. We lit incense, did some chanting, bowed, and then started to circumambulate. We went round three times, and on our third circuit, a tourist bus pulled up on the road and disgorged a party of Southeast Asian people led by a Mahayana Buddhist nun. With shaven head, a long grey robe, and a dark brown cloak over it clasped at her shoulder, she made her flock, dressed in Western clothes, look very ordinary. She led them to the stupa, where they performed an elaborate puja with a lot of chanting of high-pitched voices and big bundles of smoking incense. We stood quietly behind them until she noticed Ajahn Sucitto and had him join her at the front. I stayed at the back, moving off to take some photographs. It made a great scene.

After the puja was finished we were asked in halting English where we were from and about our pilgrimage. They were from Malaysia, mostly Malaysian Chinese I suspected, and were very taken with our intention to walk round the holy sites. The nun was particularly enthusiastic and tried to give Ajahn Sucitto some money. His explanation that he did not use it only resulted in her being even more impressed, and once she had worked out that I could receive the money, she had her disciples shower me with Indian bank notes. Then they had to leave—they were on a tight schedule, taking two weeks to do what it would take us most of six months.

As they drove off we turned to walk back to the Burmese Vihara. I was still clutching the bank notes and I could not help but reflect on the effect of money; it was so hard to use it skilfully, it was such sticky stuff. The generosity of unskilful pilgrims resulted in monks begging and chaukidars trying to sell flowers they did not own. Although the Burmese Vihara was set up as a service for pilgrims it now seemed to seek out the wealthy ones. On the other hand there was such joy to be had from the giving of money and the blessing that it could bring. I resolved to give all our new bank notes to the Chinese Temple. They needed it more than we did and they weren't hassling for it.

AJAHN SUCITTO

On the last morning I tried walking for alms with my bowl in the village. To my surprise at first, there was no devotional or hospitable response from the local Indian population. I didn't even receive a stare. Here bhikkhus were part of the scene: they were either well endowed with cameras and money and arrived in deluxe coaches at the head of a pilgrim entourage, or they were the caretakers of the temples, or they were the beggars who patrolled the sacred ruins or sat patiently with little cloths sprinkled with coins in front of them. No cause for devotion, faith, or generosity to arise in that. A quixotic gallantry stirred me: for me to be here as a pilgrim in the Middle Country meant to serve it by living as the Buddha told us. Maybe that would cause faith and wise reflections to arise—but really there was no point in having expectations. My dharma was to live as a bhikkhu; whether anyone responded to that was their business.

November 20th: it was time to leave Kushinagar. We took leave of U Ñanissara and paid our last respects at the Nirvana Temple in the morning. We left in the middle of the afternoon, after the midday heat had abated a little. Nick planned a nearby destination for us for that day: Fazil Nagar, eighteen kilometres due east. There, according to Bhante, was a stupa and the site where the Buddha ate his last meal, the fatal dish that set off the violent colic and dysentery that brought his life to an end. The straight and obvious route was along the main road that connects Lucknow and Gorakhpur with a new bridge over the Gandak River. On the other side of the river, the road would lead south to Patna and thence connect to Calcutta or the industrial towns of southern Bihar. A high road at the time of the Buddha, it was now a trunk road, hard going for wayfarers like ourselves.

On the road to Tuthibari, trucks had passed us quite frequently—but here the traffic was continuous in both directions. The heavy lorries and buses thundering in both lanes competed over the central two metres of the road which was the strip that had unbroken tarmac on it. A walker had to stay engaged with the flow to negotiate his own passage in the pitted margins and ditches on the fringe of the pavement—the zone shared with teetering bullock carts, bicycles, and motor scooters. Apart from the effect of the physical weaving and bobbing and the stench of dust-laden diesel fumes, the nerve endings were further seared by the continual welter of harsh sound: a truck or bus driver in India drives with one thumb almost constantly rammed on the horn, and the small fry mimic the leviathans. In India not many bikes had lights but they all had bells; ox carts had the whoops and calls of their drivers, scooters had hooters, lorries had klaxons. They were like the four castes; Nick and I, inaudible, marginalized and shoved to the worst part of the track, walked hunched and harried in the way of the Untouchables. "I feel as if I have been liberated from hell," said Ambedkar immediately after his conversion: by the time we arrived at the outskirts of Fazil Nagar, I had an inkling of what he meant.

Nick had some vague indications of a Jain *dharamsala* (pilgrims' resthouse) in Fazil Nagar where we could stop for the night. The idea of a Jain resthouse was intriguing. The things I'd heard about Jain renunciation made us bhikkhus look soft. Apparently they didn't shave their heads: the monks (nuns too?) had every hair on their bodies pulled out. They didn't have almsbowls; instead they had to collect food in their hands and were only allowed to go to a limited number of houses to glean alms. Of the two Jain sects, one wore white robes, the other, "sky-clad," wore nothing.

Jainism had formed at the same time as Buddhism, and like the Buddha, Mahavira, its nominal founder, claimed to have had many enlightened predecessors. For both these teachers, their predecessors and their disciples were *samanas,* people who had abandoned caste and avowed no allegiance to gods. In the samanas' tradition the realisation of truth came through direct gnosis in a life styled on purification through austerity rather than rite. Probably predating the Aryan conquest, the tradition was incompatible with the Vedic system; it must have been sustained by recluses in forests and caves over the centuries, but it gained a broad focus through the popularity of the Buddha and Mahavira. The two masters apparently did not meet, and their teachings are actually quite different. Mahavira, like the Buddha, rejected animal sacrifice and all destruction of life but, unlike the Buddha, made even unintentional killing a hindrance to liberation. Harmlessness was taken to the point where one couldn't scratch oneself because of the violence one would commit to one's own flesh. The underlying rationale behind all this asceticism was to avoid being involved with any unwholesome action, however minute: root vegetables were forbidden, for example, lest the earth or creatures living therein be disturbed by the cultivator in providing food for the monks. At least that's what I'd heard. People will do some extreme things for the sake of purity.

A chai stall, the only sane place in India, received us in the dusk. Inquiries took us a little way back from the main road to an large and imposing set of metal doors with silence and darkness behind them. They seemed to be locked. We took it in turns tugging and pushing on the doors or rattling them with some hesitation: what if they were up to some esoteric mortifications beyond in the gloom? Less than ebullient after the events of the day, we wandered up and down a little—was this the right place? The man who had pointed it out to us came by, surprised to see us still out in the dark street: after affirming to us that this was the dharamsala, he walked up to the doors and effortlessly pushed open a smaller door within the left-hand door. A little embarrassed, we stepped through into the darkness.

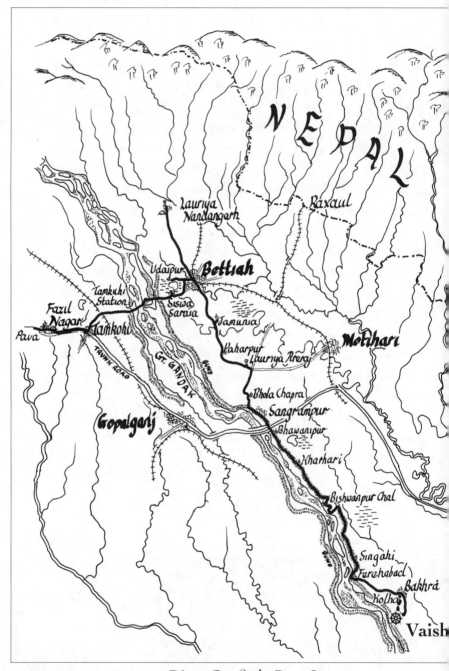

River Gandak, Part 2

6

Spiritual Friendship

AJAHN SUCITTO

The man who had helped us, his function fulfilled, disappeared. There were a lot of these people popping up on the pilgrimage. Thinking back, we'd sometimes speculate, "What would have happened if that man hadn't shown up?" and a glow of gratitude and wonder would arise. In that glow these friends in the darkness could be seen as a main thread of the pilgrimage: it was as if the frequently irritating experiences were just there to provide the scenario within which some benevolent being could arise to guide us through. But the glow was brief: we soon dropped back into darkness again.

This time, the darkness was actually a gloom slightly illuminated by light from a building a dozen metres ahead. In between was some kind of a garden—a few stunted trees, scraps of dry grass, a low block that must have been a latrine and washing area with a few buckets dotted around it. The yellow patch of light at the end of the garden drew us in. Beyond the door arose a startled caretaker, an old ledger to sign in on, garbled attempts at conversation, a fumbling with keys, a rickety door that unlocked, and a simple room to sink down in.

The room was bare except for a single large table-like structure that was the sleeping platform. It nearly filled the room. The day's walk was

ebbing out of my blisters when the door banged open and some bedding came in with a pair of arms around it and a couple of legs carrying
it along. I made the reassuring satisfied noises *"Ahchaa, ahchaa, thik,
thik,"* "Yes ... right, that's fine...," and reverted to a woozy meditation for
a while before stretching out on my half of the platform.

Sleeping on hard surfaces goes in phases: first is the hour or two of
near-coma, and then, as the mind begins to revive, comes awareness of
the uncomfortable impression of bone on something that does not
yield. Limbo sleep takes over—drifting in and out of the nether world
prompted by the need to roll over. Eventually the snatches of sleep
become so brief that you get up. But that first draught of oblivion is so
sweet ... I should have known that a Jain resthouse would snatch it away.
All too soon, the crash of the door and a flash of light summoned us to
the surface world, blinking ...

Three men wrapped in plaid blankets, one with a shaven head, all
with tense expressions: something wrong? Some phrases jostled around
but the waving of another book indicated that what was needed was
more signatures and ... passport numbers. When the brief business was
concluded, they continued looking around, commenting to each other,
occasionally proffering a gentle inquiry in our direction; then they
brought over the blankets that we hadn't used and put them on our table
... I realized that they wanted to be sure we had everything we needed.
We were guests, Westerners as well, and therefore instinctively to be
looked after. Not knowing quite what to do, they settled for just sitting
watching over us attentively.

My little clock said eleven o'clock. *I* knew what to do. So I made to lie
down with "that's it, I'm going to sleep" smiles and sighs. They sat back
quietly to watch. This obviously wasn't working. Nick, man of action,
bundled them out of the room, drew the bar across the door, and put
out the light.

After the early morning meditation, we paid up and, having left our
bags in the resthouse, set off in search of Pava, the site of the Buddha's

last meal. Somehow we had ascertained it lay down the side road beside the resthouse—a stroke of luck, that. We walked about a kilometre with rising uncertainty—no sign of anything special. After a while we turned back and wandered down the road looking around us. Nothing but fields and trees. Then a magical stranger came along who pieced together our mysterious presence and garb, and my inquiries about "Buddha Bhagwan," and pointed vigorously at a nearby patch of land—it was uncultivated with a few cows meandering around, and the outskirts of a village on its far side. But he kept pointing vigorously ... there *was* a regular-shaped white block on the far side, but nothing that you could call a shrine. Still, having come this far, we felt obliged to investigate.

The land on the edges of villages is of course the most convenient place for the villagers to defecate in; so apart from the cow dung, there were liberal scatterings of human excrement to be mindful of as we picked our way over to the mysterious white block. Next to it stood the now familiar blue enamelled notice of the Archaeological Survey of India, whose white lettering informed the reader that this was an ancient monument and defacing it would render the culprit subject to a fine of 5,000 rupees or three months' imprisonment. That was all. The white block was rectangular, about the size of a small desk, concrete and unadorned. Apart from the notice, only a few remains of incense sticks confirmed that, yes, this indeed must be the spot commemorating the place where Cunda the smith offered the Buddha the fatal meal of "pig's delight."

The story goes that the Buddha had felt that the mysterious dish— perhaps pork, or perhaps something that pigs feed on, like truffles, or even as totally unrelated to pigs as "toad in the hole" is to toads—was bad to eat. Still he hadn't wanted to disappoint the humble smith by rejecting his offering, so he took some himself, while telling Cunda to ditch whatever remained of that dish and not to give it to any of the other monks. However, his own stamina was now considerably reduced by age and a recent severe illness, and soon the bad food brought on a violent attack of dysentery. With his loyal attendant, Ananda, the Buddha had slowly and painfully made his way onward to pass away in the sal grove outside of Kusinara. Of his last acts, one of the most generous was to tell Ananda to absolve Cunda from any blame. The smith's intentions had been good, and after all, the Buddha's body was old and painful: "kept going by being bandaged up" as he put it. In fact he reflected that Cunda's deed could even be seen as a blessing: it was allowing him to pass into the Ultimate Nirvana that he had guided so many others to over forty-five years.

I had to admit the setting was appropriate. The dung-strewn field and the buzzing flies befitted a place of dysentery and death. The warmth of the morning wafted excremental odours over the fragrance of the incense that I lit and offered. Nick produced some yellow sponge cake with a cheerful remark. It was wrapped in greasy paper and tasted like it had been steeped in ammonia. I felt like keeping the Buddha's resolve to eat on, no matter what, but Nick, munching some himself, was coming to the same conclusions: the mysterious "pig's delight" must be none other than this rancid cake! Not being ready to follow the Buddha's example yet, I ate half, spat some out and gave the rest to the flies. For them it would probably make a change from excrement.

We picked up our bags from the resthouse and moved on into Fazil Nagar. Down a back street, a strange hill (with another blue enamelled notice beside it) could only have been an ancient stupa that had become grassed over. There was a Muslim shrine on it now. Past that and across the fields we went; a farmer offered us a meal in a tiny village, and then we were on a small road leading back to the trunk road.

NICK

That morning as we had walked into Fazil Nagar we had talked about Venerable Ananda, the Buddha's faithful companion. We would get talking like that sometimes, hit on a new topic of conversation and spend an hour or two mulling it over as we walked along. It would happen in the morning, before the walking got too unpleasant, and usually after we'd left some stop that had injected something new into our world. Ajahn Sucitto had spoken of the sense of pathos he felt in the descriptions of the Buddha's last years. Reading between the lines it appeared to him that the days when the Buddha was accompanied everywhere by many monks were gone. He was old, in his eighties, and presumably most of his disciples were now much younger and off practicing on their own. Ajahn Sucitto imagined them all thinking, with the arrogance of youth, that the Buddha was past it, only Ananda staying with him until the end.

Ananda spent many years with the Buddha and is mentioned throughout the scriptures. It was he in fact, who memorized many of the teachings and the incidents which led to them. These include many conversations he had with the Buddha himself. He comes across in the scriptures as kind and enthusiastic if sometimes a bit foolish, someone constantly more concerned with others than himself. One conversation I remember us discussing was the time Ananda was enthusiastically praising spiritual friendship and said that surely spiritual friendship must account for half of the holy life. The Buddha replied that no, spiritual friendship was all of the holy life. Ajahn Sucitto pointed out that the Buddha's reply could also be translated as a play on words, "No Ananda, *friendship with the spiritual* is the whole of the holy life." Another extract from the suttas that Ajahn Sucitto quoted were the words the Buddha consoled Ananda with when he was overcome with grief at the Buddha's imminent death.

> *Enough, Ananda, do not weep and wail. Have I not already told you that all things that are pleasant and delightful are changeable, subject to separation and becoming other? So how could it be, Ananda—since whatever is born, become, compounded is subject to decay—how could it be that it should not pass away?*

That topic lasted us most of the morning. It was a delight when we could talk like that; Ajahn Sucitto could be such a mine of information. We were still discussing Venerable Ananda as we walked on after the meal but the heat of the afternoon and the trunk road soon put an end to that. Instead we went back to trudging along with our heads down, in our own worlds—mine soon a fog of fatigue and negativity as I trailed some way behind him. The brief feeling of companionship had evaporated. I found, though, that however fed up I got with everything I could never get that angry with my companion because of the basic respect I had for him. We were just both in this together, come what may.

A motorbike pulled up as we walked on. "Excuse me, what is your native place?" The question was there before we were aware of the questioner, now dismounting.

"We are from England."

"And what is the purpose of your visit?" A small crowd began to form.

"We are on a walking pilgrimage."

"I am asking why it is that you are walking?" Our questioner stood in our path confident that he had the right to interrogate us. It was is on the trunk roads that we met such educated Indians, and some could be so arrogant. "And what is your opinion of India?" Ajahn Sucitto patiently answered the questions as a larger and larger crowd coalesced to stare at us. The problem with this kind of man was that he did not want us to leave; having us answer his questions fed his feeling of self-importance. He simply replied to my suggestions that we must be moving along with another question. This time, after some fifteen minutes of questions, I hit on the solution.

"It has been most enjoyable speaking to you. Thank you so much for your very interesting questions." The flattery stunned him momentarily. "Goodbye." We managed to turn and escape before he could recover.

The trunk road was the most direct route to our next holy site, Vaishali. It led southeast, crossing the only bridge over the Great Gandak

River, and heading for the city of Muzaffarpur in Bihar. There was an alternative, though. In very small writing on the old map I had with me was the word "ferry" and it was on a part of the river that is to the east of where we now were. If we could cross there we would be able to visit two other Buddhist sites, Lauriya Nandangar and Lauriya Areraj. Both had pillars that had been erected by the great Buddhist emperor Ashoka, and Lauriya Nandangar also had a large Buddhist stupa. It would also mean that we could then follow the river south instead of the road, and rivers usually meant lots of wildlife.

We reached Tamkuhi around five. It was a small town that had grown up along the trunk road. The road was the main street and was lined with transport cafes, stalls selling snacks and fruit, figures squatting on the ground behind small piles of produce, and lots of people milling about. The small road we were looking for led off to the north and on its corner was a tea shop with a group of young men sitting outside. We stopped for tea and to ask the way. The young men spoke English but were hazy about whether we could go to Bettiah, a town on the other side of the Gandak, this way. So I got them to ask the people in the crowd that had gathered about us. Their question, in the local dialect, set off an animated discussion with one old chap seeming particularly agitated. "This old man says there is a ferry this way." The old man nodded and gave us a betel-juice grin.

As we walked on some of the young men joined us, walking abreast, and started asking questions about our journey. They were wearing the standard Indian version of Western dress: black shoes, black nylon trousers, and a white short-sleeve shirt with a pen in the pocket. Every young educated Indian male we met was dressed that way; the only variation I ever spotted was in the quality of the pen and whether they had a wristwatch. Our new companions had proper fountain pens, not ballpoints, and they all had good-looking watches, so they must be from better-off families. After a while one of them suggested that we could stay at his house. We were reluctant but he was a nice lad with an open friendly face, and persistent, so eventually we decided to accept tea and see what we thought then; after all his father might not be quite so keen to have two such unusual guests for the night.

We need not have worried: the father turned out to be just as friendly as his son. We were made at home on the veranda of a big brick house in the centre of the village, served with tea and again pressed to stay. They wanted to feed us too, and, when we explained we could not eat after noon, we had to agree to breakfast. We spent the evening on the veranda talking to the men of the family and others from the village, now wearing the more comfortable clothes of village life, sarongs of simple checked cloth topped with a white T-shirt or vest. A young daughter peeked at us from around the door to the house, ducking inside if we looked her way; the other women made do with furtive looks from the safety of the kitchen. We sat and talked late and then slept the night on their veranda on bedding made up by the son and his younger brothers.

In the morning we woke before first light to the sound of activity in the house. We sat in meditation until dawn when tea arrived—but no breakfast. It would be here soon, perhaps we would like to wash at the village pump first? But when we returned there still was no breakfast. It was getting late, and I was fretting for the loss of the cool morning's walking, but it did no good—they were determined to do us proud. When eventually it did come, it was better and more elaborate than any of our midday meals.

It was an open road that day with few trees to shade us, and the walk through the heat, laden with a heavy meal, was taxing. The road led north to Tamkuhi Station, the local railway station, where we turned east onto a smaller road. It was all very open country with nowhere suitable to rest or to sleep the night, so we pressed on in the hope that the other side of the river would be better, both of us getting more and more weary. By late afternoon we knew we were getting near to the Great Gandak by the way the road was changing. First the quality of the tarmac had deteriorated, then potholes appeared and then the tarmac steadily decreased until there was none. The road still had lots of activity, no lorries or cars, but people walking, flights of bicycles, and the occasional rickshaw or cart. The road was raised on a slight mound above the fields, its surface now red-brown dirt, the colour we were slowly turning. As we went farther it became more uneven, rutted, and dusty, and then suddenly the fields just stopped, a cliff fell some twenty feet, and there was a very wide, very sluggish, river. Here it was steadily eroding away slices of someone's land.

A collection of huts—one selling tea—some government signs, and then steps down the cliff and a landing stage. We sank down onto a bench outside the tea hut, and I ordered tea. As we drank we watched the wooden ferry slowly make its way back across the river, the ferrymen leaning into long poles. Once it had beached we clambered down and got on along with a dozen others and half a dozen bicycles. That filled the boat completely, the bicycles leaning against each other in the middle, and us and the other passengers on seats along the sides. I felt very close to the water sloshing against the boat, which rocked and sank under the weight of its cargo as the last passengers and bicycles found their place.

The four boatmen were dressed in the working clothes of the poor: a dirty sarong, a vest, and a piece of cloth wrapped about their head. One of them clambered around collecting the fares, deliberately discreet with the other passengers so I could not see how much they were paying. When he got to me, he boldly stuck out his hand and demanded *"das rupee."* But I had seen the official prices displayed on the government sign and knew that ten rupees was eight too many. *"Do rupee,"* I replied. *"Das rupee,"* he demanded. I had to make out as if I was leaving the boat, rocking it and the passengers as I did so. Then he became more reasonable, *"Cha rupee"* (four rupees). He pointed to the two of us in turn and then to our luggage, which was taking up the room of a passenger. I countered with *"Ting rupee"* (three rupees). He accepted with a tilt of the head, and I paid up.

The boat was then towed up river by the ferrymen. They bent forward, hauling on ropes over their shoulders, and grunted their way along the bank until we had gone some several hundred yards. Then we set off, steered and pushed by them straining on the poles against the surge of the current. Despite this the boat steadily moved downriver as we crossed. The river lapped at the sides, a dirty grey, full of sediment from the Himalayas. From our low perspective the river looked vast as it slipped away beneath us.

The boat landed on a grey sandy beach and we had to clamber out into the shallow water. Beyond was an empty expanse of sand heaped up and channelled, deposited there by the river in flood, with tall waving grassland some way beyond it. A couple of grass huts sat at the edge of the grass, presumably homes for the ferrymen, and from there a path went on. Ignoring the path—and the warnings about bandits and crocodiles we had received earlier—we trudged across the sand heading downriver and let the increasing gloom of the approaching night hide us. We sat that night by the river feeling it quietly surging by, laden with the sediment that created the Ganges plains we were crossing.

India was once, 45 million years ago, a separate land mass. Having broken away from Gondwanaland, much of which is now Antarctica, it sailed majestically and imperceptibly across the ocean to come up against the rest of Asia. India, true to its disruptive nature, is still moving, pushing north and forcing up the Himalayas as its crunched-up leading edge. Because India is being forced under Asia, there was at first an inland sea at the base of the Himalayas, much like the Mediterranean today, but bigger. The erosion of the new mountains filled the sea with sediment until it became a vast river plain, known now as the Indus-Ganges plain, running from the Afghani hills in the west over three thousand miles to the Burmese hills in the east. The Himalayan mountains are still being eroded as they continue to be pushed up, filling with sediment the big rivers that flow out of them: the Ganges, Brahmaputra, and Indus with their tributaries, such as the Gandak.

The rivers snake across the plain, ever shifting their position, eroding one bank and depositing sediment elsewhere. When the monsoon comes, the rivers rise and spill out over the land, depositing silt over everything. This fertilizes the land but also causes a lot of destruction—and it slowly buries the history of the people who live there. That is why all the Buddhist archaeological remains have been buried, covered with up to four metres of silt. That is just the last two thousand years' worth.' In places the silt is as deep as four thousand metres. Looking out over the Great Gandak laden with silt like some vast, flowing mud bath, makes you realize how integral the rivers are to the plain. It's no wonder the Indians worship them.

AJAHN SUCITTO

Night by the Gandak letting the day end. It was good to look up into the huge sky and see Orion, an old companion from Britain, standing overhead. The great hunter was refreshingly silent. At the end of the day, I just wanted to sit with the Buddha and let the rest of it pass over. It was strange spending so much time with Nick but hardly having a conversation. To my mind, his bounding spontaneous style seemed insensitive. Or maybe not being able to do things *my* way was the problem. Well that was my friend: loyal, generous, exasperating Nick. I could feel myself getting moody toward the end of each day, what with the blisters, the heat, the fatigue, the grime, and the jangle of India; and I realised that I was probably irritating him in return. We were probably helping each other through all kinds of attachments if we could only realise it!

At the end of a day, Nick would be looking for "a good spot to spend the night," a concept that meant little to me. So we would stumble around in the darkness until we sank down somewhere as "not good enough" as anywhere else. So it was beside the Gandak—how can one stretch of sand be better than another? Well why argue, especially as it was time to fumble around in the dark trying to find a level patch of ground, then unpack the lantern and try to get some light going.

One in every ten Indian matches will light when struck. The others are there to wear out the striker and build up exasperation so that, as you furiously scratch the lucky match against the side of the box, the head flies off, sometimes igniting to land in your eye or burn a hole in your sleeping bag. In case you get over that hurdle, the candles either lack wicks or are made of ill-burning wax. Occasionally, my grim, almost bloody-minded, resolve would raise a flame. By the Gandak, the river breeze playfully snuffed that out.

So the end of the day was hardly the mellow space in which to sort out personality conflicts. I was too tired out and saturated with dissatisfaction to want to do anything but sit there, with my Buddha image somewhere in the dark in front of me. Or lie down, feet stretched out to cool in the wind until it was all right. A night beside a great Indian river, off the beaten track in the middle of nowhere, should have been amazing. But, sitting quietly and opening to the way it is, it was in a way more than that: despite the blisters and dullness and human jangle as constant companions, everything was all right.

NICK

Next morning we woke to find ourselves covered in heavy dew. People were coming off the ferry and we were able to follow them as they pushed their bicycles across the sand and through the grasslands. One man without a bicycle was dressed all in his best white. White baggy long cotton shirt hanging down and half covering his white cotton dhoti. A dhoti is created afresh every morning from a long piece of light cloth wrapped in a complex way that has always intrigued me, with the material passing a couple of times through the legs and giving the effect half of skirt, half trousers. Apparently the longer the piece of cloth, and so the more baggy and elaborate looking the assemblage, the better the dhoti. The Indians wearing these would walk along with the end pieces flapping slightly and, when outdoors, one corner held in a hand to keep the bottom from getting dirty. Without any conversation that I can remember, our all-white guide showed us the way, walking ahead like some guardian angel. The sand undulated, and much of it, as we got farther from the river, was covered in a mixture of tall grasses and scrub. There was standing water in places and small tributaries of the main river to be waded through. Then our guardian would hold his white skirts up higher and indicate us to follow his route through the shallowest parts. He had no need to take off his plastic shoes but our leather sandals had to come off and then be put back on for each crossing, while he waited patiently. Every so often we would come upon a patch of what must have been better soil, which someone was cultivating.

Eventually the path climbed to a higher level and we were not on sand any more. Ahead of us the bicycles were mounted and ridden off, Our guide, having pointed out our path, had to leave us. We found ourselves alone walking on a wandering dirt track through fields, trees, and small villages. My map told us that we were in fact on an island but gave no idea how to proceed. I had to go on into the unknown, trusting the guide's directions. The path eventually brought us of its own to the other branch of the river. Past undulating desert-like tracts of sand in which the poor villagers were trying to grow a crop of some leafy green vegetable, each plant sitting in its own hollow in the shade of a large, cut banana leaf placed above it on sticks. There were long parallel lines of them with the occasional toiling cultivator carrying water from the distant river in old cooking oil drums slung from a pole across his shoulders. When we reached this branch of the river, we found it was much smaller than the first, and we were able to wade across, following the tracks of the cultivators and up to our thighs in water. So we returned to the land of metaled roads and the motor car. We were also now in Bihar.

7

The Kingdom of the Law

AJAHN SUCITTO

Homage to the Buddha. "Homage to all the Buddhas, the great sages who have arisen in the world." Thus ran one of my much-repeated mantras: the recitation of the names and virtues of the twenty-eight Buddhas of whom Gotama was the most recent. This chant was supposed to have a protective influence. At least reciting it while fingering the twenty-eight-bead mala did cast a benevolent mood around the mixed bag of mental states and sensory impingement coming my way.

We were leaving Uttar Pradesh and entering Bihar. At the time of the Buddha the Gandak River was also a boundary—to the west lay the republic of the Mallas, a vassal state of the powerful kingdom of Kosala; to the east were the federation of republics known as the Vajjian confederacy. Shortly after the Buddha's death, the whole region was conquered by Ajatasattu, who subsumed it into his kingdom of Magadha, the heart of what under Ashoka in the third century B.C.E. came to be the first and greatest Indian empire.

I had woken up cold in the dark with my legs aching from the hard ground. Orion had gone and my mind was full of mud. In that fuddle and gloom we lost something most every morning—candles, items of clothing, whatever. India took them all in exchange for the mud and grit she bestowed upon us. This morning it was sand, pasted on our sleeping gear by the heavy dew, that we packed away and carried in our bags. We struggled east across the dunes and into a harsh sunrise. Through squinting eyes a new land eventually appeared—a village, cultivation, and a road—and that feeling of returning to more welcoming ways. So it seemed at first, as we stood on the road from the river and people came rushing toward us ... but no, they were following two cantering horses dragging a cart our way, to the riverbank. Drums were pounding—the men running behind the cart were beating drums—and as the cart rattled by, we were greeted by a pale thin hand hanging out from beneath the white cloth bundle on the back of the cart. Welcome to Bihar. The heavy odour of the corpse was unmistakable. I gently put my hands in anjali and bowed my head. Our pilgrimage had arrived at Death, one of the principle gateways to the realm of Dhamma.

NICK

The road we were now on led to Bettiah, the local big town, but we were looking out for Udaipur Nature Reserve. The road was quiet, with just a few bicycles and the occasional vehicle. We walked along it till ten o'clock, the time we usually stopped for food, and then turned off at the next huddle of houses.

We found ourselves in a comparatively large and prosperous-looking village, and as we walked slowly through, an old man called us over to sit on rope beds on the veranda of his house. Small and slightly stooped, he was a quiet and gentle soul who smiled at Ajahn Sucitto's attempts at Hindi. Instead of replying, he went off and returned with a much younger man who spoke good English. The old man had him find out if we would take food and what we could eat and then withdrew to leave us to talk.

The young man was a very different character. Robust and confident, he was the old man's nephew and home on leave from the army.

A sub-lieutenant in a regiment posted to the Punjab, he had recently married and was here to visit his new wife in their small house round the corner. He came from one of the wealthier families in the village, and we were introduced to some of his older and more important relations who began to accumulate while the old man we had first met sat in the background.

The army officer told us that the nature reserve was nearby, just behind the village. There was a lake, and some of the villagers had boats that they used to cross to where the rest house was. He had not been into the sanctuary for a long time, as it had become the base for a gang of local *dacoits,* Indian bandits. The poorer villagers could go, and he thought we would be all right, but if the dacoits saw him they would take him captive and demand a ransom from his family. There was nothing to be done but pay up, as the local police were bribed by the dacoits to leave them alone. The dacoits turned to kidnapping when the bank was built in the village and they could no longer rob the landowners directly. The bank was pointed out to us, a one-room building across the village—closed when we arrived, the steel-shuttered front had since been opened.

Dacoits are common in this, the most lawless and corrupt state in India. After Independence the new Indian government tried to do something about the unequal distribution of land, taking some from the big landowners to give small plots to the poor. In much of India they made at least some headway, but not in Bihar. This state was already known back then for the corruption of its officials, and it was they who frustrated the government's good intentions. As a result the only way out for the poor, and here that meant the Untouchables, was either to go to the towns and cities, or turn to crime. The dacoits are the revenge of the Untouchables.

We were fed with food brought to us by the old man. He still said very little, being more concerned with our welfare than with who we were. First there was water, poured over our hands into a bowl, then big stainless steel platters, placed in front of each of us to eat from. We sat on mats on the dirt floor and ate, as one does in India, with the right hand. Then after more water for washing our hands again we could return to the rope beds as our plates disappeared back to the kitchen and to the cooks we never saw. Having sat and talked for a while, we thanked them and left the village following the nephew's directions. The possibility of going by boat had been mentioned, but nothing came of it, and so we had to go the long way round by the road.

I had discovered Udaipur Nature Reserve in a typically Indian leaflet on the wildlife of Bihar. This simply listed all the state's nature reserves with a line or two of information on each, including the district name and nearest railway station. "Udaipur Sanctuary 6 sq. km wetland and forest with resident waterfowl and migrants. Best time to visit Nov.–Mar. 1 Rest house 5 Rps." I knew India well enough to take that with a pinch of salt. Still it seemed a good idea, as we would be passing, to check it out. The idea of a roof over our heads with a bird sanctuary outside was appealing to both of us, and if it really were there, we could stop for a day's rest.

We knew we had reached the sanctuary by the forest department sign...and the sudden absence of trees. Up until then we had been passing groves of mangoes and occasional trees on field edges and beside the road. These trees were all owned by someone and thus protected; the trees in the nature reserve were owned by the government and had become fair game. Ahead of us each side of the road was a wasteland of dead tree stumps and bare ground. The forestry department had been trying to rectify this lack recently, and there were some newly planted trees amid the stumps of the old ones. As we went farther into the sanctuary things got better, and the stumps became stunted regrown trees. It was about then that we met one of the forest guards coming down the road in his uniform of green rough cotton trousers and jacket.

The guard escorted us to the rest house, which from a distance looked like a great place to stay. It must have once been a shooting lodge and was built in the grand style of the British Raj, a large bungalow with a wide veranda. As we got nearer, it became clear that the lodge had been as well looked after as the forest. All was decay and lack of care: doors and windows were broken, gutters and pipes gone, and the woodwork had not seen paint for many years. Still the roof was mostly there, and the guards were happy for us to stay. There were three of them, and the senior one insisted that one of them would stay the night to protect us. They told us that the sanctuary had once been the local Raja's *shikar*, or hunting area. Like so many shikars it had fallen on hard times with the coming of the Indian state and the end of the local Raja's control. It was now used as the guard's base during the day, but it obviously had not been used for sleeping in years.

Once we had settled in, laying out our things on the floor of one of the bedrooms, mindful to avoid the rotten parts, I went off looking for wildlife. The lodge was beside a small lake that was fringed with reeds and surrounded by trees. The trees were in a better state than those we had passed on the way in, but of the resident waterfowl and migrant birds there was no sign. I did find a noisy troop of rhesus monkeys swinging about in a lakeside tree but none of the birds mentioned in the leaflet. Next morning I found out why.

I had set off early with my binoculars to see if anything more could be found at first light. There were still no birds about, but what I did find were the dacoits. I walked round a bend to come across ten of them, young, dark-skinned, and tough-looking, but well dressed and sporting thick black moustaches. They had rifles on their shoulders, bandaleros full of bullets across their chests, and, rather incongruously, black Indian bicycles by their side. They were as surprised to see me as I was to find them, and for a moment we all just stood there. Then one of them said something in Hindi and gestured. I think he meant me to come nearer, but I felt best staying where I was. A man with them had a little English, and through him they demanded to know who I was, what I was doing, and whether I had companions. I played it as confidently as I could, looking stern and answering their questions in a perfunctory manner. And I told them "No!" they couldn't see what was in the belt under my trousers (both passports, our traveller's cheques, and all our money!) when they asked.

One of them was obviously the leader—he was doing most of the questioning, was the best dressed, with a richly brocaded waistcoat and rings on his fingers, and had the best rifle. It was a proper modern rifle, while most of the others had ancient-looking muskets. When he pointed at my binoculars and had the English speaker ask what they were, I let him use them. He had never used a pair before, and once I had shown him which way round to hold them, he was very impressed. That reduced the tension. I explained with sign language about bird watching, showing him the birds in my bird book. He nodded and indicated, using his rifle to point at the trees, that these were the birds they shot. After that things got quite friendly and I told him about our pilgrimage. When I bade them farewell, the man with the little English told me not to tell the guards we had met him. Then I walked quickly back to the resthouse, vowing never again to go off walking alone with all our valuables!

At the resthouse the head guard had returned with flour, rice, dhal, and vegetables and was cooking us a meal. He acted surprised when I mentioned the dacoits. Later, during our meal, the man who had been translating for the dacoits turned up. He appeared to be some kind of assistant to the forest guards. He looked furtive and said nothing to us. I did not believe that the guards did not know all about the dacoits—I had met them only a few hundred yards from the resthouse—but they would not admit it.

We spent two nights there, both of us using much of the time to sit alone by the lake enjoying the feeling of not having to go anywhere. It was a lovely stop, or at least it was for me. Ajahn Sucitto had dysentery, it was his turn; he had been feeling bad for a couple of days, but he had not told me. For him the stop at the nature reserve was timely, a chance to get over the worst of it. He also used it to catch up on writing his diary, which could get days behind when we were on the road.

The last morning the guards made us *parothas*, flat round breads fried in ghee, for breakfast, and we gave them one of our photos. The day before they had refused my offers to pay for the food, and the photos seemed a very small gift for their hospitality. We made our goodbyes, and the same guard who had led us in now led us out, onto the road to Bettiah.

AJAHN SUCITTO

> *Even so have I, bhikkhus, seen an ancient path, an ancient road traversed by the rightly enlightened ones of former times.*

> *...this Noble Eightfold Path, that is: right views, right intention, right speech, right action, right livelihood, right effort, right mind-fulness, and right concentration. This, bhikkhus, is that ancient path, that ancient road traversed by the rightly enlightened ones of former times. Along that I have gone, and going along it I have fully come to know decay-and-death, I have fully come to know the arising of decay-and-death, I have fully come to know the ceasing of decay-and-death, I have fully come to know the way going to the ceasing of decay-and-death.*

Dhamma practise often entails confronting the unpalatable until one's reactions have cooled; then by holding the attention steady it becomes clear that "things" are actually only "the way things appear," an appearance compounded by reactions and assumptions, reinforced by the resistance to change and letting go, but observation alone is not enough when the mind's eye is clouded. Heart-centred action is needed so practise becomes a moving thing, a pilgrimage. Keep going, says the Buddha, hold steady, relax the will-to-be, and you arrive at a place of peace... *"an island which you cannot go beyond...a place of non-possession and of non-attachment...I call it Nibbana."*

While I was meditating by the lake at Udaipur, November 25th made an appearance, and Nick said it was time to go. It was early morning, and we were off to see the Ashokan pillar at Lauriya Nandangarh, some distance to the north of Bettiah. We arrived at Bettiah a few hours later, as the day was heating up and my energies were melting into a groggy puddle. There were blackened buildings, some in Mughal style which must have been grand palaces once, and some Victorian-style Raj buildings also going to dissolution, cracked and crumbling with neglect, their gardens overgrown. Meanwhile, the streets bustled. We reached a bus station throbbing with revving old biscuit tins, swathed in divine titles like "Lakshmi Express." Their charioteers were bellowing "Chalo! Chalo!" and we bought into that urgency, hastily scrambling on a half-empty bus that was making every appearance of moving out of the station. But it was only an appearance. The game was this: the bus does not leave until it is crammed full to overflowing with passengers; passengers on the other hand are only going to board the bus that is leaving first. Hence a bluffing tactic ensues whereby several buses pretend to be leaving, moving slowly forward with a lot of revving and hollering and "Let's Go!" while people mill around undecided. A courtship dance.

The virtual reality of departure becomes actual at a critical moment when conviction occurs that a certain bus really *is* leaving, and its forward juddering and hollering brings about a quantum leap in passengers. As with mental events, an irrational conviction in one of a series of choices occurs, and then the reasons and events back it up. Suddenly we had action. The bus was leaving and crammed full at the same time, with the conductor shoehorning flailing bodies and bags around or on top of the seats and the engine, then clambering up onto the roof to arrange the human cargo and somehow collect fares.

The avalanche had swept me into a seat next to the aisle; Nick was on top of the engine, having an argument with the conductor through the latticework of bodies as to how many person-spaces his bag was taking up. The conductor was managing to get into high dudgeon, refusing to accept any fare at all when Nick would pay for only three. The duel was settled by Nick shoving the money into the conductor's shirt pocket.

After an appropriate time in this mass of flesh, we were delivered to Lauriya Nandangarh. The scene was of a huge fair—about ten acres of canvas-covered stalls and pavilions around the great Ashokan pillar. Even with my weak eyesight, I could see the Ashokan lion on top of the smooth column, looking like he was trying to escape the mayhem around him. The dusty road at our feet was lined with the usual melange of stalls and vendors, men on bikes or squatting by the road, and women always in that characteristic pose—one arm raised to support the pitcher or bundle on the head, the sari falling in drapes to the ankles with their anklets. Out of this timeless Indian cameo stepped our latest friend, a teenager wearing Western clothing. He invited us for a meal and led us through the fair...although I was feeling too sick and dizzy to want to focus on what was being sold. Nick kept up the conversation as we hovered by the Ashokan column.

The emperor Ashoka, having converted to Buddhism, had erected stupas, stone tablets, and pillars all around his vast empire. The tablets and the ten pillars remaining today have inscriptions on them that generally outline some aspect of the emperor's policy of righteous rule. Sometimes these edicts are quite specific—prohibiting the slaughter of animals, or proclaiming the establishment of imperial officers to ensure for the well-being of the populace—but more consistently they express Ashoka's sincere wish for Dhamma, religiously based law, to prevail. Although his own inclination was toward the Buddha's Dhamma, Ashoka—referred to in the edicts as "Beloved of the Gods"—displays therein a paternal benevolence toward the other religions of his empire.

It was a short-lived episode in Indian history, remarkable in that, despite the size of the empire and its high degree of order and integrity, Ashoka's reign was subsequently forgotten. The mainstream of Indian culture swung against a religion that had no place reserved for Brahmins; in the historical records that the Brahmins preserved, there is only the briefest cryptic mention of the great Buddhist emperor. As Buddhism died out in India, legendary accounts of Ashoka by Buddhists in other countries were the only records—and they could be dismissed as fanciful parables. Even the pillars and edicts could not hold out against ignorance. The "Brahmi" script that the edicts were inscribed with was forgotten, even by the time the indomitable Chinese pilgrim Fa Hsien came through at the beginning of the fifth century C.E. In later years the pillars were worshipped as Shiva lingams, probably ensuring fertility, or occasionally conjectured to be the walking sticks of Bhima, one of the heroes of the Hindu epic *Mahabharata*. It wasn't until 1837, when James Prinsep translated the script, and George Turnour connected them to the Ashoka of Buddhist legend, that the legends were held to encase a historical core.

History had not yet arrived at Lauriya Nandangarh. Here the pillar was the object of an unenlightened, though considerable, devotion. People were fervently throwing paisa coins, rice, and flowers at the column: women with ochre pigment daubed in their hair, nose rings flashing; the scent of perfume and mild delirium. Behind the railing surrounding the pillar, small boys scampered to gather what they could. We didn't stay long: I needed to get out of the tumult, and headed for a nearby Rama temple. There I could sit on the cool stone with my back against the wall to wait for Nick who had stayed to look at the fair.

NICK

The fair was a large bazaar of tented stalls and crisscrossing alleyways, all covered over with canvas, which radiated out from the Ashokan column, the excuse for everything else. The alleyways were narrow and crowded, so I soon lost any sense of direction. There was a system to it though; all the stalls selling the same thing were together. We had eaten at one of several selling cooked food, and we finished the meal with tea and milk sweets I bought from one of the stalls farther down the alleyway, which had piles of exotic-looking sweets in a variety of colours. Beyond them were stalls selling cloth, stalls selling toys, and even stalls selling travelling trunks. Everything that could be bought in a city bazaar was there. I supposed that it all must travel from fair to fair around the countryside serving the country people.

There were none of the game booths and rides we have at fairs in the West, but what I did find, at the end of an alleyway that brought me back to the main entrance and the Ashokan column, were two marquees, the canvas doorway of each flanked by men dressed in colourful costumes with white greasepaint faces. Each pair was dressed as man and woman and was calling out to people to come into the marquees. There must have been a play inside—I could hear the voices of actors and laughter. Although I wanted to go in, I thought better of it. Ajahn Sucitto had looked slightly disapproving of me going round the fair in the first place.

Instead I collected the young man, left Ajahn Sucitto to rest at the temple, and went off to have another go at repairing his sleeping mat. I had tried to fix his mat several times using glue and patches bought from bicycle repair stalls, but each time the patches had come unstuck. The glue was for rubber and the mat was nylon. They might work for one night, but by the next the mat was again slowly deflating, leaving Ajahn Sucitto lying on hard ground by morning. He was resigned to it—it fitted his view of the world as an innately unsatisfactory place—but I was determined to fix it.

I had suggested before we left England that an inflatable mat would be a liability, but it had been given by another monk specifically for the journey and so he wanted to bring it. Inflatable mats are meant for domestic camp sites and not for sleeping outdoors in India, where it was soon punctured by thorns.

I showed the lad the mat, and he suggested that we take it to a shoe repairman. They are everywhere in India, ready to polish shoes, to repair them, or to repair anything else made of leather or canvas;

squatting on the pavement with the tools of their trade in a box by their side. The first one we stopped to ask was a young lad. He took the mat when I produced it, and I pointed out the two bicycle patches, now peeling off, and the small holes revealed beneath. I showed him how the mat inflated so that he could see why the holes were a problem. What he thought the mat was used for is anyone's guess. He lifted the patches and looked at the holes, felt the material, and then said something in Hindi pointing down the road. All I got was a word that went poly-something-or-other. The young lad explained that this was the glue we needed, and that a shoe repairman in the market had some. So we went to find him.

He was an older man squatting on a bit of pavement near where we had got off the bus. I went through the same pantomime, and then he produced a small battered round tin, which must once have had some foodstuff in it, but now had a couple of inches of dark treacly glue in the bottom. He took the patches off, cleaned them with a flat file and then spread some of the glue with a stick and his fingers around each hole. He waited for the glue to go tacky and then put the patches back on and for good luck walloped each of them with a hammer on a small anvil, which he held between his feet. I asked if I could buy the rest of the glue as insurance against future holes, but he was reluctant. I suppose he would have been parting with the small part of the local shoe repair market he had cornered.

I returned to collect Ajahn Sucitto, still the object of attention of several locals despite the fact that he had not moved for over an hour. We thanked our guide and set off for the stupa, which we could see looming up beyond the town. It was like the cremation stupa at Kushinagar, but bigger, a great dome of dull red bricks. There must once have been a surface layer of facing bricks, but they had now gone, and the exposed underlayers stepped upward haphazardly, with gaps of earth and grass, to the top.

The first thing I did when we got there was climb it. It was higher than the surrounding trees, and there were views all around. A slight breeze rustled the tree tops, the sun was about to set in the west, and the slanting light picked out a pair of nesting storks in the tree opposite. It was the half moon, and I reckoned this was going to be a great place to sit up until midnight—I wouldn't fall asleep here!

AJAHN SUCITTO

"Namo Buddhaya, Namo Dhammaya, Namo Sanghaya." Circumambulating the stupa, the syllables of the mantra of homage chiming in with each footstep, the still point reestablished itself in my heart; I felt grateful and refreshed as the bodily sensation and the mental giddiness ceased. Here, where the mantra turns, is the stupa, the sacred axis that is both the beginning and the end of the world, and the indicator of the path beyond. Around this axis three times the mantra led us; three times around the blackened brick mountain, and then into meditation on one of its terraces.

The stupa was higher than a large house, and must once have been higher to judge from the width of the base. Currently the grass that had covered it for centuries was being gradually picked off by workers from the Archaeological Survey of India. From the round summit that was the present peak of the stupa, I could see over the surrounding flat expanse of fields. India looked golden and benevolent; a slight breeze added to the softness of the late afternoon sun. The Ashokan pillar, a mile away, with the fair spread around it, looked like a set of toys abandoned by a child after play.

Why create monuments? Why drag fifty tons of pillar through two hundred miles of forest and erect it here? But why also the massive stupa—who built this here, some six or seven hundred years after Ashoka? Why the massive temples of ancient Mesopotamia, Egypt, or Mesoamerica, why the colossal stone Buddha images of China and Afghanistan?

"How?" is easy enough: as the Buddha commented, *"volition is action"*—what the will determines becomes a reality. What is significant is the view that determines that will. Nowadays our view is that sensory existence is the reality of life. Accordingly our technology shapes the world to make this sojourn on the planet as comfortable as possible. But in some societies mortal life is held to be essentially imperfect and part of a divine order that goes beyond death. The technology develops accordingly. Ashoka, a man, touched by nobility, attempted to establish his view in proclamation and edicts carved in stone.

> Beloved of the Gods speaks thus: Happiness in this world and the next is difficult to obtain without much love of Dhamma, much self-examination, much respect, much fear (of evil), and much enthusiasm. But through my instruction, this regard for Dhamma and love of Dhamma has grown day by day, and will continue to grow. And my officers of high, low, and middle rank are practising and conforming to Dhamma, and are capable of inspiring others to do the same...And these are my instructions: to protect with Dhamma, to make happiness through Dhamma, and to guard with Dhamma.
>
> ...noble deeds of Dhamma and the practise of Dhamma consist of having kindness, generosity, truthfulness, purity, gentleness, and goodness increase among the people.

For a pilgrim at least, India is still capable of manifesting Ashokan officers. At this juncture, it was Mr. Chaudry, the superintendent of the stupa. He was duty-bound to politely remind us that it was not allowed to spend the night on the ancient monument; however, when we had completed our evening meditation, he would put us up for the night. "I am house," he said modestly with a waggle of his head (Hindi has no word for "have," and uses the verb "to be" instead). We thought he would wait up for us and so cut our half-moon vigil short at ten-thirty. The smile and the waggle of the head were indeed patiently waiting by a small house near the stupa. They indicated some stone slabs for us to recline on outside the front door. In the morning they appeared in the company of glasses of hot tea.

It was Mr. Chaudry who retrieved my cantankerous sleeping mat. Having proved its unswerving hostility by deflating again in the night, the thing decided to make a break for it during our circumambulation following the morning puja. We returned to the terrace to find it gone. It was a relief to have one less performance to go through every day. But Dhamma rarely lets you off the hook so easily. Mr. Chaudry lined up his gang of blank-faced workers and made gentle enquiries. After a pause, somebody's arm came from behind his back with the wretched mat in his hand. Much smiling and head-waggling ensued, with Nick showing them the photos of England that we had brought (and handing over a photo of ourselves to our host). We noted Mr. Chaudry's name and address—it would be good to send him a letter when we returned to England. The mat promised to present further repetitions of the cycle of endeavour, expectation of comfort, and disappointment. But before it had the opportunity, we hitched a ride on a truck back to Bettiah in order to continue our walk south. There we met another officer of the law.

Mr. Mishra was the manager of the State Bank of India in Bettiah. As such, he arrived in an unhurried manner at the bank an hour or so after it opened. It was unusual to have two Englishmen in the bank, especially one with red hair and a beard and the other shaven-headed and wearing a brown robe. The bearded one, Dr. Scott, wanted to change a traveller's cheque—which was impossible as the branch was not authorized. It had been authorized once, but now it would be necessary to take a bus to Muzzaffapur, or to Patna. Dr. Scott however only had two rupees.

Mr. Mishra told one of the clerks to bring tea and listened to us talk about our pilgrimage, nodding slightly. Yes, it would not be possible to get to Muzzaffapur, let alone Patna, by means of two rupees. Occasionally throwing queries in Hindi to various clerks—who responded by bustling around with sheets of paper, which he stirred on his desk—he slowly and regretfully reiterated that the bank was not authorized to change traveller's cheques.

"You will be walking for six months? On foot?" "Yes, on foot. We have walked from Lumbini, in Nepal." "Ahchaa..." But my attention was resting on the Roman numerals of the office clock. Eleven o'clock: feeble speculations on food. However, Mr. Mishra's eyes, peering through the thick-rimmed spectacles, had a calming effect, and the scene seemed to be unfolding in some way; the scurrying of the clerks indicated that. There was some debate about exchange rates, while Mr. Mishra examined one of Nick's cheques. They used to be able to change traveller's cheques, he commented, but...and more, slightly heated, exchanges with the clerks...now it was not possible. When the hands of the clock moved past twelve I relaxed; we could forget about eating for the day. Waiting eventually cuts through the tendons of personal motivation and lets things take their natural course. Mr. Mishra's pen methodically wove across various papers, and a figure was produced. Nick signed his cheque and received the two hundred and something rupees. The conversation continued on various topics. Mr. Mishra, chin resting on one hand, woollen hat neatly balanced on his head, regretted that the bank was unable to change money, therefore he had given us two hundred rupees of his own money. He would try to get reimbursed by changing the cheque via the branch in Patna. Meanwhile, he wished us good fortune on our pilgrimage.

We walked out of Bettiah in the heat of the day, heading more or less south toward Lauriya Areraj, site of another Ashokan pillar, and Vaishali, the old capital of the republic of the Licchavis and a place much loved by the Buddha. The presence of the two Ashokan pillars suggests that this route might have been a pilgrim's way between Patna, Ashoka's capital, and the Buddhist holy places of Vaishali and Lumbini. Fa Hsien and Hsuan Tsiang might have proceeded along this very route in search of scriptures to bring back to China. To me, buoyed up spiritually by human benevolence and light-headed from the lack of food, it felt like a pilgrim's way. I let the mantra in my mind carry me along.

8

Cycles

AJAHN SUCITTO

November 26th. Another dark evening and we were still walking. Not that I was eager to get anywhere; everywhere we arrived seemed to display the same characteristics as the place we had just come from. Progress itself was more psychological than geographical: the land always looked much the same, in paddy fields stretched out and scantily decked with clumps of mango, banyan, and bodhi trees. On its stage the pujas, walking, going for alms, and occasional halts for tea came round repetitively.

Progress was a matter of being undone and swallowed by the forces around me: the bantering inner and outer voices, the sweat and grime, the grit in the throat. The balance came through simply focusing on these things. Through yielding into the dullness, my plodding assumed an oxlike doggedness, pushing steadily forward. Walking wove a net of assurance, giving me the semblance of control over my destiny. Even as the world flooded through me, I could take refuge in the appearance of being able to walk through and away from it. Rationally I knew better; there would be no getting away from the heat, the "Where are you going?"—the psychological chafing, bodily discomfort, and fatigue—except by ceasing to resist them. But such abandonment takes time.

When I contemplated the urge to keep going and questioned it, all the reasons and needs came down to one point: I want to escape being vulnerable. Let me find a place where I can close a door.

But on the open road of a pilgrimage, all the doors are open, and they do not open onto shrines and sunsets and peaceful places, only on more doors that gape as vacant as the stares and questions that you pass through. *"Kaha ja ra hai?"* "Where are you going?" The question penetrates. So you keep walking. Maybe the night will hide you.

The pivot of the day for us was the alms round, commenced by the ritual of adjusting my robes and slowing the pace. Alms faring makes you completely vulnerable to the unknown scene around you; it is time for realising humanity in a way that few people can. There was a kind of dignity in the humility of the lifestyle that the Buddha espoused.

> *They do not brood over the past,*
> *They do not hanker after the future,*
> *They live upon whatever they receive*
> *Therefore they are radiant.*

More than at any other time, on alms round I tried to walk the balance between the palpable agitation of Nick behind me and the uncertain attention of the village ahead. I centred on the bhikkhus' rules for alms gathering:

> *I shall go well restrained in inhabited areas, this is a training*
> *   to be done...*
> *I shall go with downcast eyes, this is a training to be done...*
> *I shall go with little sound in inhabited areas, this is a training*
> *   to be done...*

Sometimes we would leave the village only to be called back; sometimes the movement would naturally take us to a centre point beneath a tree or beside a shrine and leave us there. Sometimes the movement turned into chanting before it left us sitting in stillness. It could take a long while for the mind to give up and go still, but when we did, the bright signs appeared, and the event happened: bustling, beckoning, a hut, elders, a burlap sack on the earth floor and plates of leaves. A new anonymous friend emptied flakes of some grain *(chula)* onto the leaves and then ladled curd onto them from a goatskin bucket with his hand.

> *I shall accept the alms food appreciatingly...*
> *I shall eat the alms food appreciatingly...*
> *I shall eat the alms food with attention on the bowl...*
> *I shall not make up an extra large mouthful...*
> *I shall not eat stuffing out the cheeks...*
> *I shall not eat scraping the bowl with a finger, this is a training*
> *to be done.*

After the meal, we gave the blessing chant and a few words on peace, generosity, or on what we were doing. It brought me again to brightness, to the place of belonging to what is good and recognising its universality; and a little more of the hide around the heart would wear away. Because of this, it got easier to rest for a brief period in the middle of the day with a bunch of children squatting around me exchanging loud whispers, pointing at my heavy leather sandals and occasionally venturing into a few inquiries: "Where is your house?" Then we would just gaze at each other, though they could always stare longer than I: after all they had an answer.

We moved past Lauriya Areraj, an Ashokan pillar set back from the road with a sign that had completely rusted. Next to the untranslated Ashokan edict, a few people were hacking the limbs from a mango tree. The Ashokan ideal, with its exhortations to plant and protect trees, had long since gone. We stopped walking for a few minutes, but there was no stillness.

Night in a Shiva temple; a dusty windowless room was unlocked for us. Here Shiva was addressed as Pashupati—Lord of the Animals—a recollection of his pre-Vedic origins when he was Rudra, a fertility god in the ancient Mother Goddess religion of India. He was part of the old order that the Aryans overturned: they brought with them gods not born from Nature but subduing it. Yet the cycle always turns: as the Aryans settled into the agrarian culture, warrior deities lost their relevance, and their images could no longer command. So it was easy for the Buddha to mock and dethrone them all, condemning the sacrifice of animals and worship based on mere superstition. Even more humiliating, he allowed the Vedic gods a few walk-on parts in minor heavens of his cosmology of *samsara,* the realms beings cycle through while ensnared by dukkha. For a determined Buddhist, the heavens—of which there are many— are merely a phase in the cycle and grant no final release. The old gods died not from persecution but from ignominy. As part of the same movement away from the gods, the earliest of great spiritual poems called the Upanishads were already being recited in the Buddha's day. In a similar turning inward that placed the self-sacrifice of austerity above the sacrifice of animals, the Upanishads proclaimed a simple dualism between a transcendent God (Brahman) and Soul (Atman). Devotion to God was a primary means of attaining the bliss of transcendent unity; and by leaving the structure of family and caste undisturbed, such devotion was acceptable to the orthodox. But the cycle turned again: devotion and ritual require gods with forms, and so the formless God acquired many. So gods returned, though they were essentially different from the old Vedic deities. Brahma, and more vigorously Shiva and Vishnu, are transcendent and immanent: they are the creators of the cycle of existence as well as manifesting in forms that participate in it. As such they are aligned to that feminine power that gives birth, is sought after by its creations, consumes them, and gives birth again. Virgin, Madonna, and Dark Goddess. Shiva and Vishnu are male, though sinuous, forms, but their activities are characteristic channels for Goddess-energy.

Vishnu is the recumbent dreamer from whose navel a lotus buds and opens to reveal Brahma, the creator of the universe. Brahma opens his eye and a world system is born; he closes it and the world ends. A thousand of those births and deaths constitute a day in Brahma's life; 360 of those days make up a year; after one hundred of those years and a vast carnival of world systems, of heroes and wars and glory and decay, the world-play is over. World-creating Brahma, and the lotus, are drawn back into the body of Vishnu, until the next dream sends forth a new lotus. Meanwhile Vishnu manifests in the world, in mortal male forms—such as Krishna and Rama—whose purpose is to defend, or reestablish, true dharma.

Some of Shiva's roles display the same female knowledge, and his consorts are powerful and greatly revered. Shiva is the turner of the cycle of creation and destruction, of fertility and death. Shiva is Nataraja, the supreme dancer, whose dancing brings the created world to its end. In another turn he is trampled under the feet of his ferocious consort Kali, who represents time, death, and destruction. Shiva's forms are *maya*, illusion; Shiva's energy, his *shakti*, is the weaver and destroyer of the play, and it is female.

After a night in the utter, windowless dark, morning came, and with it this flowerlike world and the new celebration. The temple priest, freshly bathed, in spotless white dhoti and groomed hair, lovingly attended Shiva's image like a bride, bathing it with pure water and decking it with blossoms as he rang the god's bells and sang a lilting hymn. I knelt nearby, watching. Could it be that to celebrate the play of the world is the way to transcend it?

NICK

Our daily alms rounds were a very good learning experience for me. Day after day, I'd fail. I would try to walk into the village, five steps or so behind Ajahn Sucitto, slowly and calmly keeping my eyes on the ground. I would try, but in no time I would be looking over his shoulder trying to spot the best possible place to stop. I had quickly learned that we got better food from the big brick houses in the middle of the villages with the T.V. aerials on their roofs than from the mud huts on the village edge. My mind would start yammering, and I would often end up trying to give advice. "Ah, Bhante, that looks a good place over there," mentioning a little temple or tree that just so happened to be in the middle of the village and next to some big houses. Afterward I would resolve to show more restraint next time, usually to no avail.

Once we had stopped and sat, my mind would calm. There was nothing left to do, we could only be open and wait. My mind, so intent on the outcome, would be right there in the moment. Waiting, not knowing, is powerful. When someone did offer us food it would be such a beautiful blessing.

The offering would manifest in so many different ways that my mind could never predict how it would be. There was one infallible rule, however: whoever first asked us would be the one to feed us. No matter if there were a hundred people around us, or whether the asker was rich or poor. No matter if all they did was ask if we had eaten—even if others asked whether we ate rice, chappatis, and so on—it was now that person's duty, and duty is a very powerful thing in India.

To begin with we weren't having breakfast, for Ajahn Sucitto had wanted us to live on one meal a day, as the Buddha had recommended his followers to do when possible. So that one meal was often it! Whatever we were given would have to last us the next twenty-four hours. As we went on, that resolve slowly got worn away by my offers to stop at a tea stall in the mornings and then perhaps to have a little something with the tea. If there is an Achilles' heel in Ajahn Sucitto's ascetic armour, it is his fondness for tea.

Tea stalls are everywhere in India, erected wherever there is the opportunity to make a small living from passing trade. Cobbled together out of planks, plastic sheeting, and anything else that comes to hand, they do not seem much to us, but to the owner they are their life. They live and work in them, willing to make tea at any time of day or night. At least one member of the family, if not all of them, will sleep there to protect their meagre investment.

There was a tea stall that morning. It may well have been because we had been living on such meagre rations for the last few days, but to me it seemed a fine example of the genre. It was neatly turned out with two benches either side of the main table and protected by a blue plastic awning. The table had a clean blue-and-white checked plastic cloth on it and a neat row of small dishes containing brightly coloured snacks. Everything was tidy and the ground round it had been recently swept. The owner sat with a welcoming smile at one end, his son beside him stoking the small clay fireplace with a few sticks. We ordered two teas.

It comes as a surprise to us English that in India, the land of tea, they do not make it the way we do. Instead, water, milk, sugar, and some fine tea dust (presumably cheaper than the tea leaves India exports to the rest of the world) is brought to boil in a small saucepan over a fire. A little spice is usually included as well, cardamom or perhaps a small piece of ginger. Once boiled, the mixture is strained through a muslin cloth into small glasses. All over India the price for a glass of tea was one rupee; what varied was how much tea one got and how good it was.

The tea at this stall was particularly good, as were the small plates of curried chickpeas that Ajahn Sucitto agreed to have with it. The father and son were friendly and attentive, and when we left I was so taken with their little stall that I wrote out a sign which read, "THE BEST TEA SHOP IN THE WORLD" and showed them how it should be fixed to the front of the stall. They were pleased—even though they could not speak a word of English.

The tea stall was where a road came up and over the bund. On the way from the river to Udaipur sanctuary, I had noticed this huge dyke built by the British to retain the Great Gandak in flood. It was my map which called it a bund, and showed that it followed the river south to where it joined the Ganges some five days' walking away. I suggested we could try walking on it, as it might be better than the road and it should give some great views of the river and its wildlife. I was right, it was good walking. The bund meandered through the paddy fields, its sides planted long ago with trees that gave us shade, and there was a well-worn path along the top, which was used as a local highway by people on foot and bicycle. There were no noisy lorries or buses, no need to map read, and there were even mile posts for counting off our progress. It was the best walking we had had. Ajahn Sucitto was obviously enjoying it, the simplicity of it allowed him to use the walking as a meditation. He would get so absorbed and reluctant to stop that he would even miss someone offering us tea. For me though there was only one problem. The bund, more than half a mile from the river, offered no view of either it or its wildlife.

As we walked along the bund, we had an overview of the surrounding land. We were some thirty feet up on the only piece of higher land, passing through a vast flatness of chequered fields, villages dotted everywhere. Most of the villages were on the side of the bund away from the river, protected from its flooding, and tracks came up and over the bund to their fields on the other side.

There were also occasional small communities on the top of the bund, which we would pass close to throughout the day. At first light there was the pungent smoke from small fires lit outside front doors, with much of the family squatting around them warming themselves, their tethered animals snorting plumes of white vapour. No adult women were to be seen though; presumably they were inside preparing the first meal. Later we would see the people making their way to the fields, herding their cows and water buffalos ahead of them. Around ten-thirty the people returned alone for their midday meal, and they would be back again with their animals well before sundown. Each hut would then have at least one cow or water buffalo outside munching and snorting at raised troughs made of the same grey mud as the huts and filled with chopped green straw—the stalks of the last harvested crop—mixed with water. The animals were such an integral part of their lives and so important in extracting the maximum from the land that I could see why the Hindus had come to worship the cow.

The land we were passing now would be very productive, the soils fertilized every year by the silt left by the flooding Gandak, and with water readily available from the river or from a water table near to the surface. It all seemed very green and prosperous, looking down on it from the bund. The only wildlife we saw though were birds: a few small birds in the trees, and little egrets and paddy birds in the wetter fields. Both of these are small herons that stalk the rice fields of India hunting small fish. The little egrets are all white, while the paddy birds look a dull brown in the fields, but when taking off, their white wings give the same effect as those of the egrets—a flutter of white looking like large white handkerchiefs suddenly caught in a breeze.

Walking on the bund was enjoyable, but I could not get out of my mind the idea of the Great Gandak so near by. I kept looking for a glimpse of it but to no avail. The idea of this big river I imagined full of wildlife was calling me, and on the second day I could not resist any longer. I suggested we try walking by the river; the excuse was that the bund took a couple of turns and by cutting across to the river we might take a shortcut. The suggestion did not go down well, but Ajahn Sucitto reluctantly agreed. We set off across the fields on a path that was going just the right way...at least initially. After a bit it took a turn, and then a while later a couple more. And slowly, creeping up on me, came this feeling that we were lost. I could find neither the river nor our way. Unlike rivers in England, the Gandak's edge was undefined. There were wetlands, grassland, and sandbanks, but no path wandering along the bank as I had imagined. Eventually, with me suitably chastened, we had to double back to the bund having lost half a day's walking.

The third day on the bund we stopped at sunset to do our puja and meditation before dark. We sat on the grassy bank with a view across fields to some vultures that had collected near the carcass of a dead cow. Village dogs were at the carcass, snarling at the vultures if they came too close. So they stood, stared, and waited, hopping backward when growled at. Thus ends the lives of all farm animals in rural India. In the same way that animals ignore their dead, no longer relevant to the living, Indians abandon their dead and dying farm stock to be recycled by the dogs, hyenas, and vultures.

Despite the interest of the distant scene we were facing and the sinking sun beyond it, I was disturbed as usual. On this pilgrimage I never got that sense of oneness with nature that I associated with walking in England. I heard the murmuring of voices this time behind us up on the bund. I stopped myself looking round but I could not relax. When we finished and turned to climb back up the slope, a small crowd had assembled, including two better-dressed men with a moped between them. I walked up to the path in a negative state. Why do they have to stand there and look at us? Can't they see that we want to be left alone!

AJAHN SUCITTO

November 29th. At the end of a shining day, the red sun was swollen and sinking on the horizon; its final gaze was cast over the life-death business of some dogs disputing the remains of an ox or a buffalo with a gang of vultures. It was time for us also to sit on the earth and be gazed at. We were just off the bund, so obviously we were going to attract people, and, anticipating Nick's reaction, I thought that chanting the Metta Sutta might create the kind of space that would keep things tranquil:

> Whatever living beings there may be,
> Whether they are weak or strong, omitting none,
> The great or the mighty, medium, short or small,
> The seen and the unseen, those living near or far away,
> Those born and to-be-born—may all beings be at ease!

The suppressed chattering behind us and the agitation beside me became more turbulent; so we turned. Up on the bank a gaggle of youths and men were looking on with excitement. Two men dressed in the Indian "Western" style were wreathed in smiles, one supporting a moped, the other jigging up and down in rapture:

"We are very happy to see you! We are very pleased to see such devotions that you are doing! It makes us very happy, very, very happy!" His cycling companion's smile widened into a beam spreading across his smooth bespectacled countenance. It was the dancer however who was the man of words—a torrent in fact, a rhapsody of delight:

"We are very much appreciating such noble activity and expression. It gives us such great happiness to see you!" He actually wriggled with glee; infectious stuff that brightened even Nick's tetchy reactions. The dancer introduced himself as Naval Kishore Singh, and his friend on Hero-Honda motorcycle as Mr. Teewali. Mr. T. was silent, but affirmative smiles underlined his broad glossy brow. They were both schoolteachers. Mr. Singh taught English and very much admired Shakespeare —he was certainly too large in gesture to be properly savoured offstage. Mr. Teewali taught science and was, we were dramatically assured by Mr. Singh, "of very noble character. He has *great* affection for his children! He is very, very affectionate toward them!"

Mr. Singh's body seemed to operate in a different gear from his words. Although each sentiment was proclaimed with great emphasis, his body, head lowered and thrust forward, brows puckered, adopted the posture of someone imparting a confidence. But when I slipped in an enquiry as to whether he had a religious practise, whether he did pujas or worshipped God at some times, the covers came off. "I am *always* worshipping my Lord! All day I am praising my Lord! I sing, I dance!" Sympathetically, the body squirmed with consummate glee.

Fortunately his partner of glowing brow, whose beam broadened to the point at which the lower part of his face seemed in danger of falling off, imparted a moonlike serenity to the dance. In fact, it was Mr. Teewali who by some slight gesture and inaudible phrase got us moving: myself, Nick, with Mr. Singh importuning us to stay at his house, himself and the Hero-Honda (which turned out to be in some minor state of disrepair), and a dwindling group of lesser characters ambling along the bund in the evening. Nick kept declining the offers firmly and explaining with calm authority that we were pilgrims and that meant sleeping outside; this only served to heighten the rhetoric that accompanied the invitations. Eventually Mr. Teewali dropped off with the bike, and Mr. Singh disappeared. We strode into the dusk looking for a tree to camp under, not very far before Mr. Singh returned solo with redoubled pleas—it was his *duty*, he must perform his *duty*, otherwise he would be a disgrace. But we were bound to homelessness. Nick's ploy was adept and delivered squarely and with majesty. "You have done your duty! We are very grateful. You have offered us your hospitality. You have done your duty very well! We thank you! Now we must go." Turning back to the path and striding on he seemed to have stopped the show.

Until the next morning, as we passed through a village: Mr. Singh was at the gate of his house, ecstatic and calling us in with siren songs of food. The love of solitude and homelessness capsized with the first few bars of the song. After all, we were alms mendicants, and our duty was to receive offerings. On the veranda in the front yard of the large house was a group of Mr. Singh's associates, fellow thinkers and philosophers, and a pot of milky tea. Here was Mr. Singh's nephew, voluble but bitter—a commentator on the political scene. Another seemed to be dozing in a chair until Nick began inquiring about plants, and he reeled off, in a monotone, the name of every species in the surrounding landscape. Then entered the smiling wife ("We have great affection for each other! Great affection!") bustling in from the kitchen area with two plates of hot, tasty parothas and mango and lime pickles ("She is very *cunning!*")—enough to give any homeless wanderer serious doubts about the alleged unsatisfactoriness of the household life. Down went those parothas four apiece, and as the plates emptied before our appetites, the daughters, correctly interpreting the feebleness of our protests, appeared, to top them up with more even fresher and more succulent parothas straight from the pan; five, then six, and more tea, while the thinkers and Nick exchanged ruminations on plants and land and the state of India.

It was the transcendent Mr. Teewali who appeared again with moped and smile to signal the end of the cycle. I never heard him utter a word, but whispers were made in the ear of Mr. Singh, who realised, ecstatically, that he was late for school. Rather than precipitating action, this lateness seemed to be recognized merely as a state of being as worthy of celebration as any other. Perhaps it was Nick who brought down the curtain by having Messrs. Singh and Teewali pose for a photograph standing on either side of the repaired motorcycle. Bringing the Hero-Honda into the picture turned the balance: devotion to the formless now turned into right action as, waving enthusiastically, the pair roared out of the gate and back up the bund.

NICK

As we went on that morning I thought over what had been said by one of the teachers, the one we later agreed was the dormouse in this mad hatter's tea party. Mr. Singh had introduced him with the same enthusiasm he had for everything; he was a teacher of biology, "and a most splendid one," he told us, but I could get little out of him. That was until I hit on asking him if he knew the names of any of the plants. Then, as he recited the names of everything we could see, I was struck by how he could also say what everything was used for. I began to realise that we were looking at an entirely manmade landscape.

The land we were walking through was some of the most fertile land in India. It was beside one of the big rivers, and it would have been cultivated since well before the time of the Buddha, perhaps for five thousand years. As a result everything I could see growing was there for a purpose. Maybe not everything had been planted, but it all must have been tolerated for a very long time. That, I realised, was why there had been so little wildlife about. The Indians may have a good attitude to living creatures, not killing them unnecessarily and not eating them, but their intense management of this land meant no wild habitat remained for the wild animals to live in. In nearly two weeks of being outdoors every day and night, we had seen just one small group of chital and a mongoose. I would see much more than that walking for a day anywhere in England. The only wildlife in any numbers were birds—they are able to live with so much human activity.

I could not help but notice on the map that just before we left the bund, after four days' walking, we would at last be right next to the Great Gandak. That morning, an hour or so after leaving Mr. Singh, we came round a bend and were suddenly on a cliff being eroded by the river, trees behind, for once no one in sight, and the Gandak slipping slowly and mightily, full of silt, past us. It was the time of our normal morning stop, and Ajahn Sucitto agreed that this would be a good place. So we sat overlooking the great river. Downstream sailing boats were hauled up on a wooden jetty, and across the river, on the distant bank, grazed flocks of ducks and greylag geese. This is what I had been looking for. My heart trembled. At last. Sitting by the river feeling at one with it all…

"Shall we go on?" We had had our standard fifteen-minute stop it seemed, and my companion, as ever a chap of unwavering application, knew it was time to set off. I could have asked to stay, but that kind of thing is never the same if one tries to hold on to it. So we got up and went on. After just a few hundred yards, our route led away, and we turned inland never to see India's Great Gandak again.

We joined a small road heading east and were soon engulfed by a flock of boys on bicycles. There were thirty or more of them coming home from school, and as each caught us up they slowed to stare. As usual with lads of that age, they were not really interested in trying to interact with us, just curious about us as objects. They discussed us, laughed at us, and occasionally one of them would try out one of the English questions they had learned in school. We tried to ignore them, but it's difficult to ignore thirty boys trying to cycle along with you. They were bumping into each other and regularly wobbling across our path. It was midday, my most intolerant time, so I began to get annoyed. We tried walking more slowly. In response they slowed to our new pace, wobbling even more. So we slowed to little more than a crawl, and they started to really wobble and bump into each other. They kept it up for a while but it wasn't much fun, and slowly ones and twos began to break off and cycle on.

Eventually all had gone and it seemed we could walk on in peace. Then we came round a corner to find one of them outside his home, calling all his family and neighbours to see us go past, and for the next half hour each group of houses along the road would have one or two of the boys outside calling out to everyone to come see the two strange men walking down the road.

The last of the spectators were at the junction with a more major road. Our road continued on the other side, but it was no longer covered with tarmac and there were no houses and few people on it. With a sense of relief we crossed the major road and took to the dirt. By mid afternoon we were walking along a quiet slightly meandering track and passing through what must have been poorer land, as it was rough grazing dotted with shrubs and small trees. There was a glade amid it and amazingly no one in sight. It looked an ideal place to have a short rest, so we turned off the road and tucked ourselves into a corner that could not be seen from anywhere. We thought we had finally done it. Found somewhere we could be left alone. Ajahn Sucitto got his diary out and I got out some sewing that needed doing, and we settled back. No one would find us here!

Within three minutes, one man had somehow seen us and stopped. He was then spotted by others passing, and within fifteen minutes we had a crowd of a dozen plus two bicycles and a water buffalo one of them had been herding. They stood in a half circle and at a respectful distance discussing us quietly, while the water buffalo stood munching and letting out the occasional burst of urine.

Nowhere in this land was away from people. The analogy we came up with at the time was walking across a city park on a sunny Sunday afternoon: you might think you had spotted a quiet corner with no one in it, but when you got there, someone was always there. To make it worse we were like the ice cream van—wherever we went the people clustered around us.

We gave up on our peaceful glade and made our way on. We still had a long way to go to get to Vaishali that night. Sitting in the shade of the glade, the afternoon autumn heat of India had been pleasant, but back on the road it was oppressive. My mind turned to the idea of tea, as it so often did in the afternoons.

By this point in the walk the lovely Indian milky tea I had been buying in the afternoon was coming to an end. Milk was quite clearly classed as food in the monastic rules and so not supposed to be consumed after noon. Faced with the difficulty of getting tea without milk in India, other Western monks had given in. But not Ajahn Sucitto. To begin with he went along with their precedent but then discovered with his growing Hindi and enough effort he could get the chai wallah to make black tea. I dutifully followed his lead but could never quite summon the determination in my efforts to get the man to understand, and as a result it often still came with milk. My heart was obviously not in it.

The way Ajahn Sucitto would accept milky tea without a fuss was when someone else offered it; he did not want to reject their kind gesture. So I was often looking out for possible offers of tea. That afternoon as our dirt track passed through villages I started looking for invitations. I walked along attuned to any possibility, smiling at any likely offerers. Amazing how my attitude to the local people could change! The same people who could vex me so with their repetitive questions would seem completely different were they likely to offer milky tea.

AJAHN SUCITTO

Writing it all down helped to keep the events experienced within some wholeness, some continuum. Without something constant to refer to, we'd all go crazy. I suppose most people use their homes, relationships, or self-image as the stable reference point. In order to have some stable reference through the many changes of the pilgrimage, I tried to encompass every effort, and every person involved, with a blessing. Every day, I would devote the effort of the walking to all the people that I had contact with so that something in us would move together on this journey for a while. My way of engaging with the changing hosts would be to take them into my mind and heart and record a few images in the little ochre-silk-bound book. That act connected them to the circle of Sangha that I was writing for. In a way it hardly mattered how accurately anyone else could receive those images; at least the cycle of watching and connecting encouraged my heart.

Here are a few fragments that still remain: "30. Meal with Naval, +nephew +dormouse. Saw Gandak. Bike mob. Devata Bakhra > Vaishali."

The day's events hit us in different ways and brought up contrary responses. I'd slow down and talk when Nick felt like speeding up and getting away, he'd sit and linger when I felt like moving on. We were like a bike whose wheels were turned by different gears. But in the evenings the gears had stopped whirring—there was less happening and we were tired out. The road had worn the two of us into a kind of dumb unity; again it was just the darkness and the walking. Yes, the evenings: the feeling that the challenges of the day were nearing an end, and the possibility of finding a place to stop and re-centre ourselves. And this end-of-November evening, as the pilgrimage came toward another full moon, Vaishali hoved into the reach of our fond expectations of peace and reason.

Another man with a bike, a scooter this time, was waiting where the road wound through the ruts, crumpled straw, and buffalo dung that signified a collection of human lives called Bakhra. At the sight of duty to be performed, he turned his scooter in the opposite direction to the way he had been going and insisted on guiding us, accompanying us for the best part of an hour, taking us to a chai shop for tea, and setting us on the good road to Vaishali. "Here there will be no bandits," he proclaimed, and turned back again, leaving us to the ongoing way. The moon glowed like Mr. Teewali's brow, surely growing fuller by the minute.

9

The Deathless Drum

AJAHN SUCITTO

Vaishali was the site of many of the Buddha's teachings and where, at the Capala shrine, he determined to let his life finish. They say the earth quaked. The accounts say that he would have held on to his life force "until the end of the aeon" if requested, but the faithful Ananda missed the chance. Here the Buddha, having just recovered from a severe illness, eighty years old and worn, said that he would pass away after three months.

> *Ripe I am in years. My lifespan's determined.*
> *Now I go from you, having made myself my refuge.*
> *Bhikkhus, be untiring, mindful, disciplined,*
> *Guarding your minds with well-collected thought.*
> *He who, tireless, keeps to Dhamma and Vinaya,*
> *Leaving birth behind will put an end to dukkha.*

To us, Vaishali seemed like a good place for a rest, and for the all-night meditation vigil of the full moon of December. We reckoned on needing a day or so to regenerate some energy for the vigil. Therefore, we had pushed the pace a little to get there a couple of days before the full moon. Nick had the information that the only vihara in Vaishali was a temple of the Nipponzan Myohoji sect. Being Japanese, it was bound to be quiet and clean.

The last miles on the road seemed endless; we had been going vigorously with only brief pauses for about eleven hours since Mr. Singh's protracted breakfast. We hadn't even stopped for food. The sun had long gone down and the monotonous road and the rhythm of walking had merged into a hologram of fatigue in which the mind lost the ability to measure time or distance. There was just the pounding of the road and the mantra leading onward like some unstoppable dirge. We were so numb and Vaishali so small that we might have stomped past it in the dark but for a rectangular expanse of dark water wherein blazed the great moon. And the small white temple was right beside it, white and cool and still, a neat notice on its gate, and inside an immaculate shrine with great glowing Buddhas and a photo of the founder of the Nipponzan Myohoji, Reverend Nichidatsu Fuji, on the shrine. A broad smile beamed over his hands joined in anjali to greet us; fluffy white eyebrows danced like cirrus clouds above a face shining with well-being. The drum that played a central part in their ritual stood to one side of the shrine. We paid our respects and waited for the host.

At the time of the Buddha, Vaishali was the capital of the Licchavi republic, which together with the republic of the Videhas made up the Vajjian confederacy. They say that the Buddha was impressed with Vaishali—it was a beautiful spot, and the people who lived there had a form of government that was democratic by nature, being made up of leaders elected from the aristocratic class. It probably reminded him of his homeland, which was ruled in a similar way. However, although the Buddha had no illusions about the pride and stubbornness of his own people, he had nothing but praise for the Licchavis. Unlike his own people, they had offered him hospitality at the numerous shrines in their republic, and had taken to heart his advice on statecraft:

*Once...when I was at the Sarandada Shrine in Vesali, I taught the
Vajjians these seven principles for preventing decline, and as long as
they keep to these seven principles, as long as these principles remain
in force, the Vajjians may be expected to prosper and not decline.*

The Buddha also directly related the "seven principles" to the har-
monious functioning of the spiritual fraternity. Briefly stated, that
advice was the following: to meet frequently; to meet in harmony, carry
out business in harmony, and depart in harmony; to refrain from author-
izing what had not been authorized, and not to abolish what had been
authorized; to honour and respect the elders, and listen to their advice;
to maintain good conduct with regard to women; to honour and respect
their holy places; and to look after spiritual sages. These "seven principles," the Buddha assured the chief minister of Magadha, would make
the Vajjians impossible to defeat should Ajatasattu, the aggressive king
of Magadha, wage war on them. For the Sangha, the Buddha modified
these principles to include exhortations to live simply in the forest, to
sustain mindfulness, to avoid getting caught up in building projects, to
avoid too much social chitchat, to share whatever one had with fellow
samanas, and so on. With this way of living, the Buddha reminded his
disciples, the Sangha might be expected to prosper and not to decline.
With these principles established, and the many teachings he had given,
the Buddha felt that he could pass away, with encouragement to his disciples to *"live as lanterns unto yourselves, with no one else as your refuge, with
the Dhamma as your lantern and refuge, with no other refuge."*

Soon after the Buddha's demise, the Vajjians were conquered by
Ajatasattu. Paying heed to the Buddha's words to them, the king
employed a strategy of infiltrating agents who stirred up discord
amongst the Licchavis. With their harmony gone, they were easy prey.
However, the Sangha is still around, at least in an outward form; the
Vinaya's requirement that the Sangha discusses its business in an assembly and makes its decisions by unanimous consent has held it together.

There are also large-scale meetings: a hundred years or so after the death of the Buddha, a Sangha Council met at Vaishali to come to a agreement over some matters of discipline, and this, which has subsequently been called "The Second Buddhist Council," continued a tradition of large-scale meetings on such matters that has gone on ever since (the Sixth was in 1954). So despite the fact that gaining support from established secular powers throughout Asia has rendered the Sangha vulnerable to the corruptions of wealth and power, wherever there is a teaching and a training in accordance with the "seven principles," a Sangha community manifests in an authentic way.

The Vinaya training was something that I was particularly conscious of and grateful for, having spent the first couple of years as a bhikkhu with very little understanding of Sangha life. Ajahn Sumedho, whom I subsequently met by chance in Northern Thailand, had on the other hand received a superb spiritual education from the forest master Venerable Ajahn Chah, and it showed in terms of patience, kindness, and the ability to let go—things much easier said than done. Our paths had crossed again when I returned to England and found him carrying out the traditional bhikkhu training in a town house in London. Strangely enough the Vinaya made even more sense there; outside of a Buddhist culture, if you don't fully understand the aims of the training, life as a bhikkhu seems a meaningless anachronism. You lose perspective on what the symbol of the renunciant stands for and brings into the world. Most bhikkhus who have not cultivated the discipline reflectively go off the rails or disrobe when coming to the West, and I got pretty close myself. If it had not been for Ajahn Sumedho's example, I would never have developed the scope of my practise beyond that of meditation exercises. But the Buddha taught a complete way of life. The Vinaya's steady light had made it possible to live this uncertain life as a pilgrimage; now it was guiding us around the Buddha's land: the scrupulousness, the renunciation, and the fellowship that it engendered were the reason and the means whereby I came to be here. Vinaya was a way of enhancing beautiful qualities: care of the sick, respect for the elders, support of lay followers, the honour of serving the Dhamma.

The Sangha at Vaishali was currently Reverend Reiji Nakazoto and an Indian attendant. The Japanese monk's English was not great, but about as good as ours was in our evening, brain-dead state. Polite silences and gestures and tea seemed very pleasant. He had received my letter from Lumbini. It seemed that people did not normally stay at the temple, but as I was a monk ... Unfortunately the temple was about to undertake a seven-day regime of refraining from eating and drinking, so there would be no food as of tomorrow. According to Japanese tradition, the Buddha was enlightened on December 8th, and so they fast during the immediately preceding week.

Well, that was great timing on our part. Not even *water!* No water, he explained, but on the fourth day they took some noodle mush and green tea to clean out the system. And the regime would include continual drumming and mantra recitation from an hour before dawn until an hour after sunset. Of course, we were not obliged to join in ... but next morning we found that joining in was hardly a matter of choice.

WHUMP! WHUMP! WHUMP! WHUMP WHUMP! WHUMP! WHUMP! WHUMP! "NAM MYO HO RENGE KYO! NAM MYO HO RENGE KYO!" The shrine room of the tiny temple was on the other side of the wall from our beds. Drumming being the support for the principle practise of Nipponzan Myohoji, the drum was huge and attended with all the fervour it takes to sustain a seven-day fast, or a thousand-mile peace pilgrimage (also a major part of their practise), or to construct beautiful peace pagodas in places throughout the world— all done with total self-sacrificing commitment. People pointed askance to the huge scars that many of the monks bore as a result of strapping bundles of incense to their arms, setting fire to them, and sustaining the burning of their own flesh by fanning the glowing joss sticks. This apparently, was an act of penance or of offering of their lives to the Buddha.

Not what the Buddha taught, people say. But the drum and the mantra override that. WHUMP! WHUMP! WHUMP! WHUMP WHUMP! WHUMP! WHUMP! WHUMP! "NAM MYO HO RENGE KYO! NAM MYO HO RENGE KYO!" WHUMP! WHUMP! WHUMP!

And when your head is a few feet away from it, there's not a lot of room for thought. The skin vibrates with the rhythm, whether the thinking joins in or not. According to Nichiren, the monk-teacher who established this mantra practise in thirteenth-century Japan, *Nam Myo Ho Renge Kyo* (Homage to the White Lotus of the Good Law) is the heart of the Buddha's teaching, you can forget the rest. Drumming certainly makes forgetting very easy. During our stay in Vaishali, Buddhist activity could be summed up as the dawn breaking with the mantra and the sun setting to the pounding of the drum.

For the first day, activity of any kind was minimal. We lay there being pounded for a few hours until Nick dredged up the motivation to go and search for food. He returned some hours later, having had to sit down and rest every hundred yards or so, with snacks that he had bought in the nearby market. I don't remember the rest of the day, except that, as a gesture of harmony, we decided to join in the mantra sessions for the hour before dawn and the hour after sunset every day. It helped us maintain a fitting forgetfulness.

The drummers were still going strong into their second day as we made it out of the temple to a chai shop down on the main road. The drumming, although resounding over the entire area, was less dominant there, and Indian life was meandering along oblivious to the spiritual energy that was relentlessly resounding. There was a tourist information office with old posters on the wall and a few brochures about Varanasi and Uttar Pradesh. We had seen that there was a museum on the other side of the tank, and we already had a map showing the site of an ancient stupa. The museum was closed, and we didn't have the energy to get out to the stupa. Nick ambled off to survey a mound; I slowly made it back to the temple to write a letter to the

Sangha at Amaravati. Until after sunset, salutations to the white lotus continued to pour forth.

NICK

The afternoon of the second day I wanted to write some letters home. The constant drumming made it impossible in the temple—it was hard even to think, let alone compose a letter. So I went off to find somewhere quiet and out of the way. The mound I headed for had one of the small blue enamelled signs that say in English and Hindi that the site is of archaeological importance and is not to be damaged. It seemed a very inadequate defence against the forces of destruction: the sign was dwarfed by the large flat mound and so worn that most of the Hindi part could not be made out. Not that many of the local people would have been able to read it anyhow—Bihar has the lowest literacy rate in India.

The mound was covered with archaeological excavations. Most of them were old, and the exposed dull orange brickwork was beginning to crumble away. A few were apparently still in progress with fencing round them, though no one was to be seen working. In the distant corner a small group of trees sheltered a building that looked like an abandoned temple. Built of brick, it had a large wooden door covered with carvings, so worn that I took it at first to be simply rough wood. I sat in the shade of the trees looking across the plain to the south and west. The mound was at most only twenty feet high, but in the Ganges plain that is ten feet above most anything else, and the views were excellent. It was a great place but I still could not write. I was feeling lethargic and uninterested in anything that required the slightest effort. At the previous holy sites we had been like that, but this time it was much worse, and it was taking much longer to pass.

Eventually I got out a leaflet from Vaishali's one-man tourist office. I reckoned I could manage that; there was little to it, just a title for each place of note, with a line of information. It told me of a mound called the Raja Vishalka Garh, which had once been the great assembly hall of the Vajjians. It dawned on me that I was sitting on the meeting hall of the oldest known democracy in the world. This was where the 7,707 representatives of the Vajjian confederacy had met at the time of the Buddha to discuss the problems of the day.

When the confederacy fell to Magadha, the mound I was on became a palace (the present name means House of Vaishali's King) and finally a fortress. Last century, Sir Alexander Cunningham recorded towers on the four corners, but they were gone by my visit—to make more houses in the local villages I expect. Around the mound must once have been the city of the Licchavis; the ruins were probably still there buried under the twenty-five centuries of deposited silt. But there is so much history in India: the tourist leaflet, as well as describing the Buddhist remains, also mentioned that Vaishali had been the birthplace of Lord Mahavira, the founder of the Jain religion, and the temple that I was sitting beside was in fact the tomb of a famous Sufi saint. It in turn was on a slightly higher part of the mound that had once been another Buddhist stupa. And this was just one place: there are so many ruins scattered about the Ganges plain. Sitting on that mound looking out over that vast plain, I got my first real sense of the enormous weight of history that had passed. For tens of thousands of years people have been living there. Empires have come and gone, invaders have conquered and been assimilated. Cultures have flourished and died. Each has built, and their buildings have crumbled, the remains slowly being buried in layers of silt.

The stark landscape with just the occasional tree contrasted so much with the description of Vaishali left in the Buddhist scriptures. In that era, to the north of Vaishali lay the Mahavana, the Great Forest, which extended to the foothills of the Himalayas, covering much of the cultivated land we had spent the last month crossing. Vaishali had room around it then, so that the land need not be so intensively used. The scriptures describe the city as being "charming with beds of flowers in her numerous gardens and groves." Vaishali must have been beautiful. Now the mound was just a piece of communal grazing land, and the locals were so crowded together and mostly so poor that it is all they can do just to survive.

On my way across the mound I had passed women out collecting grass for their animals. I had trouble at first making out what they were doing, as they were not using knives but trowels. Then I realised that the grass was so closely cropped that the only way they could collect any was to scrape it up. So they were squatting, bent over, and scraping up the few small grass plants left, while slowly making their way crablike across the ground. The results of their efforts followed behind each of them—a small pile of grass on an opened piece of cloth, which would eventually be wrapped up and carried home on their heads.

AJAHN SUCITTO

"NAM MYO HO RENGE KYO! NAM MYO HO RENGE KYO!" WHUMP! WHUMP! WHUMP! WHUMP WHUMP! WHUMP! WHUMP! WHUMP!

We were all sitting in the shrine room before the glowing Buddhas. It was not yet dawn on the third thumping day. The Japanese monk was at the big drum, the Indian, apparently training for the monkhood, was using a small handheld disk over which a skin was stretched; the mantra painted on the skins in beautiful Japanese calligraphy danced to the rhythmic pounding. You had to hand it to them, they weren't holding anything back. The drumsticks lunged into the skins as the mantra roared, rasping out of their throats time and time again. The pounding was in unison; the drawn-out moan of the mantra gripped now the Indian, now the Japanese, while the other sucked in air. Were they chanting for World Peace or for Enlightenment? Whatever the apparent purpose, it justified itself as a manifestation of single-mindedness and energy. Whether it led to transcendence, you'd have to find out for yourself. I found the implications of that resolve, and the unreasoning energy behind it, rather frightening. The kar sevak we had seen at Lucknow station had that kind of energy in a less organized way; then there were the suicide squads and martyrs who made a purpose into a cause. Human will has an alarming power. Nick joined in, but to me it wasn't the kind of thing I could do without meaning. So I sat in my Theravada non-alignment, listening, feeling the energy, and meditating on it.

Meditation, wrote Most Reverend Fuji in one of the books around the temple, was a self-centred waste of time; the real practise was the mantra and the bringing forth of Buddha energy into the world. This was what would bring around world peace. The reverend master had undertaken incredible austerities, was greatly admired by Gandhi, and had presided over an order that was responsible for the construction of dozens of peace pagodas throughout Japan, Europe, India, North America, and Africa. However, my little Theravada mind sniffed that it still didn't seem like Buddhism to me.

But to each his own. For us, December 2nd was the day of the full-moon observance, the end of our first month on pilgrimage. I managed to rally my Theravada principles and strike out of the numbness to fare for alms in the next village, Cakramdas. It wasn't difficult to walk in the slow composed manner prescribed by the training rules; actually it was quite pleasant to be gently wading through eddies of children. When I had made it to the end of the village and decided to give up, they beckoned me on—to a house where a young man wearing Western clothes came out to meet me. Ah, I understood: he was the one in the village who spoke the best English.

"Come into my house and I will put something into your pot." It was more than something. After tea and a long conversation, it was a whole meal, specially cooked and served on a stainless plated dish. Some of the advice to the Licchavis seemed to be in good working order. But in general, the picture was of decay. Like many educated Indians, he had no job, but had enough education to know of the appalling economic statistics of this part of the world. Eighty million people in Bihar, with nearly half of that population "below the poverty line" (defined as the amount needed to buy food giving 2,100 calories per day) was an example of the figures that occupied my host's mind. And having no equation for happiness other than the one that materialism presented, he was in a more depressed state than the poorer villagers. It was good that my presence at least revitalized his dharma in terms of hospitality and presented a different way of measuring life. "Tomorrow, you must bring your friend. I will show you around the sites."

I returned to the temple feeling rather pleased with this small boost for the practise of a samana. Nick was also more invigorated, and reckoned that, as tonight was our all-night meditation vigil, the intelligent thing would be to get an hour or so's rest. We moved out into the backyard, to stretch out somewhere where a clump of bushes offered meagre shade and the drumbeat was less tangible than inside. It didn't work. That was as far as my Buddha energy could go. Another afternoon of being pounded left us with the vigour of a couple of aged teddy bears. So much for the all-night meditation. My stuffing was all out even before midnight, leaving me just enough wit to recognize that being slumped against the wall was no more of a vigil than lying on a bed. You could call that a direct realisation. At times, Most Reverend Fuji's assessment of meditation practise, although not in accord with the scriptures, summed up my attempts quite well.

NICK

To get anywhere in Vaishali we had to walk around the tank. Big and oblong, the size of several football pitches, it had steps leading down into the water and here and there a tree hanging over it. There were kingfishers: the pied kingfisher, its striking black and white markings a chequered flashing as it hovered above the water, beak pointing straight down, and the common kingfisher, the same one that is such a delight to see in England, flying across the water, a streak of metallic blue. Both could be quite mesmerising, and I would often stop to watch them on my way somewhere.

The tank was once the coronation tank for the kings of Vaishali and would then have been surrounded with important buildings. Now on one side there was just the Japanese temple and on the other a small piece of modern-day India. The contrast between the two sides was as great as between now and the bygone greatness. The temple was a land of order, dynamic effort, and cleanliness. On the other side the small tea stall where we had our morning breakfast had a table covered in cracked plastic with flies crawling over it. The government museum next door was never open when we tried to visit, and no one seemed to know when it would be. And the village beyond was overcrowded and poor, the dirt tracks lined with litter and excrement, the children in rags. In Vaishali my fatigue amplified just how bad this part of India really was, and how different it was from its past.

For surely when Vaishali was great India must have been dynamic, orderly, and clean too. Societies like everything else go in cycles. That which arises passes away. And there is a theory of societies which says that when young they are expansive, militaristic, and dynamic. There is room for development, and so they are socially fluid. Later, if they are successful, they reach a maturity of confidence with a flowering of the arts and religion. Their morality changes from conquest to sharing, and their influence is great. Then they go into decline as they become overcrowded, and conservative. Socially they become rigid, and class, or caste, becomes important, as those with more of the limited resources protect them for their offspring. Societies may be temporally revived with the imposition of another social structure, like Communism, or with India Islam, but they are really on their way down because there is no new space for the society to expand into. That day to my jaundiced view it made a lot of sense. At the time of

Vaishali's greatness the society was young and fluid. It was militaristic but also open to new religious thought such as the teachings of the Buddha. Social maturity could be seen to have started for this part of India with the time of Ashoka and his empire. The standard of the carving in such as the Ashokan columns is exquisite and today seen as the peak of Indian art. That was when Buddhism flourished and it was also when moral standards such as vegetarianism started. From then on for several centuries Indian social conventions, along with Buddhism, were exported throughout Asia. But then the society went into decline. In modern Bihar it seemed to me that we were looking at the very end of the cycle.

The morning after our failed attempt at an all-night sitting the drumming stopped. It was the rest day. We left them to it and went to an archaeological site a few miles away with the young man Ajahn Sucitto had met the previous day. It was a pleasant enough walk along paths across the paddy fields, but I was tired and looking at modern India with a jaundiced eye.

On the far side of the tank was a small carpet factory. It was just a one-room building, the size of one of the houses, opening along its length onto the path and the tank. Above was a long, hand-painted red and white sign proclaiming The Mishwal Carpet Manufacturing Cooperative, or something to that effect, and inside were two long looms, intricate arrangements of wood and white string with men sitting behind them, two to each loom. They were working foot pedals that pulled the wool down through the loom, and with their hands they were pushing a long wooden shuttle back and forth, tightening the wool against a growing carpet. We stopped briefly to watch while our guide explained that the factory had been set up using a government grant designed to encourage carpet making in the region. I already knew about that. I had read how a campaign by Western charities was forcing the government to do something. Carpet making was usually done in the cities by children bought for cash from poor parents in the backward regions of India—particularly Bihar. And I recalled that carpet making was not all the children were used for. The best-looking children were sold to become prostitutes.

Not much farther along, we came to the archaeological remains at Kolhua. Our guide found the chaukidar in charge of the site, a local, wearing the usual worn khaki uniform denoting the lowest class of Indian bureaucracy (which would reflect his caste), and we were shown round by the two of them, our guide asking questions in Hindi and then relaying the replies to us in English. There was a column that we were told postdated the other Ashokan columns we had seen. It also post-dated the flowering of the Indian arts; it was a very poor imitation, shorter, squatter, with the lion on top looking more like a cloth replica stuffed with straw. There were also the excavated remains of several small Buddhist monasteries: oblong buildings each with a central court-yard with some dozen small monastic cells. These were the first we had seen of the viharas that give Bihar its name; hundreds of others have been found, nearly all following this same simple design. These must have dated from the peak of Buddhism in northern India, when Bihar would have had the density of Buddhist monks they have today in Thai-land and Burma.

On the way back we were brought for our meal to the house of a local landowner, or *thakur*. Although his home was bigger and grander than the rest in the village, it was not much by our standards. It was a square block of concrete no bigger than a small English house. And it was unfin-ished: some doorways had fancy wooden doors while others had noth-ing, and the concrete rendering on one of the walls was incomplete. Through our young friend I found out from the slightly portly and middle-aged thakur that he was the village's largest landholder. This allowed him to have several lower-caste *charmer* families working for him, both in the fields and helping around the house (they served the meal). His total holding, however, was only twenty acres, the size of a typical field in England. I asked how much other thakurs had. "Some have nearly as much as this man," the lad replied, "but most are having less." And the charmers? "They have one acre, but this they are not own-ing, they must work for it." They were the ones in the small mud huts toward the edge of the village.

Landholdings can be so small in the Ganges plain because the land is so productive. Our host told us he grew three crops a year: rice planted with the rains, then wheat, which was being planted now, and then legumes, mostly lentils and chickpeas. He had several cows and water buffalos (most families had only one), and these were grazed on the stubble of the cut crops and fed with chopped fresh straw. No one kept chickens, as to good Hindus eggs were seen as impure, not as bad as meat but getting that way.

Of course the other reason they could live on such small amounts of land was that everyone lived so frugally. We were in the house of the biggest landowner in a big village. He probably had a radio and televi-sion, but he did not have a car, and there was little ostentation, just the fancy woodwork doors and the metal plates we ate from instead of banana leaves. The workers had nothing but their mud hut, their one cow, and a few bangles for the wife. And the Untouchable castes would not even have that.

When I got back I looked up some statistics. There are 843 people per square kilometre in the Vaishali district of Bihar, not the highest in the Ganges plain, but then Vaishali is purely rural and the others have cities. A square kilometre is about 140 football pitches, so there would be on average six people living off the production from each pitch. Just imag-ine a countryside divided into plots the size of football pitches, on and on in all directions, and six people standing on each one. No wonder we could never get away from people and no wonder, with that bleak life, they found us such an interesting event.

It is this population density that is the reason Bihar is so different today from what it once was. The vast tracts of forest left at the time of the Buddha were steadily cleared over the subsequent centuries as the pop-ulation grew and, for many centuries, flourished. By the time the British came, however, this land was crowded and poor. The culture had become deeply conservative as the haves clung to their position, and it is this resistance to change that is now the real problem in Bihar. India's attempts to limit its population have only been successful in states where there has been reform. There the birth rate has markedly declined and the life expectancy doubled. But there the land has been distributed more equally, literacy is now high, healthcare widespread, and women enjoy a much better status. In the northern states of the Ganges plain, and particularly in Bihar, where Indian society is thought to be the oldest, things have not changed, and population growth continues relentlessly.

Later that day, having returned to the Japanese temple to rest, I pondered the differences between Japanese and Indian societies. Here was a contrast between the order and wealth of a young society against the chaos and poverty of an old one. But could that all just be put down to population change? It seemed there was something else: their attitudes to social conventions and rules. In the temple, as in Japan, individuals were subservient to rules, but out in India it was the reverse. Every Indian asserted his unique individuality, and rules were there to be ignored. This is how it proved to be at the museum when we at last found it open with a sleeping caretaker sitting on a chair in the entrance. We climbed the steps and entered quietly so as not to disturb him. Facing us was a most sublime Buddha image, carved from black stone with a beautiful serenity to its features. I reflected on how different the culture must have been to have produced that. It stood alone against the plain white wall, facing everyone who entered. After it, the rest of the museum was a disappointment. As usual the museum seemed to miss the point of the religious things it was exhibiting. The halls on either side of the entrance lobby were lined with archaeological remains: bits of different Buddhist ages, acts of devotion now exhibited in ordered rows. We were the only people there and we were not there long.

On the way out I suggested to Ajahn Sucitto that the serene Buddha was well worth a photograph, and he agreed. The trouble was that there had been a notice proclaiming "Photographs Are Forbidden" at the entrance. Still, I reckoned if I used my little camera no one would notice. So as we were taking one last look I slipped the camera up to my eye and adjusted the focus...

"Excuse me sir, photographs are not allowed." It was the museum caretaker we had passed on the way in. He was now standing behind us.

I gave him my most pleading look. "But this Buddha rupa is *so* beautiful, and I would *so* like to have a photograph of it to show people in England."

With a slight waggle of his head he replied, "How can I stop you?" And with that he walked back to his chair.

AJAHN SUCITTO

The day the drum stopped was a sad day. When I could actually think more clearly, Vaishali struck me with a kind of pathos. The fact that it had been a place where the Buddha gave some seminal teachings on the survival of his Way in the future meant that I kept relating the city's decline to the decline of the Triple Gem in its birthplace. This was the place where the Buddha first summarized his teachings as *sila* (morality), *samadhi* (meditation), and *pañña* (wisdom), the definition that is the bedrock of Buddhism. And here, worn out, and encouraging his disciples to take responsibility for themselves to practise the Dhamma for their own and others' welfare, was where he left his alms bowl and began the journey north to his death place.

Now the barest relics are left. The Buddha's bowl had occupied a hallowed shrine until the Emperor Kanishka removed it in the second century C.E. According to the sutta, the Licchavis obtained an eighth portion of the Buddha's remains and enshrined them in a stupa in Vaishali. The sutta's account was confirmed by the pilgrim Hsuan Tsiang, who visited when Vaishali's ruins were more extensive. He even added that the emperor Ashoka had opened the stupa, taken out nine-tenths of the relics to put in other stupas, and left the tenth portion and rebuilt the stupa. Nobody made much of all that until the remnants of the stupa were discovered in 1958. In the heart of the rubble was a small soapstone reliquary containing burnt bone. The ruin itself, which we visited after the museum, consisted of an ancient earth core that had been enlarged with bricks on several occasions and showed signs of having been opened about 250 years after its construction. But now even that reliquary had been taken away from Vaishali. According to the museum, the relics, along with anything of archaeological interest, were now in Patna Museum. All that remained here were a few lumps of stone delineating where the stupa had stood. It had held the Enlightened One's remains for two thousand years, and now it looked like the decayed molar in the jaw of something long since dead. In the falling dusk, I placed some of the offerings I had brought from England into the empty heart of the stupa, then circumambulated it with lit candles and incense.

Tea with our host on his rest day was a pleasant relief for everybody. Nick and I talked to him about Buddhism in Britain, and we were excited to hear that the relics from the Buddha's cremation, although not on show, could be seen if one obtained special permission from the director of the museum in Patna. Strangely enough, he had never got round to pursuing the possibility himself.

The next morning it was back to the drum. We sat in for the last time, and as the night sky paled, left the throbbing temple and headed over the long bare mound to the southeast. Nick was telling me all about it, but I wasn't interested. All this dead stuff seemed beside the point.

There was a story the Buddha told about a drum, a great drum that had not been properly looked after; eventually the drumhead rotted and only the pegs remained. The drum was unable to sound. This will happen to the Dhamma, the Buddha had warned, if the Sangha does not keep the teachings in the suttas well learned. These teachings and the Vinaya were his bequest. Leaving Vaishali for the last time, the Enlightened One had turned and given it a long, fond look: his final blessing.

Striding across that mound in the grey dawn, I couldn't bring myself to do the same. Better to keep going and stay with the walking.

And how does a monk live as a refuge unto himself...? Here, Ananda, a monk abides contemplating the body as body, earnestly, clearly aware, mindful, and having put away all hankering and fretting for the world, and likewise with regard to feelings, mind, and mind objects.

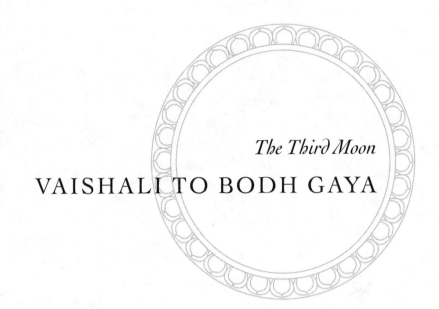

The Third Moon

VAISHALI TO BODH GAYA

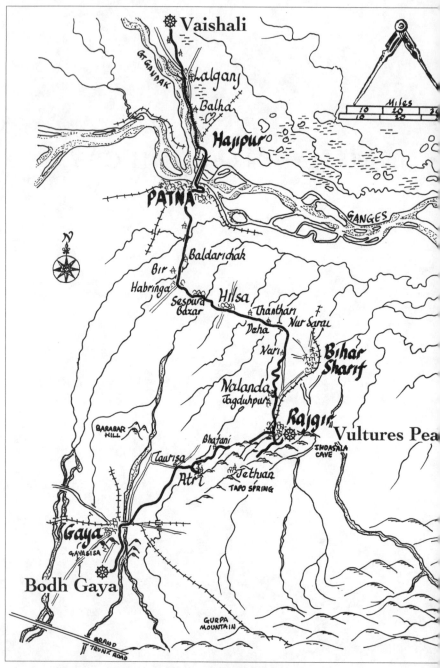

Mid-Bihar

10

The Treasure House

AJAHN SUCITTO

Onward to Hajipur. "Hajipur, Hajipur!" Some crazy man was jabbering at us, and I threw the words at him as a desperate offering. He wasn't the only one accosting us of course. "Kaha ja ra hai?" they asked. "Hajipur!" That dumbfounded them for a while. My Hindi wasn't that good, but probably the next question meant "Why on earth are you going to Hajipur?" We just grinned: that's where the bridge over the Ganges began ... maybe. Nick couldn't get the maps to tally.

Onward our path narrowed in the darkness as it wriggled between baked mud walls—the walls that defend the backyards of villagers' houses against thieves and wild animals. And still we crept onward, feeling like fugitives because of those walls (beyond them evening oil lamps and smoky smells mingling with cooking and burning dung), looking for somewhere to lie down in the darkness. Funny the details that stick: we both remember the cycads where we unrolled our bedding: "How do you call them again, Nick?" "Cycads, Bhante. Cycads [pronounced *sigh cads*]. A very primitive form of plant. Them, or something pretty like them, would have been around with the dinosaurs." "Really! Cycads. Cycads."

I think I was starting to crack up. Fixing all these details in my memory seemed important: it gave a brief mooring to an attention that is losing its customary bearings. Like my mother. In my last anxious visits before leaving England, her mind was deteriorating: "What time is it?" was her constant refrain, repeated every minute or two. Age is brutal at exposing our instinctive need to hold reality in a mesh of words. "It doesn't matter, mum." But it *did*. Each time would be carefully written down, relating to nothing but the need to keep track.

Younger minds can put a little more flesh on the bones of our insecurity. They can go onward to the next memory.

NICK

It was forty-eight kilometres to Patna from Vaishali, and we had reckoned on getting there in time for the meal the next day. We walked south on a minor road heading for Hajipur. It was a pleasant enough road with little traffic and trees to shade us, but we soon found it hard going. By the afternoon we were feeling as tired as we had upon reaching Vaishali. Our stop there had obviously done little to alleviate our rundown state. The fatigue gradually closed in, numbing the mind and reducing my awareness to little more than the road stretching ahead.

We were no longer trying to do the puja and meditation late in the afternoon, leaving it for after dark when we could be alone. Every evening at about six I would start to yearn for a place to stop for the night. But I was plagued with the need to find somewhere nice. I still had associations from other walking trips, of pleasant evenings by campfires out in the wilds, finishing the day in time to enjoy sitting in meditation under the stars. So I would start looking for this ideal camp site, which of course didn't exist. Ajahn Sucitto wouldn't mind where we stopped and just wanted to keep going; his response to adversity was always to plod on. Eventually it would get too dark to find anywhere in particular, and we would end up stumbling into some mango grove or other where we would collapse, sort out our stuff, and then try to do the puja and meditation.

That night we had walked around Hajipur on the bund and had gone as far as our old maps could take us. Ajahn Sucitto accepted that we would have to leave the next bit till the morning. I enjoyed ending the day with a salutation to our two small Buddhas, sitting on some rock or tree stump that Ajahn Sucitto had found; it was the meditation that was painful. There would be such cramp in my calves, and the soles of my feet and my mind would be so dull with fatigue that all I could do, as a way of coping, was to shuffle from one position to another. That evening, as usual, my meditation did not last that long. The call of my sleeping bag, the one reliable comfortable experience in the day, was too great. We were a bit apart, each under a different tree, and I quietly sank to the horizontal—quietly, not so much to avoid disturbing Ajahn Sucitto, who was still perfectly upright and unmoving in the lotus posture, as to hide the fact that I was giving in so soon.

The next morning we were up and away very early, intent on reaching Patna by midmorning. We walked into Hajipur as dawn was beginning. The inhabitants were just stirring, and the streets were empty of the commotion that would later fill them. Our intentions were frustrated, however, as we tried to find the right road out. Twice we asked and twice we were assured that we were going the right way, but I knew the road must be a larger one if it led to the only crossing of the Ganges for a hundred miles, and it was far too quiet even at that time of the morning. It was a problem I knew from the last time I was in India. If you ask whether you are going the right way, people can so want to please that they are likely to say "yes" whether they know or not.

Eventually we did find the main road—a bypass on the other side of town. There were big long-distance lorries thundering along it, the kind of lorries I used to hitchhike in India when I was twenty and nearly penniless. They looked to be mostly the same model as then: made to a 1960s Mercedes design by TaTa, the big Bombay engineering corporation. (I had assumed at first that they were Mercedes and that the TaTa name on the back was an Indian English "goodbye.") In those days

I had learned to look for these long-distance lorries when I was after a lift. They were slightly bigger and more important than the other lorries, and on them the painted designs, which cover all Indian lorries, were always Sikh. The Sikh spear symbol was on either side of the company name above the windscreen. The Sikhs seem to run much of the big merchant business in India. That, combined with their affinity for things mechanical, had allowed them to corner the long-distance transport business. Those lorries were a great way to travel. Sitting with the crew of driver, co-driver, and a boy who would be out at each stop cleaning the windscreen, we would thunder across India, stopping only for meals at Sikh transport cafes. The lorries did not go that fast, maybe fifty miles per hour at the most, but they would drive them all day and then all night while I slept above the cab with one of the drivers on the two rope beds, under the rocking stars.

The same lorries rumbled by us as we made our way along a straight road rising slowly to the bridge. The Indian government is proud of this bridge, which, to cope with the Ganges in full flood, is one of the longest in the world. We had seen it mentioned as one of the highlights of Bihar in a tourist brochure. For us though it was the famous river that was important, and we had decided to have a little ceremony to acknowledge the crossing. However, we were very tired, and as we had been walking since early that morning without breakfast, we were also getting both hungry and weak. Once on the bridge we seemed to cross for ages with no sight of the river, over miles of cultivated land that presumably became river during the monsoon. The bridge just went on and on, and we got more and more tired. Finally sand banks appeared below us, and there, at last, was the Ganges, even bigger than the Gandak, and even more full of silt.

Looking down from the bridge as we walked out over the river, I watched men filling four sailing junks with river silt from the bank: carrying it in baskets on their heads as they walked up planks to tip it into the holds. I was wondering where it was going (I have since discovered to be made into bricks) when what I thought was an enormous fish surfaced. Then it did it again and a few more times, each time farther downriver. I like to think it was a Gangetic dolphin, partly because, although they are now so rare, it really might have been (it was behaving like one), but just as much because I think they are such amazing creatures that I would like to think I have seen one. Living in the murk of a river so full of silt, they are nearly blind and have to rely on echo-location to find their way about and to find the fish they eat. The silt also makes them difficult to see, which is why so little is known about them.

I turned to Ajahn Sucitto to point out my discovery, but he wasn't interested; all I got was a grunt.

AJAHN SUCITTO

That interminable bridge. "Hey, here's the bridge already," chirped the mind. "Patna's just over the other side—nearly there!" What other side—for the first hour, we didn't even get to the river. By the time the shimmering goddess appeared way below us, everything in me was dissolving and bobbing together—the shaking legs, the breath, and the mantra, driven onward by a flagging will. Mother Ganga was flowing effortlessly and timelessly east, west to east, the way in which the earth's turning creates our time. Boats rocked peacefully in her jewelled hands—not onward but *on,* borne on the ceaseless tide. Staggering onward—onward to what? But still: "Better not stop now; at least get halfway over...then we'll have a rest."

Halfway along that uncaring treadmill was the stop. We were midway between the banks. "Stop"—I rolled the delicious word around my mouth, savouring it like water-ice. Get the bag off ... sit down on the pavement beside the lane. Here at the intersection of time with the timeless: Buddha puja. We laid down mats, set our Buddha images on the lower step of the parapet in front of us, and offered incense to the Awakened One. Offered it also to Mother Ganga and the eternal cycle—a vast interweaving mandala of mud and refuse, and of a light so dazzling my eyes could hardly look at it. From her, people derived their livelihood and faith; it was the place of their spiritual purification, an open sewer, and a graveyard. Ganga, a goddess descending from Vishnu through Shiva's hair, was the span of life itself. No wonder she was hard to cross over.

The few minutes of meditation were terminated by something thumping into me; it was Nick scrambling to his feet—an oxcart was bearing down on us, only a few feet away. "Jai Ram!" bobbed into focus again, as we jumped onto the lower step of the parapet clutching our bags, and a train of oxen trundled by, the driver clucking and whooping at his beasts, probably wondering where we had sprung up from.

So onward, more as fugitives than devotees, but onward. A white onion-shaped dome, bluish in the morning light and misty, shone from the other shore. "That must be a Sikh temple" the mind chirped again, "rest ... hospitality ... food ... not far now." But the road marched on and Ganga knowingly danced.

Because, having crossed over the river, the bridge was in no hurry to merge into the maze of streets—it soared disdainfully over the rooftops that clung to Mother Ganga's sleeve and continued heading south. We had to abandon it. Finding a blocked-off stairway winding down the side of one of its legs, we ignobly clawed over the barrier to climb down to the world below. The white dome had disappeared.

We had decided to stay in a Sikh temple, or *gurdwara,* while in Patna. Religious places seemed far more appropriate than cheap hotels. There were dharamsalas in the city, but local people had repeatedly and emphatically warned us against using them—they were dirty and were full of thieves, and Patna was a lawless city—we should be very careful where we stayed. Sikh gurdwaras, however, have a reputation for hospitality, and Patna had the largest outside of the Punjab. Nick's simple guide to the city indicated "Shri Harimandir Sahib," the main gurdwara, somewhere off in the east. So there was another journey, more churning in the flow—

buses, rickshaws jangling at one's heels, scooter taxis rasping like frenzied ducks—until in a wall, way beyond the hope of getting anywhere, a
gate lay open. Here was the gurdwara, "the gateway of the Guru."

It was an impressive place: huge gates opened onto a vast plaza of polished white paving surrounded by the stone walls and balconies and gal-
leries of what must have been offices and lodgings. Onion-shaped fluted
domes rose above the gateways in each wall of the square. The eye's
attention however was rightly drawn to the centre, to the temple building itself, square and built in the Mughal style, with characteristic domes
and with windows with balconies that looked out over the plaza. The
Sikhs must be well organized; there was an order everywhere that
seemed "un-Indian." It was shocking to see a set of buildings so homo-
geneous and in good repair, with plenty of space in the square, no
chaotic crowds, no dogs, cows, or tea stalls, no rubbish, no strands of
hunched bodies squatting over wares, no blaring Bollywood sound-
tracks. We stood for a while and took in the space. It looked like a good
place to rest.

Furthermore, the little chap by my elbow, looking up with shining
eyes from his mass of beard and turban, couldn't have been nicer. He
wore the uniform of a guide and welcomed us in, presenting his card:
"Ram Rattan Singh, Temple Guide." We covered our heads with cloth
and removed our sandals, as was expected, and explained our interest in
the holy place and our wish to stay a couple of nights. He beamed and
indicated the nearby reception, outside which he would wait while we
booked in, and offered to show us around afterward.

The man inside was larger and less affirmative. He took us to the
Director, who was larger still and distinctly negative: "No. Foreigners
are not allowed to stay."

Back to Ram Rattan Singh; then back in again to witness a heated
debate between David and Goliath. Nowadays Goliath wins.

Well, we'd look around anyway with Ram Rattan Singh. He was muttering about the injustice and un-Sikh-like behaviour of the Director all

the way across the plaza; but when we entered the temple—an interior like a mosque but with a central shrine room like a Hindu temple—his stream flowed more lyrically. Dates, histories, names.... We walked around the shrine, looking through its windows at memorabilia, old, mundane objects that reverence had made sacred: here remnants of the Guru's clothing, here other objects that I can't remember now; all treasures of Sikhism. Our guide was filling in the details of a picture that I didn't have an outline of: "You can drink some of this water, it is coming from the spring that Guru Gobind Singh drank from." Here Guru Gobind Singh was born; here was a picture of Guru Gobind Singh as a beatific child; and so on up the white marble stairs, onto the next floor and the next, reviewing the Sikh memory bank. More cases and pictures: ghastly images of powerfully built bearded prisoners (Sikhs surely) being sawn apart by bald, scowling, and heavy-browed captors; here mighty-thighed heroic Sikhs with grim ardour in their eyes urging others on to battle and martyrdom; and then up another flight, wondering "What do Sikhs believe in anyway?" "There is one God with many names. All men are brothers." I might have guessed.

And who *was* Guru Gobind Singh?

For the Sikhs, there were ten great teachers, or gurus, and Guru Gobind Singh was the tenth of them. He was born in Patna in 1666. Guru Nanak was the first. Their sayings, poems, and devotional songs were collected in the Sikh holy book, the *Adi Granth*. That was the thing downstairs that we came back to, placed on a cushion with a canopy over it, and attended by immaculately dressed priests with long white flywhisks. Horsehair, I supposed in a mesmerized stupor that I hoped passed for reverence. My legs were going wobbly again. We hovered in silence for a while, consciousness flowing across the hallucinogenic pattern of white paving squares, a serene lake on which burly turbaned devotees floated among soft white light and gold brocades.

I needed to sit down and eat, and made suitable noises. Ram Rattan Singh took us to a cheap hotel across the road, muttering about the

Director. Nick was explaining that we would have liked to stay in a temple and absorb some of the religion; we were pilgrims, his companion was a monk, and a monk should stay in a holy place. The hotel manager, the new ear for Ram Rattan Singh's tirade, waggled his head sympathetically. I got into the unmemorable little room and sat down. Nick had the energy to operate in terms of purpose. He determined to go off and do business-like things, first of which was to get a bag full of takeaway snacks from the street and offer them to me. Then, with an "I'll be back later," he marched off to duty.

NICK

In Patna I went off for the rest of the day in one of the three-wheeled taxis prevalent in all Indian cities. These ran a kind of bus route through the old part of town and then on to the centre of modern Patna. The taxis used a scooter as their basis but with two wheels at the back supporting a compartment that could hold four small locals. The driver sat in a cab at the front on a seat designed for one but onto which two more passengers might squeeze on either side. That is where I preferred to travel; sitting on the edge of his seat, hanging slightly out of the cab, and holding on to the frame just above my head. It doesn't sound that comfortable, but it was much better than trying to cram my big Western body into the back. I never had to wait; they were always coming toward me—winding their way through the traffic, the crowds, and past the occasional cow—whenever I wanted one. Despite there being so many, they were always full by the time they got to the city centre.

I went into New Patna after some things we needed, Western things we could only get in a city, like colour slide film or the special small batteries for Ajahn Sucitto's torch, and to collect our mail from the post office and visit the bank. I made a point of seeking out the main branch of the State Bank of India as I wanted not only to change some traveller's cheques but also to acknowledge the kind action of their bank manager in Bettiah. I had written out a formal letter of commendation addressed to the bank's president. At the bank, the official in charge of the foreign exchange department already knew about Mr. Mishra's action. He explained that he had recently been authorized to accept the cheque and to reimburse Mr. Mishra. He took my letter, solemnly assuring me that it would go to the president and that "it will be very much to Mr. Mishra's credit," and I left the bank feeling I had returned one good deed with another.

It was from the bank that I began the quest which led, via a series of dingy offices, to the Patna Zoological Gardens and the small office of the wildlife division of the state forestry department. That was a good afternoon. The gardens, to me, were a treasure house, as they had many of the species that I might see as we crossed the forested hills of southern Bihar. There was an enclosure with most of the native species of deer, which would have been great for learning to identify them, but the list of the names displayed on the fence gave no way of identifying which was which. Luckily a passing janitor was able to help. Elsewhere, there were tigers and leopards, and an aviary with birds of prey and owls. It was a weekday, and the better-off locals who would visit the zoo were in their offices. I had many of the exhibits to myself, and I never had to queue even once at the tea rooms, to which I returned several times for a new discovery: wonderful chilled cartons of mango juice called "Fruitees."

There was no one at the wildlife offices—not unusual for Bihar state offices I had already discovered—and I was able to wander round, studying the big wall maps showing the forest areas, the distribution of different forest types, and pictures of the wildlife. On my second visit, two junior officers turned up. They were very enthusiastic about our plans and gave useful advice. They knew personally all the forest officers in the regions we were passing through and threw in details about each of them. The field jobs went to junior officers like themselves, and they had all been to college together. They told me which forest resthouses would be on our route and to which of the district forest offices to write to get permission to stay. It would only cost ten rupees a night, but I must first get a chittee signed by the district forest officer. Although both were trained as foresters, they were very keen on wildlife. They warned me though that much of the forest we were going through might not be in good repair, being so near the overcrowded Ganges plain. They insisted we should go to the south of Bihar, where there were big areas of unaffected forest. I promised we would try and promised to pass on their regards to their fellow junior officers when we met them. Then I wandered back through the zoological gardens to take one last look at some of the animals we might get to see in the wild. I was excited about the prospect and looked forward to getting to the forests ahead.

AJAHN SUCITTO

My afternoon ritual was to unpack the bags, sort the stuff out, then write some memories in the diary. Unpacking wafts perceptions into the mind. The Buddha rupa from the Cambodia Trust; I placed it in the only high place, the ledge where the brick wall was capped by a wooden window frame, and the ravages of Cambodia drifted to the surface. Here was the small stainless-steel alms bowl that Jayasaro had sent me from Thailand for the trip; here the bag that the bhikkhus at Amaravati had sorted out, with all kinds of straps and buckles with which to hold on my sleeping mat; Vajiro's sleeping bag; the belt pouch that Suviro had made for me; the shiny stainless steel mug that a novice had given me; the sandals revamped with old motorcycle tires glued to the soles to sustain a thousand miles of walking. And the relics—tiny crystals, fragments, and icons from shrines, those revered crumbs to offer to the shrines at holy places, so that the aspirations of my fellow samanas would merge into this paying of homage.

But the rubbish—there were no cupboards or shelves, so everything was awash on the floor: rubbish and valuables distinguished only by emotional resonance. Here next to the relics, a fragment of a Hindi newspaper that the snacks had come wrapped in; here a crushed empty matchbox; here the mangled stub of a candle. Indian hotels never have wastepaper baskets. You just throw the rubbish on the floor and someone sweeps it up every day or so, or when you leave. It's hard to throw things on the floor, the mind is so used to setting things apart—this is valuable, it goes here; this is rubbish, throw it away. But here there is no throwing away, because there is no "away." In India, it's all here. All rubbish, all sacred.

And so with the perceptions and memories. What makes up a pilgrimage; what do you put in a diary? The gritty grey stone shower stall (water was available when no one else had a tap on); the two men wearing Nehru caps slouched in armchairs behind newspapers in the foyer; or between Vaishali and Hajipur the traditional graffiti-like paintings on the sides of the houses; or on the bund huge banyan trees, often with a simple shrine: a stone, a swash of red paint, a strand of dead flowers; or some more momentary ripple—a white ox shaking its dripping muzzle at its feed, the light scattering through the drops of water, or the groan and clatter of a pump where we squatted to wash, or a small boy solemnly talking about Charles Dickens as he walked along with us. Or the smoky sunsets that we lumbered through as people withdrew into huts and houses and women's voices murmured through the walls, and the chilly evenings, two mats around a tree somewhere and a faltering puja to introduce us to the spangled night's darkness.

So many wavelets of memory; so many fragments borne on the tide—on, but not onward. When I caught some and put them in the diary they became so much debris. All rubbish, all sacred. I doubted whether Nick's hundreds of photographs had done much better. You might as well try to net a river.

But even a poor man has to have his treasures. Later in the afternoon, I returned to the gurdwara. Ram Rattan Singh took me around to his room: maybe two and a half by three metres of space, containing his smiling wife and four sparkling-eyed children; a bed, a stove, a cupboard;

and under the bed a photograph album. Here was Ram with the president of India, also a Sikh, here was Ram solemnly with other VIPs who stirred no memories in my mind. I gave him one of the photos of Nick and myself, and one of the cards that someone had given me as a joke: "Venerable Sucitto Bhikkhu" in copperplate, and underneath it in small capitals: "alms-mendicant." He was pleased; I was pleased. You realise you need this stuff in order to be able to make the invitations and the blessings, the gestures that count. And to see the richness. For him what was unnoticeable, but which I carried away like a jewel, was the invitation into his life; and the perception that here was a family of six, cheerful and bright, yet living in one room—most of which was bare.

In the evening I was with Nick in the white space of the gurdwara. The place was gently throbbing with the evening kirtan; two men, one on a harmonium and one playing tablas, singing verses from the *Adi Granth*. The attention of a scattering of human forms was held in its flow. Wrapped in so much cloth, the men and the women all looked huge, and their relaxed stillness gave them dignity. Nick, red-bearded, his head wrapped in a cloth, looked like a Sikh, albeit some cousin from Mars. They all seemed easy, flowing along in the spirit (and maybe even in the verses) of Kabir, Guru Nanak, Guru Angad, Guru Amardas, Guru Ramdas, Guru Arjan.

As with Buddhism, this spiritual outflow had started informally, not from a wish to create a new religion, but simply to purify and point to the truths—and to the false grasping—in current practices and ideas. Like Buddhism, the way of the Gurus had sprung from the mystic source of personal revelation that keeps bubbling up through the crust of Vedic Brahmanism, and from which religious forms get deposited like silt.

Sometimes it's the conflict between religions that cracks the crust. In the first half of the fifteenth century, when Islam was establishing itself in Northern India, Kabir, a Muslim by birth, took discipleship from a Hindu guru and saw beyond the form of established religion:

There is nothing but water at the holy bathing places; and I know
that they are useless, for I have bathed in them.
The images are all lifeless, they cannot speak; I know, for I have
cried aloud to them.
The Purana and the Koran are mere words; lifting up the curtain,
I have seen.
Kabir gives utterance to the words of experience; and he knows
very well that all other things are untrue.

That was the beginning of the flow. A few years later, Nanak had a
revelation while immersed in a river, and picked up the same theme—
God is formless, not Muslim, not Hindu—then wandered, singing it.
Those who heard and took Nanak as their guru became his disciples,
learners, or in the Punjabi language, "sikhs." For five hundred years
since, the sayings of Nanak and subsequent gurus had been recited and
venerated as the Sikhs' contribution to India's treasury of teachings. But
the next day we went in search of another kind of treasure.

Jalan House was what we had come to see: a private museum that
one could only enter with the permission of Mr. Jalan himself. And yesterday, the incomparable Dr. Scott had tracked him down to one of his
jewellery stores. "Yes...and if I am not there, my son will show you
around."

The son was fourteen years old, from St. Paul's School, Darjeeling,
courteous and accomplished. And the house? Probably a hundred and
something years old, struggling against the corrosive effects of nature
and the Indian state. It had been fine under the British, but since Independence, some of the collection had been grabbed by the state, then
there was tax and the cost of servants...it was hard to keep it all going.
And surely there was a lot of stuff there to hold on to: wonderful old
instruments—sitars and tamboura and vinods; coins from all ages; a
sizeable collection of Chinese porcelain; and ivory Kwanyins. Here
(with a nonchalant wave of the hand) was the fine-tooled silver scabbard

of Emperor Akbar's sword, here Napoleon III's bed, here George V's dining set—matching plates, bowls, saucers—and so on ... carved chess pieces, old manuscripts ... the *Prajnaparamita Sutra* in Devanagari script ... time's fragments. And really now there wasn't time to see it all; various daytime duties, school, work, and so on, were dawning. Outside the house we said goodbye ... "And we have an old Daimler from before the war ... but the servant lost the keys so we can't get in it anymore."

Slimy lanes seethed around the stump of the wealthy estate; they had deposited contemptuous mounds of refuse—human, animal, and vegetable—against its grand ageing walls. Patna was weary and under curfew—too many deprived people in the city. Ayodhya was still simmering.

NICK

The next day was to be our final one in Patna, and we had set the afternoon aside for our planned visit to Patna museum and the attempt to see the Buddha's ashes. I had been for going earlier, but Ajahn Sucitto had insisted that we were to make just the one attempt to see the ashes. Ajahn Sucitto approaches the material world with an expectation of disappointment. He rationalized that we were unlikely to succeed and therefore would be causing ourselves unnecessary suffering if we tried too much. I had been for making a campaign of it.

We went into New Patna, crammed in the back of a three-wheeled taxi. The museum was one of the grand Victorian buildings left by the Raj. They were all together on several wide tree-lined avenues that had once been the British part of Patna but that had since been colonized by India. Now there were stalls along the pavements, little tea shacks built around the trees, beggars propped up against walls, the odd cow meandering down the road, and people bustling about everywhere.

If you looked above this sea of India, the frontage of the museum, rising out of it all, still looked imposing. Inside, however, it was obvious that India had taken over here too. The stuffed animals in the large glass cases in the centre of the main hall had the occasional bit of fur falling out, and the tiger was stalking through long grass bent and tattered with age. The collections of traditional weapons (which for some reason were amidst the animals) were dusty, and the tribal costumes were faded and slightly moth-eaten. Directed past all this and the knots of people looking at the various exhibits, we made our way up some wide stone stairs, flanked by more models of tribal people wearing more costumes, to the small office of the assistant curator in a back corner.

He was a pleasant young chap, but although delighted to see us, he could not help. "Regretfully the curator is not here at present, and so it is not possible to see these ashes." I tried telling him how far we had come and how much we would like to see the ashes, but all we got was his sympathy and an invitation of tea. Over the tea he told us about his university thesis, which had been on some aspect of Buddhist history, and then, after at least half an hour of this, and without anyone coming into the room, he suddenly announced, "The curator is now here and you may see him with your request."

We had no idea why it was suddenly possible, but we did not object. With our hopes rekindled we were taken next door into a larger room and through that into another, where the curator, grey-haired and portly, sat behind a desk taking tea with two cronies. His two companions had the same unhurried air as the curator (it goes with being employed in the government service), and the three appeared as if they had been there all along.

I repeated our request to see the Buddha's ashes. The curator listened politely and then explained, "First you must write a letter to me outlining your request, and then it can be arranged."

"But this is our last day in Patna."

"To see the Buddha's ashes I must first have a request in writing." My hopes began to sink but then I had an idea.

"Could we write the letter now and give it to you?"

"Of course." So the assistant curator took us out into the room next door, brought us paper from his room, and we sat down to compose a formal letter of request, which Ajahn Sucitto was concerned to get just right. It had to explain who we were and what we were doing and to be written in the humble rhetoric of Victorian English that he felt the curator would like. It took a while but eventually it was done, written out neatly with lots of flowery phrases. We were taken back in, and the curator received our crafted letter without even glancing at it. He just put it aside on his desk and announced. "Now we can go to see the ashes. You are most fortunate. To see the ashes you must have two sets of keys, and for that you must have both myself and this man here." He indicated a uniformed employee who must have been called to the room in our absence.

Our party then set sail behind the figurehead of the curator, who passed majestically through his museum. We went through the outer room and past the assistant's room, then past the stairs and various archaeological exhibits in glass cases, until we came to a distant storeroom. The uniformed assistant stepped forward to unlock the door, and we all entered. Inside was a dusty room full of cupboards and wide chests with long drawers. There was only one window, high up on the far wall, and from it a shaft of light slanted down into the room. The curator got his keys out, unlocked one of the cupboards, and lifted out an old flat wooden box the size and shape of a thick pencil box, which he unlocked with a small key. Inside the box, nestling in deep blue velvet, was a simple but delicate off-white soapstone casket, and beside that an ordinary screw top glass phial like those used in hospitals. The phial was half filled with grey ashes. The remains of the Buddha! He took it and the casket out and placed them on his hand for us to look at more closely. I asked him to raise his hand so that they were illuminated by the shaft of dusty sunlight and then I took a photo. My heart was singing with delight and awe.

AJAHN SUCITTO

Everything was bright for that moment, everything was still. Nothing was said, nothing thought. The Buddha's ashes. His last words tolled in my mind: *"all conditioned processes are transient, practise with diligence."* But for a few precious moments there was the light. That's all I needed to see.

After the Buddha's ashes, who could be interested in looking at more remains? Apparently somewhere in Patna various sites had been excavated to reveal its glorious past as the capital of the Mauriyan empire, but such things seemed irrelevant now. All conditioned processes are transient: and the deepest irony was that in India the incarnate had lasted longer than the Sangha of the Buddha's heirs. And the legacy of his teachings. Pointlessness descended: here I am, a lone bhikkhu following a long dead history. Where am I going?

Now my right foot asked for attention. The blisters had all gone, but the strap of my right sandal had chafed a sore on the upper surface of the foot. Before we set off for our trip to New Patna, I had put a sticking plaster over it but inadvertently created a slight tuck in the skin. In the course of the afternoon, the skin had torn open (you don't think that skin does that until you live in India) and opened into a sore about a centimetre across. No big problem; but I knew from past experience how slowly things heal in India. It requires a sustained effort to keep the flies out, and a regular bombardment of medicines to prevent further infection. And this was a foot, bound to get dirty and required to do a lot of duty in a hostile environment. Hence I wound several layers of white cloth around it and, suitably turbaned, returned to the gurdwara.

In the cool of the following morning in that holy space, a renowned preacher was expounding the *Adi Granth*. As the preacher was blind, a priest would beautifully intone a few verses from the sacred text, always about the same length; as he completed his last phrase, the preacher began his commentary in less formal cadences, but also softly modulated and of equal length. No, this was no talk; it was a dialogue, a few threads of the Sikh epic woven with the rhythm and harmony of a song, between the main theme of the priest's intonation and the counterpoint of the preacher's commentary. The congregation was rapt. When you have harmony and attention, songs don't need music. For me it was like witnessing two late-night jazz musicians soulfully exchanging phrases of one of those standards that reach back into a shared place of feeling. The audience was right there with them, sharing in the much-heard song of their people. Occasional smiles, keen attention; we've heard it before, but tell it like it is.

Upstairs, above the flow, the vision was less convivial. Many of the exhibits came from the time of the conflict between the Sikhs and the Mughals in the seventeenth and eighteenth centuries. This conflict had moulded much of Sikhism, giving it its characteristic forms and identity, and through that formalisation fixed it as a separate faith. Without the antagonism of the emperors, Sikhism would probably occupy the same position in the culture as Sufism in Islam.

Emperor Akbar, renowned for his religious tolerance and statesmanship, seemed genuinely to admire the Sikhs; during his reign, the Sikh Jerusalem, Amritsar, was built, and some of the verses of Kabir and Nanak were collected as the forerunner of the Adi Granth. Fortunes changed with the emperors. Under Jahangir, Arjan, the fifth Guru was executed, and consequently the Guru's son, Guru Hargobind, started marshalling the Sikhs into a fighting force. Once they had become established as a political and military entity, further antagonism was inevitable and continued through the reigns of Shah Jahan and Aurangzeb. Aurangzeb was probably no crueller than any other emperor of the time, but he was more single-minded and long-lived than most. His personal determination to establish India as an Islamic state through the sword as well as through his own prayers, fasting, and veneration of the Koran, made life difficult if you didn't share his views. While Muslims regard him as a saint, in the annals of Sikhism he is a bigoted monster. It was during his reign that the tortures and persecutions of Sikhs began on a large scale. The ninth Guru kept to his dharma at the cost of his head.

Martyrs throughout history will testify that there's nothing like receiving a hammering to give your cause some shape. The ninth Guru's son was a warrior: "The ultimate test of truth is to die fighting for it." However, Guru Gobind was not only a warrior, but also the author of much of the outward form of Sikhism. In 1699, he established the fraternity of the *Khalsa,* an orthodoxy of followers identified by always wearing uncut hair, a comb, military-style underpants, a steel bangle, and a dagger. And, significantly, Guru Gobind proclaimed that the true Sikhs of the Khalsa should subsequently carry the surname "Singh"—"lion."

Guru Gobind Singh is therefore held in reverence by Sikhs, second only to Guru Nanak. He is typified as a hero of true Hindu culture in the face of Muslim intolerance, an heir of Lord Ram even. He lost his four sons (two walled up alive; two in battle) and a wife in the struggle for dharma and was finally assassinated, leaving the Holy Book, the *Adi Granth* or "Shri Guru Granth Saheb," as the next and lasting Guru.

So that sealed things off. A book, however sacred, has no way of developing. Sikhism since has retained its identity through emphatic reruns of the warrior-saint theme. The saintly aspects are their rejection of caste distinction, their refusal to steal, lie, or take alcohol or drugs, and their avoidance of sex outside of marriage. But what gets remembered are all the heroic struggles against an oppressive majority. As the power of the Mughals declined, the Sikhs fought against the British, and then, having been defeated but favoured by the British, fought for them against the sepoys in the Indian Mutiny. Separated from Muslims and Hindus alike, they have been fighting over the Punjab since it was divided by Partition—fighting against rival factions in their own group, and fighting against the Hindu rulers of the Republic. Memories are still fresh of the armed Sikh occupation of the Golden Temple at Amritsar and of terrorist activities in the early 1980s: the siege and the army attack on the temple, the assassination of Indira Gandhi by her Sikh body-guards, and the subsequent rioting and murder of Sikhs by Hindus. Memories—the hypnosis of history fixing the future into the pattern of the past.

Opening into the present is the only sane ground. Fittingly the last scene in Patna was back on that lakelike ground floor of the gurdwara, where Ram Rattan Singh met us and steered us into the dining hall for the *langar*, the communal meal that is one of the oldest Sikh traditions. Roti and dhal were served to all, and we sat on the floor in the sacred fraternity of eating. A Sangha of sorts. Through the gateway at last.

That was a suitable time for leaving. We were heading for Nalanda. Not directly, the way of the main road, but via a road heading south toward Bir. Nick felt that if we headed down that road, he could find a way of cutting across country that would make the walk more pleasant. Ram was delighted: his cousin lived somewhere down that road at a place called Baldarichak. He wrote a note to his cousin, gave it to Nick, and walked along with us for a way. We left him in a Sikh jewellery store owned by one of the elders of the temple committee, campaigning again about the lack of hospitality shown to us. Jai Ram!

By the side of the road toward sunset, another puja. Afterward I noticed how pleasant it was to be sitting in a field carefully using a needle to get a splinter out of Nick's foot. It seemed like one of the more sacred acts that I had undertaken in the last month.

After dark the walking was still flowing on; some fellow driving a tractor stopped and jabbered at us excitedly ... same old stuff about danger and bandits. "Baldarichak!" we threw at him, half crazy with walking, and went on. "Baldarichak the Beautiful, City of Our Dreams," we joked. Baldarichak! Whoever went to Balderichak?

And Nalanda, Rajgir, and Bodh Gaya—more dreams destined to become memories. Yet I plodded along, one foot shrouded in bandages and carrying a few less ideas. All right to be stupidly plodding in stupid Bihar. Was this the way to follow the Buddha? Who knows.

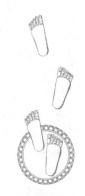

11

Dark Angel

AJAHN SUCITTO

We were now in the second week of glowing December, the time that the Indian climate is at its most benign. The heat of the day goes down to a sunny English summer (the nights are autumnal) and the light is golden; I felt grateful for its gentleness. The light no longer stabbed my eyes when I gazed over the landscape. I could even handle looking up at the birds on the telegraph wires silhouetted against the pastel blue sky. Although those more distant were just fuzzy black blobs, the nearer ones—rollers and red-vented bulbuls with forked tail—were quite pretty. I was starting to get mellow. India, for all its rough edges, had looked after us well.

Baldarichak had offered us a chilly night on a table outside the hut of Ram's cousin. In the morning, after a glass of hot milk, the family group had stood around us silently, watching us pack our bags. The children were like perching birds, bare-legged with their heads and upper bodies wrapped in blankets. All they could offer was their attention; I tried a few phrases of Hindi, which they accepted without comment. The metalled road took us a couple of miles to a warm sunrise, a small market village, and a glass of tea.

There Nick paced around, looking at a wide dirt track that branched off from the road, inspecting his map, muttering aloud "It must be ..." squinting at the horizon, looking down the metalled road, saying "Hilsa? Hilsa?" to passing strangers. All part of the conjuring act that I had ceased trying to understand. "That must be northeast ... and there's a lot of cycle tracks going that way ... It must be ..." My place was to stand poised for the decision, with an agreeable smile that I hoped was supportive rather than condescending, and then follow. Somewhere in whatever direction, we'd go for alms, there was water everywhere, and at the end of the day we would be in another field or village more or less the same as where we started from.

NICK

Trying to find our way using the maps I had with me was not like map reading in England, where you could note something from the map and then follow it. As ever in India nothing was that certain. I had three maps: a modern German one of eastern India, up to date but on far too small a scale to be of much use away from the main roads; a commercial Indian one of Bihar State, on a bigger scale but crudely made and very unreliable; and the copies of the maps from the British India Office. These were on a large scale, full of detail, but fifty years out of date. The three maps hardly ever agreed with each other and only occasionally, even between them, agreed with what was on the ground. Route planning had thus to be a tentative business. I would combine the information from all three maps with various bits of advice we got from locals as we went along. As most people had never been more than a few miles down the path, this advice was usually even more unreliable than the maps. With all of that we would try to make our way.

As we proceeded, my mind would go again and again through the same mental cycle. It would start with anticipation. We will go there, and along this path, to that place, and we will see this and that, and so on. Then for some reason or another we would not be able to. A path would not exist, or there would be a village, river, or whatever, where it was not supposed to be. So I would get annoyed, only to find that what we ended up doing was just as good and interesting as that which I had planned. India is great at putting a spanner into the planning and anticipating mind. It is that mindstate that gets in the way of being open to what is happening.

Using the maps to get away from tarmac roads did not mean we had got away from the Indian bicycle. Once we were on dirt paths, I appreciated what those bicycles were all about. Old "sit up and beg" Raleighs with that heavy build, and lots of big springs under the saddle. Thick tires, padded seats, and the one low gear meant that they could go anywhere in the country, even meandering their slow way along the small paths on the mud walls between the paddy fields.

We were trying to head southeast, but in fact our route wandered a lot—with us sometimes going east and sometimes south. It would have been quicker to follow the roads, but this way was more peaceful, and we were seeing the real rural India where everything went at a much slower and more steady pace. The landscape was dotted with people working in the fields, now with growing crops. Many were raising water for irrigation using horizontal tree trunks hollowed out to look like long thin canoes. One end of these was open and rested on the lip of the drainage ditch to be filled. The closed end was suspended by rope from a leaning pole above the water to be raised. A man stood by each one, dressed in the soil-stained, off-white cloth of a labourer. Putting his weight on the suspended end, it would drop, bending the pole, and dip into the water. When they took their weight off, the pole would unbend, the hollowed trunk would rise, and water would run out of it into the ditch. He would step on and off the trunk, over and again, creating a slow rhythmic creaking accompanied by a gentle sloshing, as the water ran into the ditch.

AJAHN SUCITTO

December 8th. Chula and curd from a few farm workers on an old estate. In the afternoon a man cycling along the track that wound around the paddy field bade us follow him and led us to within a few miles of our destination, Hilsa. He left us recommending that we spend the night in the Kali temple in the small town.

The idea caused a shiver of alarm. I could almost imagine the clamour and the reek of blood. Kali! Hideous fangs and long tongue protrude from her blood-dripping mouth; human skulls are draped in a garland around her neck; animal sacrifices are performed in her name. Trampling down the body of her consort, the supreme lord Shiva, she is Shiva's energy that eventually must destroy even Shiva's form. Call her Fate, Kamma, or all-devouring Time, she is the power that shapes and undoes lives that we long to call our own.

It was dark when we found Hilsa. What a ghost town! Hardly anyone about. Hilsa had no street lights—and no street either; the track got muddier and more well used until, out of the darkness, the forms of buildings materialized. Nick didn't favour dragging ourselves around this murk looking for a temple and asked some ghost for the dak bungalow instead. Dak bungalows were a vestige of the Raj; in the days before hotels, they were built as places where travelling civil servants could spend the night. A caretaker, or *chaukidar,* lived in the bungalow, and he would guard the place, keep it clean, and cater to the travellers. Dak bungalows still exist in many small towns, and—by some stroke of luck (although we liked to attribute it to benign providence)—there was a dak bungalow just a few minutes' walk away from where we had entered the town.

It too was swathed in darkness. Nick swung the garden gate open, and we proceeded up the path by torchlight. The heap on the veranda must be the chaukidar asleep ... deeply asleep—neither calls, nor shouts nor torchlight could wake him. Was he all right? As Nick shone the torch directly in his face, he moaned slightly but made no movement. Had he been attacked there in the darkness? Nick stepped over him, opened the front door, which wasn't locked, and began inspecting the room. "Electricity's off—do you have a candle, Bhante? ... He's drunk." I was wondering whether this procedure was ethically correct, but Nick had no doubts—"pay in the morning"—and we moved in.

A simple clean room, and it connected to a bathroom where one could get clean by splashing water from a tank—and even a toilet. There were also a couple of hard beds available for us to spread our sleeping bags on. I lit up a few candles, bathed, and then anointed and dressed my throbbing foot as preliminaries to the evening meditation. Well, well, well...fortune seemed to be smiling on our good efforts.

A few feeble moans ended the meditation, followed by the sound of the chaukidar stumbling and crashing around. He had come to, enough to realise that something had happened, but was still too smashed to know what. He couldn't find the door, and the subsiding groan indicated that he had lapsed back into unconsciousness. Poor chaukidar! He was clean out of luck. In the morning he tried to pocket the charge for the room, but Nick knew the system of payment and was too sharp for him. "See Bhante, you have to sign that book—and write in how much you have paid. When I looked in it, most people had paid thirty rupees. He's taken the book so that he can pocket the money himself." ... "*Das rupee!* I give you ten rupees. Or you give me book and I give you thirty rupees." You generally give the chaukidar ten rupees baksheesh. "No! No book, no thirty rupees!"

I felt sorry for the chaukidar: his bad night was being followed by an unsuccessful morning. But the sun and Nick were up and moving on. Within a couple of minutes they led us straight into the Kali temple, which was near where we had entered Hilsa. The temple was paradoxical. The image on the shrine, six-armed and brandishing weapons like some giant demonic spider, face split by a savage grimace, was ferocious, yet the temple was quiet and serene. The old priest, upright in bearing and mild-eyed, beckoned for us to stay and gave us a little food. His English, carefully enunciated in soft faltering phrases, wasn't up to explaining much. The only fragments of the conversation that stuck in my mind was that his brother was working in California.

But during that half an hour or so, Kali revealed herself a little. The dark goddess obviously had a bright aspect. Flowers adorned her shrine, and white cloths had been draped around her arms. A woman was making ritual offerings in little dishes and chanting to her. All was sweetness and blessings. It could have been Sunday in an English church with a village lady offering flowers to one of those gory images that symbolize the love of God for humanity.

Yes, Jehovah had no more scruples about ripping people apart than Kali. Come to think of it, following the Dhamma was no pushover either. The angels of transcendence have their dark side. If you could take it, all this getting beaten up was about giving up ownership of the birth-death thread. The impeccable few who let go come to a life beyond the web; flawed aspirants grasp wildly and go under in the darkness. In the eyes of the Transcendent, that's fair—compassionate even.

So, let it flow.

NICK

We left Hilsa on a wide dirt track heading east. It was easy walking, and in the late morning, it took us into a village. We stopped in the centre under an old Bodhi tree surrounded by a raised platform of packed earth with a small shrine at its base. The villagers who collected around us asked if we had eaten and then brought us some food. There were the usual questions about what we were doing and where we were going, and they led to other questions. Ajahn Sucitto's Hindi was now good enough to give simple answers. They asked him about problems in their lives, and for the first time he was able to talk Dhamma in Hindi. My own Hindi was still limited to practical things like asking how much something cost, so all I could pick up was the people's appreciation for what Ajahn Sucitto was saying. Obviously, the basic Buddhist teachings were just as relevant despite the very different culture; after all they were originally taught in India. Later they brought cups of tea and encouraged us to wash under the village pump. When we eventually left, I took with me a feeling of peacefulness and openness from that village, away from the urgency of the roads.

We continued along the broad dirt track that had brought us there. Although we had rested and the worst of the day's heat was now over, we found the afternoon's walking hard. I was still feeling run down, and each day a weariness would overcome me after a few hours' walking. Ajahn Sucitto was affected too. Since Patna he had stopped setting such a hard pace and now stopped at the slightest excuse. He seemed dazed, a bit like a punch-drunk boxer after fifteen inconclusive rounds. I suppose I must have looked much the same.

I reckoned we were suffering from protein deficiency. In Patna I had bought as much protein as I could—bags of cashew nuts, boiled eggs and curd—and we had felt better when we set out again. Now we were on the road there was less opportunity to supplement our diet. In the mornings, whenever we could, we would stop in a tea stall and have a plate of curried chickpeas as a small breakfast. Now I just ordered them; I did not bother asking. Although he was slightly dismissive of my concerns, he had let go of the idea of trying to survive on alms food alone. The chickpea dishes had much more protein than the runny dhal that came with the rice at midday. That was mostly water. I began to suspect that the midday meal was for Indians a meal of stodge and that they ate most of their protein at other times.

In the evening eggs were for sale from little stalls on wheels; the light from their kerosene lamps illuminating a tray of them, a flat pan for frying them on, and salt and spices to flavour them with. We were not eating in the evenings and we were hardly ever in the villages at that time, but that did not stop me fantasising about them. My body so yearned for protein that I would find myself dwelling on the thought of an egg, just a simple hard-boiled one, over and again, as we walked along.

We were cutting across country, and as we wanted to be at Nalanda in time for the meal, I was particularly concerned to get it right. First, Ajahn Sucitto asked a man taking a water buffalo to the fields who told us in Hindi that Nalanda was an hour away, and then a bit later I asked someone else, this time a chap on a bicycle who spoke English. He told us that it was eight kilometres to Nalanda, which was much more than an hour's walk. And that is how it went on. Each time we asked directions, we would get a different estimate of how far it was, often an increase on the last one, until I began to suspect that we were either going round in circles or that Nalanda was retreating before us. Finally, after walking for several hours at an ever-increasing speed as we began to worry that we were never going to get there in time, I stopped an educated-looking chap. His reply was very confident, "This road is leading to Nalanda, which is two and a half kilometres from here." The exactness of that *two and a half* convinced me that this time the information must be correct and that the others had been wrong, so we set off walking even faster as we had little time left.... We had been going for only five minutes when we came round a corner to see the ruins of Nalanda showing just beyond some trees, only two fields away.

Although we were never quite certain where we were, we knew when we were near a holy site by the change in the way people treated us: the friendliness and helpfulness we experienced as we went through the rest of the countryside would disappear. Instead of being seen as pilgrims to be helped, we were seen as a source of income. To the locals we were just more of the wealthy foreign tourists and pilgrims they got to see so often. At the holy sites the people recognized my companion was a monk, but they had seen too many foreign monks with video cameras, riding in rickshaws, and handling money to be inspired.

This time the path led us through a village where we were spotted by a cycle rickshaw–wallah who pulled up beside us to offer a lift. We said no but he kept pestering us. Then several young children came running, with their small hands outstretched, and crying out in high-pitched voices, "One rupee! One rupee!" As we turned into the lane leading to the Thai vihara, our intended destination, there was a sadhu sitting against a low wall. He had long dreadlocks tied in a gigantic knot, his face, arms, and legs were daubed with white, and he was wrapped in cloths of a variety of bright colours. Leaning by his side was a trident, festooned with red rags. He was the most impressive looking sadhu we had seen, and I thought he would make a great picture. I got my camera out and pointed at it, then at him, so to ask his permission. His response was immediate. He sat bolt upright and barked out, "One hundred and twelve rupees and eighteen paisa." Evidently he had also met tourists before.

AJAHN SUCITTO

Past Nari and Nur Sarai, we joined the road that comes from Patna to Nalanda. In the time of the Buddha it must have been the main route between Savatthi, the capital of Kosala, and Rajagaha, capital of Magadha. Along this road pilgrims would have hurried to the holy places farther south, or to stay in the great university of Nalanda, sometimes for years on end, copying sutras and studying the Dhamma. But to me, Nalanda was principally the place where there was a Thai monastery where I could rest my right foot and let it heal. I determined to do as little walking as possible. Wat Thai Nalanda would be an excellent place to recuperate.

Beyond its surrounding railings loomed a four- or five-storeyed building capped with a long roof, down the ridges of which gigantic stylized serpents stretched. Our island of peace was surrounded by swaying young trees that beckoned like nymphs...but at the gate we were welcomed by the hounds of Hell. The manic clamour of the temple dogs produced some shouting, whistling, and the sounds of sticks hitting concrete. Two dark faces appeared at the railings: the first, that of an elderly Indian man, was rapidly eclipsed by that of a Thai woman with shaven head— a nun, or *maechee,* her dark skin standing out against the whiteness of her robes. "Okay, okay, Bhante," her voice was hoarse and American-accented, "Just a minute ... the dogs." Getting the furious beasts under control took some more hollering in Hindi (the Indian man whirling around with his stick), but then she pulled the metal gate open and hurried us across the courtyard to the building. "You gotta be careful of the monkeys, Bhante" (large Hanumans gazing down innocently from the trees in the monastery compound). "They come down and bite you. Don't go outside the building without a stick! Here's a stick. They're real dangerous, Bhante!"

But they never attacked *her.* A few days later I saw her dozing in the sun in the monastery courtyard with two Hanumans in attendance, one checking her white sweater for any insects, one tenderly inspecting her scalp with careful fingers. They loved her. I found out that it was her offerings of food that had encouraged these lawless creatures to stay here. In their fenced-off area, the dogs would go wild whenever the monkeys descended from the trees, yelping in fury at the mild-faced Hanumans. But the omnipotent Thai nun had the dogs under control too...and the couple of Indian attendants who scurried briskly at her command.

No wonder she was hoarse. The daily administration depended on her voice. The main activity of the monastery was to cater to the tour buses of Thais who were undertaking a rapid pilgrimage of the Buddhist holy places and didn't want to come into contact with anything Indian if they could possibly avoid it. The monastery, or *wat,* is a familiar icon in the Thai mind; it provides the opportunity to "make merit," to create the skilful kamma through acts of generosity that will bring them good fortune in the future. The wat is also a storehouse of Thai-Buddhist culture and manners; to a Thai abroad the wat is Thailand, and is generously supported to remain as such. No matter that for most of the time the only monastic resident was one nun; the tour buses brought their own bhikkhus with them, to be accommodated overnight in the simple but well-ordered rooms of the wat and given dishes of well-cooked Thai-style food the next day before proceeding to the next Thai haven, Wat Thai Bodh Gaya or Wat Thai Sarnath. Form and merit mean a lot to Thais. Maechee Ahlee could call down the support for both; even in India. That was impressive.

After being given a room and an unbelievable meal, I made my way to the roof of the residence block. I felt I could give my wounds some air there. The sore had grown larger with the sixty-mile walk from Patna and had been joined by another; the soles of my feet and the heels were cracked and black. Then there were the other kinds of repairs that had to be undertaken at each stop: now the robes were showing signs of wear and tear, particularly the *sanghati,* the double-thick extra upper robe that is the third of the bhikkhu's allowed robes. The one I had was over ten years old, patched and repatched. Its main body was so old that mending it was like patching an overripe tomato—the sewing thread tore new holes in it, and one had to compromise with something between a darn and a lattice of stitches.

To be truthful, a certain embarrassment about my worn robes and torn feet kept me on the roof; I felt too lumbering and coarse for the graceful manners of civilized Thai society. The times that I did venture down, even with my battered robes worn as neatly as I could manage, and walking in small composed steps, I was still too big and ungainly. Compared to them, I felt like a wild ape. The visiting elder bhikkhus in immaculate glowing russet robes seemed uninterested, or perhaps uneasy, but would respond with cool politeness. Their female lay followers would kneel and bow and address me respectfully in angelic fluting tones. When they heard my few clumsy phrases of Thai, they responded in delicate English. And they were always impressed when they found out that I was a forest bhikkhu and a disciple of Ajahn Chah and Ajahn Sumedho. One of the tour guides, concerned about my wounds, offered me some orange tincture. At least it made my foot look pretty.

Retreating to the roof, I could be at ease with tears and tatters, wash my robes and bandages and hang them out to dry, sit in the sun, and look over at Nalanda in the distance. There, in the fifth century c.e., sponsored and supported by the Gupta emperors, had arisen the *mahavihara*, a "great residence" comprising several Buddhist monasteries whose sole activity was study. What was now just a heap of bricks had been one of the finest blossoms in the religion that had evolved out of the Buddha's teaching.

> *Homage to the perfection of wisdom, the lovely, the holy!…Here, O Sariputra, form is emptiness and the very emptiness is form; emptiness does not differ from form, nor does form differ from emptiness; whatever is form, that is emptiness, whatever is emptiness, that is form. The same is true of feelings, perceptions, impulses, and consciousness…where there is emptiness there is neither form, nor feeling, nor perception, nor impulse, nor consciousness.*

The patronage of Ashoka was the prime condition that allowed the Buddha's teachings to develop into a religion: earning it fabulous endowments, prestige—as well as the jealousy of the Brahmins. And despite occasional periods of persecution under succeeding monarchs, Buddhism and its many capable exponents filled a contemplative, philosophical, and devotional space with a vigour that the Vedas and the Upanishads could not provide. By the beginning of the Common Era, India was coming into a new age; trade routes connected it to the Asiatic Greeks with their philosophies, the growing Christian worldview of Rome, as well as the evolved culture of China. Grecian-styled Buddha images were created for the sake of recollection and veneration. Some argued that the Buddha was of a different nature than the merely mortal—his real undying essence had manifested a "dream" body in order to present teachings to the world. In this new divine framework, saviour figures appeared, called *bodhisattvas*. And during these, and succeeding, centuries after the Buddha's death, his teachings became the subject of an equally lively revision:

> *...there is no ignorance, nor extinction of ignorance...no suffering, nor origination, nor stopping, nor path; there is no cognition, no attainment, and no nonattainment.*

The old teachings had pointed out that what we term as "self" is in reality empty of a cohesive, consistent, and independent reality. The new teachings extended that analysis to every structure of reality, including any structure of teaching. This is *prajnaparamita*, "the perfection of wisdom," which

> *cannot be expounded and learned, nor isolated and described, nor stated in words, nor reflected upon by means of or in terms of any limited pattern of awareness.*

In the course of the next eight hundred years or so, prajnaparamita was conceived as a truth, gestated as a symbol, born as an image, and worshipped as a divinity. Over forty sutras, from the vast *Perfection of Wisdom in 100,000 Lines* down to the *Perfection of Wisdom in One Letter*, were composed around her ineffability. Even though she represents the essential emptiness of all phenomena, her form was delightful. What can be more captivating to the contemplative than that ungraspable, ever-beyond, ever-present truth? She was called a goddess and was one of the divinities who emerged to preside over Buddhism's "Second Turning of the Wheel," the "Great Way" or *Mahayana*.

Perhaps even the Gupta emperors, though Hindu, fell under her spell. They themselves were tolerant of Buddhism and recognized that Buddhist monks made very good scholars. Astronomy, logic, metaphysics, and grammar were studied at Nalanda along with the Mahayana sutras and commentaries. The brilliant expositions on emptiness by

Nagarjuna, the Yogacarin presentation of a world that is purely mind-made, and later the magical "thunderbolt teachings" of tantra—all and much more were debated through the centuries at Nalanda. In that palace, old archetypes married new symbols to produce a pantheon of deities: Taras of various hue; Avalokiteshvara, the Compassionate One, thirteen-headed, thousand-armed, and thousand-eyed the better to serve all sentient beings; and his counterpart, Mahakala, the ferocious guardian of truth, black and wreathed in flames. They may have first appeared as literary personae in one of the vast sutras or tantric rituals that were composed in the first millennium of the Common Era, but by the end of it, they had at least as much substance as the old Vedic deities. In the tantric teachings that eventually developed at Nalanda, these powerful spiritual forces were to be visualized and even acted out in esoteric rituals.

But ... Buddhism lost touch with the samana lifestyle that had connected the Sangha to the ordinary people. In some of the later teachings, the lifestyle of the Sangha is presented as a dull-witted attachment to monasticism, and the great bhikkhu disciples of the earlier texts appear as inept. Gotama the Buddha is one of millions of buddhas in innumerable world systems, not a samana subject to illness faring for alms around the Ganges Plain. His teachings in his historical form were to be interpreted as a kind of primer, a "lower path" or "small vehicle" to get people started who were too self-centred to attune to the compassion and grandeur of the higher teachings.

Nalanda grew away from the living context of the Dhamma Vinaya. The scholar monks didn't have to go on alms round or have contact with the ordinary people. And so the Turkic invaders who devastated Nalanda and slaughtered its inhabitants in 1200 hacked something that had already lost its roots. Buddhism had idealized into a vast pattern of images, concepts, and rituals that were not *"immediately comprehensible...to be seen by oneself"*—the touchstone of the Buddha's message. This meant that it had no more relevance to the lives of the majority of the populace than the evolving line of Vedic worship and Advaita Vedantic thought that absorbed it.

Philosophically you could even see the destruction of Nalanda as the culmination of Prajna's teaching: form, having been revealed as essentially void, was dramatically swept away. In a dialectic that delighted in paradox, what finer tantric consort could there be for Prajna than Ikhtiyar-ud-din-Muhammad—an illiterate freebooter with arms like an ape? He was the demonic counterpoint to the goddess. When they met, form and emptiness shattered together. The neighbouring university-monastery of Odantapuri became the troops' headquarters, from which they raided and sacked Nalanda. While a few teachers still lingered around the crippled body of the mahavihara, there were very few ordinary people devoted to the Sangha to look after any monks who might have survived, and even fewer inspired to go forth themselves. Buddhism had moved on to Sri Lanka, China, Central and Southeast Asia. In India it still lingered in a few fringe areas, but 1200 is the year that it ceased to have any affect on the mainstream of the culture.

Those who are thoroughly devoted to prajnaparamita will not die suddenly or unexpectedly, neither from poison nor any kind of weapon, nor from fire, water…nor from violence of any kind from any quarter, unless they choose to manifest such suffering as a skilful teaching or as some other form of compassionate action.

Destruction? Suffering? Compassion? In some respects the goddess's teachings bore a striking resemblance to those of Mother Kali. And wasn't that Jesus in the background somewhere? Looking down from the roof was starting to give me vertigo.

NICK

There were two meals a day at the wat: one was at seven in the morning and the other was just before midday. Both would be announced by the maechee sounding a large gong and served in a room connected to the kitchen. Both meals also consisted of the same food, white rice with lots of different meat dishes. Sometimes there was also fish or eggs and perhaps a small plate of raw vegetables. No exception to this heavy carnivorous diet was made for the breakfast, except that vegetables were less likely. We would sit on mats on the floor, Ajahn Sucitto at a large table with three Thai monks, who were also staying, and with all the food dishes, while I sat at a small table on my own with nothing on it but a plate. Thai monastic discipline is very strong on form, especially around food. This way the monks avoided any concern that the dishes had been handled by me without being formally offered back. They passed each dish as they finished with it, first the rice and then one dish of meat after another.

At meal times one of the workers would be on guard with a broom in the courtyard to shoo away monkeys as we crossed to the dining hall. At other times we had to carry our sticks. Otherwise the monkeys would gang up with the dogs and rush to attack us, driving us back to the haven of the main building, where they were not allowed. Even with a stick in hand it was a scary journey: the dogs would wake from their slumbers and start growling and then barking. This would bring the monkeys scuttling across the ground screeching loudly. Beating the stick on the ground would stop them, just out of range but still screeching loudly, until we made it through the gate.

I left the wat several times during our stay to visit the ruins at the main site. Ajahn Sucitto only went the once. He was not really interested in Nalanda.

Nalanda, though, must once have been a very impressive place. Even today the ruins are quite stunning and on a much grander scale than at any of the other holy sites we had visited. Several enormous and very solid-looking temples tower above one, their original outer ornate skin long gone, leaving tumbled red brickwork. Each of them contains a main shrine room, now empty, with flights of stairs leading up to it, and there are many smaller shrine rooms, as well as stupas containing small meditation cells, set about them. There are now walkways for visitors that go round the temples and a path that leads to the top of the remains of the largest one. In places, the temples have been excavated to reveal that they grew slowly, like the stupas we saw elsewhere, enlarged by building a bigger version on each previous one.

The rest of the site consists of eleven Buddhist monasteries set out in an orderly row opposite the temples—each built to the same basic rectangular design as we had seen at Vaishali. However, more of the walls were left here, and I could walk round and get a better feel for how the monks once lived. Although the cells were small, they were bigger than at Vaishali; and as well as recesses with a large slab of stone for a bed, there were also smaller alcoves for the monks' books. The cells faced inward onto a large pillared courtyard where once lectures and debates would have taken place, the teacher sitting on a raised stone slab at one end in front of the main shrine. At the opposite end was the porticoed entrance to the vihara. All the outside walls were very substantial; according to the Chinese pilgrims, the viharas were originally four storeys high with "spires that licked the clouds."

It was in these courtyards that Buddhist teachings and other studies were taught and debated. The level of teaching was very advanced. To gain admission to Nalanda, potential students had to answer a series of extremely difficult questions on Buddhadhamma. These were put to them by the gatekeeper, a scholar of high repute who resided at the one main gate in the wall that encircled the whole complex. Only those who answered quickly and accurately would be allowed to enter, and according to Hsuan Tsaing, "seven to eight out of every ten fail." Nalanda was thus more like a postgraduate college, and with such renown that degrees were often forged.

As well as study, it is believed that bronze metalwork was also practiced at Nalanda. Today the museum attached to the site is full to overflowing with ornate bronze statues of various different bodhisattvas, and the occasional image of the Buddha. There are rows and rows of them in a great variety of forms and flowing postures; and all with broken noses. The invading Turks did that, as they did with all heathen statues they found.

The grandeur of the site, and the complexity of the images, masked something, however. The essence of the original Buddhist teachings seemed to have gone. For all their artistic complexity, the images failed to convey for me any feeling of the sublime. The grandiose buildings were very impressive but did not move my heart in the way the simple stupas at other sites had. My favourite place was a large mound topped with a few Bodhi trees that was nearly cut off from the rest of the site; a small isthmus jutting out into the paddy fields. The distant sound of Indian pop music from the stalls at the entrance mingled with the calls of the farmers to their oxen and the sound of the gentle breeze in the Bodhi trees above me. A pair of black-shouldered kites would perch high in one of the trees, occasionally taking off to quarter the area, hovering over the fields and diving to the ground, or gliding, and then suddenly plummeting into the trees, hoping to catch small birds unawares.

From my vantage point I could see the visitors touring the Nalanda site, appearing and then disappearing among the ruins, or climbing the main temples to peer out over the surrounding land: western tourists in twos and threes, middle-class Indian families with their children scampering about, and large parties of Tibetans, mostly monks, who arrived by the coachload to be disgorged at the main gate. They would create a sea of maroon as they mingled at the entrance. Once inside, the sea would quickly disperse among the ruins. The monks were mostly young, either boys, youths, or young men, and they had a lot of restless energy. They would be all over the site calling to each other in Tibetan about what they had found. All of them, even the old monks, wore white sneakers. They seem to have become part of a Tibetan monk's required clothing, those, and watches, which are usually wound about with the mala beads they also wear on their wrists. The only Tibetan monk I can remember seeing without sneakers on is the Dalai Lama, who wears sensible-looking brown leather shoes.

It was the Dalai Lama who was responsible for the busloads of Tibetans being at Nalanda. Every winter he gives an empowerment at one of the Indian holy sites, and they were there to attend the next one. They would have come from the Tibetan refugee settlements, now all over India, or from Nepal, Sikkim, and Bhutan in the Himalayas. They were combining the two-week empowerment with the opportunity to make a pilgrimage to the holy sites. For Tibetan Buddhists, like the Chinese, any pilgrimage had to include visiting Nalanda, as it was from Nalanda that many of their teachings originally came.

Monks such as Hsuan Tsaing travelled to India not just as a pilgrimage but also to study at Nalanda and elsewhere and to return home with religious scriptures. The journey was a very dangerous one, through unknown lands, across the Gobi Desert, and traversing high Himalayan passes. From accounts in the Chinese chronicles, it is estimated that of all the pilgrims known to have left for India only forty-two are known to have returned in four centuries. Hsuan Tsaing was captured and nearly killed by pirates. The account of his journey makes much of his fearlessness and unwavering resolution, but personally I find the account of I-Tsing, another Chinese pilgrim, more moving—he seemed more human in his reactions. He came forty years later and was attacked while crossing through the hills of Bihar. Suffering from "an illness of the season," he had been forced to drop behind the large company he had been travelling with, and "late in the day, when the sun was about to set, some mountain brigands made their appearance." They robbed him of everything, including his clothes, and left him very frightened. It was then that he recalled a rumour that in India "when they took a white man, they killed him to offer a sacrifice to heaven. When I thought of this tale, my dismay grew twice as much. Thereupon I entered into a muddy hole and besmeared all my body with mud. I covered myself with leaves, and supporting myself on a stick, I advanced slowly." And that is how, at the second watch of the night, he reached the village where his fellow travellers were staying.

It was such pilgrims who spread the Mahayana teachings. Hsuan Tsaing became a great Dharma master in China, founding a new school of Buddhism based on the teachings he brought home. A Tibetan in residence at Nalanda at the same time, Thonmi Sambhota, was responsible for converting the Tibetan king, who proclaimed Buddhism the state religion when he returned. They also came from Sumatra, Java, Sri Lanka, and Korea. Great teaching monasteries arose in those countries that were modelled on the mahaviharas. Those in Tibet lasted a thousand years—until the Cultural Revolution.

The Chinese pilgrims of the seventh century describe the dedication and moral integrity of the monks residing at Nalanda, but with time this changed. Nalanda grew fabulously rich, and monks began to study for material gain, for positions at court, or for prestige. By the tenth and eleventh centuries, Buddhism in India was mostly confined to Bihar and Bengal where the mahaviharas were.

When the Muslim invasions of India came, the armies destroyed any temples they found and killed all the priests, or monks, in them. There is a graphic description by the Muslim historian Minhaju-s Sirj of the destruction of the Odantapuri mahavihara, which was near to Nalanda:

> Ikhtiyar-ud-din-Muhammad, with great vigour and audacity, rushed in at the gate of the fort and gained possession of the place. Great plunder fell into the hands of the victors. Most of the inhabitants of the place were Brahmins with shaven heads (Buddhist monks). They were put to death. Large numbers of books were found, and when the Muhammadans saw them they called for some persons to explain their contents, but all of the men had been killed. It was discovered that the whole fort and city was a place of study.

It happens to everything eventually, it all must be trampled under foot. Whether it is Tibetan culture being destroyed by the red cadres of the Cultural Revolution, British institutions being demolished by Margaret Thatcher's handbag, or Buddhism being wiped from India by the Turkic invasions of the twelfth and thirteenth centuries, Kali in her many manifestations will take them all. The good things just seem to last longer, but they too have to go, their goodness corrupted from within; sometimes they can be like old trees—still outwardly impressive but with rotting centres, waiting to fall with the next storm. The Buddha said that although his teachings would last five thousand years, they too would eventually completely disappear.

AJAHN SUCITTO

At Nalanda I felt most attuned to Maechee Ahlee. Brief conversations that we had when she wasn't attending to visitors or rushing around shouting at the attendants or the dogs (or both) revealed a sharp mind and a sincere heart. She had come here ten years ago to study at the new University of Nalanda (an academy adjacent to the wat). In fact she had gained a doctorate in Abhidhamma. But those days had gone; now she wasn't even that interested in learning meditation. "Don't want to study anything new, Bhante. Don't have time to read. Just like to sit in the sun and do nothing sometime. Sometime I'd like to live in a forest ... that'd be nice. Maybe next year I go back to Thailand, visit my mum. She keep writing to me—when I gonna come home? Been here ten years, Bhante ... long time, Bhante. Like to see my mum again. She gonna die soon."

I wondered how my mother was getting on. I'd written a couple of times to her and also to my brother who lived close by. Although I wasn't expecting a reply, the memory of her frailty nagged me. Perhaps I should have stayed in England to look after her; the last time I was overseas, living in Thailand, my father died. They'd brought me a letter from him and a telegram at the same time. In the letter he said that he hadn't been feeling too well of late but was looking forward to coming out to visit me in the monastery. The telegram was from my brother saying that dad had died that morning.

That was hard to take. Dad had wished me well in my life as a bhikkhu. He had worked hard all his life, built his own business up from scratch, and began to realise, in his sixties, with all the stress and anxiety and long hours, that he was caught in it, and that maybe his dropout son had a point. After twenty-five years of some friendship but little communication as adults, we would have met. So there was the regret.

Then, when I went back to England to visit my recently widowed mother, my teacher died in Thailand. That was Ajahn Alan—so bright, calm, and gentle in the vihara in Chiang Mai when I first met him. It was evening and the oil lamp was lit by the seat where he was sitting; the windows, having no glass, allowed hordes of flying ants to flurry in toward the light and crawl over his face and arms as he sat. But he displayed no irritation, carefully picking an ant away from his eye or mouth when its life seemed to be endangered by his lecturing. That presentation, and the strange relocation of attention through focusing on the breath, was all that was needed to set my Dhamma wheel rolling. If I could watch my thoughts and feelings and not react to them ... if I could watch my mind ... then whose was this mind and who am I?

So I went to stay in Ajahn Alan's monastery in Nakhon Sawan and became his disciple. So did a few other Westerners. That stimulated plans in our teacher's mind. Ajahn Alan had always felt frustrated by the cultural overlays that eight hundred years of Thai culture had deposited on the Buddha's words. Some of the archaic rules seemed to him to be anachronisms; nowadays he felt it was more suitable to be able to handle money in order to purchase books and other requisites for teaching, as well as to be able to travel to bring the Dhamma to those who might be interested to hear. This all made sense to me, but I did feel uneasy about his proposal to set up his own vihara in northern Thailand, and even more uneasy about his expectation that I be one of the teachers there. After three years I had no realisation to impart. Then again, Ajahn Alan, although tremendously concerned for the welfare of his disciples, and a storehouse of knowledge on all forms of Buddhism, psychotherapy, and related topics, didn't give you much peace of mind. He was always on the go; the whole practise was bound up with doing; even the meditation felt like an activity aimed at getting you somewhere. Not that he bothered with meditation himself—he was too busy reading, teaching, and writing. He was too busy to go out for alms, go to the daily chanting, attend the Patimokkha recitations, or associate with the Thai bhikkhus. Under pressure from the abbot of the monastery, he would go to a few of the monastery's ceremonies for the laypeople, but to him this was not the essence of Buddhism, it was all just custom, dead wood that kept most Thai bhikkhus complacently coasting on the simple faith of the laity. His vihara was going to be something different.

It was. He set it up while I was in England and wrote to me about it while my six weeks in England extended into a proposed five months. Alan was optimistic as usual, but the vihara was slow in getting going. For a start, it was off the beaten track, so only a few of the Westerners that he had hoped to encourage made it out there. There was no chanting or ceremonies, so there was nothing to attract the local villagers either. Ajahn Alan had to go out for alms, and walk fifteen kilometres every day with a weak ankle that steadily worsened. So after ten years in robes, he felt the way forward was to disrobe, go to Bangkok, and teach meditation as a layman.

We'd already lost contact by then. I was learning about the bhikkhu life from Ajahn Sumedho, who apparently still needed to meditate (I thought at first that he couldn't have learned very much if he still needed to do it after twelve years as a bhikkhu!), was still stuck with the cranky old monastic conventions, and still presided over morning and evening chanting and Patimokkha recitations—but felt good to live with. So Alan and I were faring on in different directions. The next I heard of him was a few months after we began to create a monastery out of a derelict house in West Sussex. A former disciple of Alan's, himself a bhikkhu just on the point of disrobing, wrote out of courtesy. Alan had committed suicide in Bangkok. The sequence after disrobing had involved difficulty in finding a means of livelihood, debt, depression, drinking alcohol, more debts, and despair—and finally a glass of bleach. There was no explanatory note, but in an earlier letter he had asked that if anything happened to him to pass everything he had to his former temple boys.

My teacher and more regret. Another good man strangled in the web that his mind had spun. Having Buddhism figured out hadn't helped him in the end. The teaching of his death was his most powerful transmission.

Who dies? Who lives? Why are we so obsessed with ourselves? It's when Death's angel comes that you see all the acquisitions, positions, and fancy games are empty. Coming out of one's own preoccupations is a matter of life and death.

NICK

The last day at Nalanda I went out for my usual walk, down to the archaeological site. The walk there took me past the small college next door. This had been set up by the Indian government for the study of Buddhism, and many of the students were young Theravadan monks, mostly from the hill states on the border with Burma, which have small Buddhist populations. The monks were out playing volleyball with the other students on a dusty piece of ground outside the college. They seemed to be having a much easier time of being a monk than my companion. So did the Tibetan monks I had seen enjoying themselves in the Nalanda ruins. But then they did not seem to be taking much heed of the rules of training, which were, after all, laid down by the Buddha. So who was right? At times I really did wonder on this pilgrimage. Why did it have to be so hard? Ajahn Sucitto seemed even to *want* it to be difficult.

I contemplated that a lot of it came down to the difference between Asians and Westerners. Left to themselves Asians will just hang out, like the young Thai monks staying in the wat who were rather aimlessly making their way around the Indian holy sites. In Thailand one of the favourite words is *sabai,* which they use in the way the Spanish use *mañana.* Westerners, on the other hand, can be driven by the need to get something done, to achieve something, and, in the spiritual life, to resolve all those emotional hangups. In Thailand they don't have the hang-ups, they don't even have a word for guilt! So perhaps it depends on the culture. For them the harshness of the Thai forest tradition makes sense as a counter; for us perhaps there is a need for some kindness to ourselves in with it. But then I've always been easy on myself.

My companion did seem to be changing, though. Since Patna things had got a lot easier. Maybe that was just because we had got so run down, but I hoped it was more than that.

Our last day at Nalanda was my birthday. I walked down to the site to get some cold Fruitees to celebrate. They were sold by some of the stalls at the main entrance, and I had got into the habit of buying them when I passed. This time I bought seven, one for Ajahn Sucitto, one for each of the Thai monks at the wat, one for the maechee, and one for me. Having distributed them I went upstairs to drink mine on the flat roof of the wat. It had been a quiet day but a nice one, and I felt the best I had since we started the pilgrimage. We had eaten well at Nalanda, and all that meat protein had got us feeling fit again. It had also helped Ajahn Sucitto's foot. The temperature was now much more manageable—in fact it felt very pleasant up there on the roof in the slight breeze—and I was looking forward to the next part of the journey. From the roof I could see the hills of southern Bihar, rising out of the plain just beyond Rajgir. Our long trek across the plains would soon be over. Rajgir was our next stop, and after that we would be in forested uplands.

AJAHN SUCITTO

December 15th. After five days on the roof it was time to get walking. There had been some healing; Wat Thai had looked after us well. Just after the grey dawn broke, I bandaged up my foot and followed Nick across the fields. We stopped briefly at a small deserted Buddhist temple called Jagdishpur, more beautiful, more sacred, to my mind, than the grandeur of Nalanda.

We had our plans—to be at Rajgir for the next dark moon, and then on to Bodh Gaya, where Nick had arranged some Christmas accommodation, and possibly to meet Sister Thanissara, one of the nuns from Amaravati, who was also on pilgrimage in India. That would be nice. Just stuff in the mind—all insubstantial and not the real thing at all, but what else is there? This is the stuff of aspiration as well as separation and grief, and it beckoned us on. Nothing much to do about that but let go gracefully. How you come out of the unknown, transfigured or destroyed, must depend on how you go into it. After all, dark angels always play fair. You can trust them to shatter your world.

12

Letting Go

AJAHN SUCITTO

By the time we reached Rajgir, we were almost running: striding very briskly into Rajgir to arrive at the Burmese Vihara in time for the meal, which would surely be occurring around eleven o'clock.

The town of Rajgir was clearly marked by a line of hills that rose out of the plain and that had been visible from Nalanda, fifteen kilometres away. At last, something to rest the eyes upon, something to give rise to the impression, however illusory, that there was somewhere to get to ... the first sign that the world might have an end to it since the glimpse of the Himalayas six weeks previously. Those blue hills promised a cool vantage point over the tangle and swelter of the world. The Buddha, born within the sight of the Himalayas must have loved this place! In King Bimbisara's capital, then called "Rajagaha," he was a welcome and respected guest: when he was not staying with the Sangha in the Bamboo Grove—the park that the king had given him just outside the town—he would have been living in those hills on "Vulture's Peak." From that crag he could have looked over the town and the forested plain, with the great birds slowly wheeling below him.

To arrive at such a serene place within oneself is difficult: for the pair of us to feel balanced and calm simultaneously for more than the occasional delightful moment was well-nigh impossible. Mostly it was like flying with a broken wing, and in that state we did absurd things. For no real reason, we had dallied on the way: with a stoned sadhu in a bat-infested temple, and later in a nearby village where a shopkeeper had implored us to stop and have tea. Then, having subscribed to the "being with what turns up" mode of thought, we switched back to "destination fever" and found ourselves hastily pounding along the main road at (Nick timed it) seven kilometres per hour.

A strange sense of foreboding accompanied the otherwise reassuring perceptions of the hills: Rajagaha had been the place of betrayal, of the struggle for power. The narratives from the Buddhist scriptures refer to two simultaneous conspiracies that came to a head in Magadha's capital; that of Devadatta to wrest leadership of the Sangha from his cousin and teacher, the Buddha, and that of Ajatasattu to take over the kingdom by disposing of his father, King Bimbisara. Having attempted and failed to take over the Sangha by implying that the Buddha was too old, Devadatta later made arrangements for assassins to murder the Awakened One. When this failed (the assassins were all converted by the Buddha) he set a boulder rolling down from one of the crags to where the Master was walking. It struck a rock and shattered, but a fragment had grazed the Buddha's foot. Rebuked and warned by the Buddha, Devadatta was ostracized from the Sangha and caused a schism by attempting to create his own Order, one that would adhere to stricter standards than those advocated by the Buddha. In this way he hoped to justify his desire to lead the Order with the need to develop a purer lifestyle, now that the Buddha was over the hill and had gone soft. This too was unsuccessful—the Master sent his two chief disciples to visit Devadatta's Sangha, and in one night of Dhamma talks they won the bhikkhus back to the original path.

Devadatta's friend, Prince Ajatasattu, had been more successful. His father had discovered and foiled one of his plots, then having caught his son and pardoned him, he abdicated in his favour. That wasn't enough for Ajatasattu. When he became king, he had his father imprisoned and later murdered. It became part of the family tradition. As Magadha waxed powerful and took over the Vajjian confederacy and even Kosala, four generations of Ajatasattu's descendants murdered their fathers.

Hatred is never cured by hatred,
only through kindness.
This is the eternal law.

It might have been partly my associations with Rajagaha, but I felt "wrong." The race along the road was so absurd it was funny; but behind the events, the vision was fading, and little things were getting at me. Nick losing things for example. Nearly every day he would lose something—a clock, a pen, an item of clothing—and he never seemed to take any steps to remedy the habit. Then there was not one day that he got the chanting right—simple things like mixing "Buddha" up with "Dhamma" and chanting "I bow to the Bumma" (maybe it was on purpose!). Sometimes I doubted whether he was really into the spirit of the pilgrimage, dismissing the local people abruptly but goggling over the birdlife. These and other little things repeated over and again would chafe me like the continual rubbing against a blister. Such pettiness would make me feel annoyed at myself and brush it all away philosophically, yet the irritations and denials were starting to merge into a dull despair. Why did it bother me? Why? It shouldn't be this way, I should be feeling light and inspired. Was any of this helping me develop toward Awakening?

In a daze I whirled into the Burmese Vihara behind Nick at eleven-thirty. Glancing around, I noticed a few buildings, a courtyard. We located an ancient Burmese bhikkhu, U Zayanta, in the main building and an Indian man and his wife, who were the manager and the cook respectively. Food was being served for Bhante, but for us no meal was available; it had to be ordered in advance, or something like that. The reason was irrelevant; it was obviously part of the Grand Plan to frustrate our every expectation. The manager advised us to go to the "Minto Hotel." Something in me wanted to give up then and there, but caught in the momentum, we strode up and down the street with the minutes ticking by and no "Minto Hotel" to be found. The frustration in my heart wanted to scream. But Nick, bless him, eventually hustled us into some eating house with ten minutes to go and got them to dish up some food. The best I could manage was to control the surge of emotion and eat in silence. Not good at all.

NICK

We went back to the vihara after the meal and the manager took us up to a room on the roof. We seemed to have the building to ourselves. Once we had washed, unpacked, and paid our respects in a less flustered second meeting with Venerable Zayanta, I went off to have a look around.

Across the road from the vihara was a large flat open area. It was perhaps five hundred yards across, surrounded by a slight mound, raised some ten feet above the road, and it had at least four games of cricket being played on it, as well as local people crossing it, and a small herd of goats trying to find something to eat in one corner. This, it seemed, was the remains of New Rajagaha, the city built at the time of the Buddha as the new capital of the kingdom of Magadha. The Buddha would have come here on alms round when it was a thriving and very important city. The slight mound circling it was once the old city walls, and remnants of the towers where it reached the old city gates could still be discerned. I only knew all that, though, from later looking at a tourist leaflet. What it actually looked like was a big barren public space—which, to the locals, is what it was.

The ruins of New Rajagaha are on the edge of modern Rajgir. Beyond the cricketers and goats could be seen the start of the shops and marketplace. On the other side of the ruins and beyond the vihara were the hills, the first break in the Ganges plain since we started walking. They rose steeply, with a narrow valley cutting into them opposite the vihara. This valley was once the entrance to Old Rajagaha—the original capital of Magadha. Old Rajagaha had been protected inside the natural fortress of the hills, but during the time of the Buddha, the kingdom had grown sufficiently that King Bimbasara felt confident enough to move the city out onto the fertile plain.

The Rajgir hills are an outlying portion of the central Indian uplands, which start twenty miles farther south. This rolling plateau, known as the Deccan, is an ancient area of worn-down mountains—much, much older than the Himalayas. On its northern edge it has been dissected by rivers flowing down into the Ganges plain. As the sediment in the plain has built up, the leading edge of the uplands has been buried, leaving the outlying higher bits, like the Rajgir hills, sticking out of the plain: rugged islands in a flat green sea of cultivation. The Rajgir hills sweep round in an arc, with the two arms trailing off together to the southwest as a double ridge. There are only three gaps through them to the flat area contained in the middle. They made the ideal protection for a capital city and were probably the reason that the kingdom of Magadha grew to prominence.

The rocks of these hills are old and the soil so poor that, in the past, the hills were left as forest. They were still shown as such on my old 1940s maps, but by the time of our visit the demands for wood by the ever-growing population had denuded them. From the vihara all I could see were bare stony slopes rising up some five hundred feet, scattered with the occasional boulder and rocky outcrop. But each evening, lines of poor people, mostly women, would come into town past the vihara with piles of wood on their heads: large bundles of long thin branches or long sticks made from split logs. They held them with one hand, the wood overhanging forward and back and rocking gently as they walked. The multitudes of the plains have to have fuel to cook their food and, as they cannot afford coal or gas, they use wood—if they can get it. The poor people collect it for sale, cutting it as long sticks to feed into small clay fireplaces. When wood disappears completely from an area, they use dried cow dung mixed with straw.

I remembered watching those lines of women each tea time when I last stayed at the vihara. That was in 1974 when I was twenty-one. I had been in India for over a year, and I was travelling alone. The friend I had come with had gone off to stay in a Hindu ashram but that had not appealed to me—I was put off by the emphasis on gurus and all that devotion. Buddhist meditation interested me, though, and I had booked a place on a meditation course taught by a man called Goenka to be held in the vihara at Rajgir. I had turned up the night before it was due to begin, as had a pleasant English public-school chap. The next morning we sat together on the terrace, drinking tea, playing chess, being ribbed by an American for being so English, and watching the course assemble around us. Old Venerable Zayanta was there, but only in the background, as the course was organized by a small group of Goenka's Western disciples. By the evening over 150 Westerners had arrived, mostly in their twenties and dressed in a great assortment of styles and colours. The early 1970s was a time when it was easy for the young to travel. There was full employment, and none of us felt any need to settle down to a career. India was a favourite destination, and if you were in India you had to learn meditation. The vihara could not have taken any more. We were sharing rooms—four in the one I was in—and we were knee to knee in the meditation hall. Goenka seemed a jolly, rotund, and wise chap, sitting at the front on a small dais beside his rotund Indian wife, and all he taught was meditation, which he presented in a very rational way. He referred to the Buddha and his teachings, but there were no Buddha images and bowing, or anything else I would have found hard to swallow.

The courses were ten-day intensive meditation retreats. Each day was scheduled with ten hours of sitting meditation, and we were supposed to be completely silent. Goenka would continually encourage us to keep at it. He would start each evening talk, in his deep mellow Indian voice, with phrases like "three days are over, there are only seven days left to apply yourselves." It was jumping in at the deep end, very difficult at first, but as long as you stuck at it, you were going to learn to swim. The meditation teaching was all about technique, three days of *anapanasati*, focusing on the breath as a meditation object. That was followed by what Goenka called "vipassana" meditation, slowly taking your awareness over the sensations in your body from the top of your head to the tip of each toe. Four times a day there was a one-hour period of "maximum determination." I was very impressed with how the "old students," as they were called, could sit perfectly still for the whole hour while I went through agonies trying and failing to do it myself. During the course we would meet the teacher in small groups to discuss our progress. I had overheard a Western Buddhist monk on the course ask Goenka what sensation he should concentrate on when speaking, to which Goenka gave a very detailed answer. When it was my turn I asked the same question in the hope that he would treat me equally seriously. Goenka was not impressed; he just told me it was supposed to be a silent retreat.

I had not been an entirely exemplary student on that first course. I had discovered, during one of the periods when we were supposed to be practising in our own room, that if I closed the shutters and lay on my back, a slight gap under the shutter allowed the reflected light from the sun to project a full upside-down faint image of the courtyard outside onto the back wall of the room, like a home movie. The room was acting as a pinhole camera. It was like that for most of the morning, and I would invite other students in and we would lie there watching the to-ings and fro-ings of this amazing upside-down world. On this visit I wanted to know if the image was still there, but the room was being used by a large family of Bengali Buddhists from Calcutta. The idea of trying to explain to them that I wanted to lie on my back in their darkened room was just too much.

I discovered something else, though, that proved just as evocative. When filling in the registration book, I looked back through it to see who might have stayed at the vihara recently. Skipping through several pages filled with foreigners' names, nationalities, and addresses from the past few months, suddenly there was a leap in time, and I was looking at the list of people on the meditation course I had been on eighteen years previously. For some reason the vihara had got this old book from somewhere and was using up the empty pages. It was eerie, one of those things you can dismiss as coincidence but leaves you wondering at the deeper reverberations in this world. There was my name, second on the list. The chap I had been having tea with came first, the Western monk had signed his preordination name, Christopher Titmuss (someone we were to meet again later), and I recognised several other names—others who like me had gone on to become "old students" of Goenka.

I must have eventually done some thirty of those meditation courses. First in India and then in England when I returned. I followed the tradition for five years with several teachers. Eventually, though, I tired of all the emphasis on technique. I had taken the meditation to the point where I was beginning to become familiar with the space of the mind, and the insights I had did not fit in with what we were being taught. So I left and explored other forms of Buddhist teaching, ones that had all that nonsense like bowing, Buddha statues, and monks that I would have had trouble with at first. However, I still feel a lot of gratitude to Goenka. He is still teaching and must have introduced tens of thousands to the Path by now.

On this visit to Rajgir my experience was to be much less benevolent. It all started with that ludicrous fast stomp into town. As with everything we tried to do at Rajgir, it wasn't that our approach was any different—we had stormed into other holy places in the same way and been fed each time—it was just that we had become complacent. This time we enjoyed the stomping along and just assumed that if we made it in time we would be welcome. It came as quite a shock when, having got there with no time to spare, we were turned away. It was a similar story on the second day when we tried to visit the Sattapanni Cave somewhere up on the side of the nearest of the hills. For Ajahn Sucitto this cave was important because it was there, three months after the death of the Buddha, that the elders of the bhikkhu Sangha met to agree on the teachings and the monastic rules. That is known as the First Sangha Council, a very important event in the Theravadan tradition, as supposedly the teachings and rules they follow to this day were all agreed upon then. For myself, I wanted to visit the Sattapanni Cave to find out if it was the cave I had visited eighteen years previously at the end of the Goenka retreat. I remember wandering across the fields with three others to climb up to a lonely black dot on the hillside. They told me it had been lived in by the Buddha, and we sat there together in silence. Then, when the others had left, I bowed for the first time, to a small Buddha rupa, in gratitude for what I had received.

So Ajahn Sucitto and I set off in the morning for the Sattapanni Cave with what we assumed was plenty of time. We climbed the flights of stairs that started just beyond the Lakshmi Narian Temple, a giant pink building that looked as if it had been turned out of an ornate jelly mould. As we got higher we could see down into the temple, its hot baths heaving with fleshy humanity. The baths are fed by a hot spring. At the time of the Buddha it ran into a secluded natural pool that he and his disciples used. It was popular then, but now it was so popular that one sight of all those people made me drop the idea of a visit. It was difficult climbing in the heat, and we made slow going. We stopped regularly to rest by the path and once in a small Hindu temple, where a priest demanded money as soon as we entered. Eventually we got high enough that the bare stony ground gave way to a scrub of low coppiced trees and spiny shrubs. Amidst it was a group of women cutting firewood, hacking at any regrown branches with long wide knives. Their saris were old, worn, and grubby, and they had cheap plastic bangles on their arms, the bright colours contrasting with their dusty dark skin. They called to each other as they worked, but as we laboured up to them they fell silent and moved off quietly, farther away from the path. Soon after that, dripping with sweat, we had to admit defeat; we were never going to make it in time to return to the vihara for the meal. So we turned and started back, on our way down passing a Jain pilgrim on her way up to one of the Jain temples that are on the summit of the seven main hills. Jains all seem to be from the merchant classes, rich enough to do a pilgrimage in style. This lady was late middle-aged, very overweight, dressed in a pure white sari, and she was being carried up by two men on a seat slung beneath a long pole that ran between their shoulders. The men doing the carrying were some of the same poor people as the women cutting the wood. They too were dark-skinned, small, and scrawny looking, and their faces were knotted with the strain as they climbed the stairs.

At that point I still had not realised that our luck had changed and I made another attempt to visit the Sattapanni Cave that afternoon. Ajahn Sucitto had the sense to stay behind. I left it till the cool of the late afternoon and did actually get as far as the cave, a big rock overhang with dark recesses and not the place I had visited previously, but I had no time to actually look at anything, let alone take in the spectacular view. Two policemen were rounding up the visitors as it was time to go back. I tried arguing with them but to no avail. Bandits roamed the hills and it was their job to protect the tourists. I had just one glance at the view over the vast plain stretching to the north. With more time I was certain I could have spotted the places we had been. Then I turned round and trudged back, along with three Japanese travellers toting video cameras, the policemen bringing up the rear. So much for the Sattapanni Cave.

AJAHN SUCITTO

The New Moon was December 16th. In the afternoon I wandered around the nearby Bamboo Grove. It was just a little way along the main road, toward the gap in the hills that separated Old and New Raja-gaha. Right next to it stood a huge and immaculate temple of the Nip-ponzan Myohoji; the monks and their supporters had done a wonderful job in restoring and caring for the ancient park. The grove had no build-ings—it never had—but there was a lovely pond in the centre of the towering stands of bamboo. It had been a very special gift—the first gift of land to the Buddha, and an indication of the devoted support of one of the most powerful kings of the region. Even before Gotama's enlightenment, Bimbisara had recognised the quality of the young recluse and had asked him to return when he had realised his goal. Within a year or two of the wakening, the Buddha returned as prom-ised, and the king brought his retinue out to pay their respects and lis-ten to the Master. At the end of the discourse, all those present declared themselves to be the Buddha's disciples. The king's proclamation was particularly moving:

> As a prince, Lord, I had five wishes; now they have been fulfilled. "If only I might be anointed on a throne." That was the first wish and it has been fulfilled. The second was: "If only I might encounter a fully enlightened One."…The third was: "If only I might be able to honour that Blessed One."…The fourth was: "If only that Blessed One would teach me Dhamma."…The fifth was: "If only I might be able to understand that Blessed One's Dhamma." And that too has been fulfilled….Lord, let the Blessed One receive me as a lay follower who has gone to him for refuge for as long as breath lasts.

It was painful to think that such devotion had not prevented the king from meeting a cruel death some thirty-five years later at the hands of his son. I turned away. Nobody was around in the nearby temple, so I drifted back to the homely Burmese Vihara. It was friendly now, and to judge from appearances, had aspired to elegance a few years ago. The meal had been served on a table with a tablecloth and old-fashioned, shiny cutlery. The Indian couple were quiet, friendly, and efficient;

Bhante was jovial and animated. Antiquated pictures of holy places in Burma decorated the dining room; but now that had all given way to the power-lust of the current military regime. Like Cambodia, and Tibet. What refuge had Buddhism provided for any of them?

The vigil wasn't so bad. We were in two rooms up on the roof. I sat outside the room with the stars and the gloom. You can't control it, you can't not care about it, you can't grasp it, you can't forget it. "Let go of it," recommended Ajahn Sumedho. It doesn't always work like that—I don't see where I'm holding on. Some moments it did all drop, and what was terribly "me" was seen as a pattern of mind created by the wish to be clear, or certain, or accepted. That wish always hindered the natural peace of the mind. When a letting go occurred, everything was light, the self-importance of despair was humorous, and you wondered how you could have forgotten that. "I'll remember and do better next time," chirps the mind, assuming ownership and authority, and thereby paves the way for the next black hole when it can't bring about the same process. The whole trap was set around "I am": the need to get life under control by figuring it out or attaining something.

"This is deathlessness: the freedom of the heart through nonclinging," said the Buddha. What was I stuck on this time? I needed to find a calm place where I could check things out.

So, the day after, we decided to go up into the hills, where things would be more conducive. There was a Nipponzan Myohoji stupa—the "Santi (Peace) Stupa" up there. It would probably have a few adjoining rooms where we could stay and thereby avoid being ordered off the hills by the police.

The climb was reasonable enough, beginning in the late afternoon. Nick couldn't bear to go round the long way via the road and the causeway, constructed, apparently by Bimbisara, as a convenient route to ascend to Vulture's Peak to see the Buddha. Instead we had to take a shortcut, which involved following a narrow stepped path through the scrubby forest up the side of the hill. We even got to glimpse some giant blue antelope-thing leaping across our path into the scrub. A nilgai, Nick said; he was very pleased, and I was pleased too. Then the path ended at a Jain shrine, and we had to scramble through the scrub and thornbushes trying to guess which direction the stupa lay in. That meant blundering around after Nick getting my legs torn, more painful floundering accompanied by inner mutterings. Eventually, just as the sun was settling behind the hills, its rays illuminated the peak of the stupa, not far off. And so we arrived at the monument. The place spoke of—no, proclaimed—Peace and Order, or at least Order, created by some impressive technology and willpower. And it was quiet; hardly anybody was about. Nick guessed that with the sun going down and the general "bandit phobia," everyone had been ordered off the hill.

Inside the temple we met the chaukidar, who had a little English. No monks were here, tomorrow the nun would come, but tonight no one was here except him and three other Indian temple workers. He wasn't certain we were allowed to stay, but as it was now dark, we could at least stay the night. We could sleep in the shrine room and ask the nun when she came tomorrow.

The shrine room was immaculate—polished wooden floor, tiers of huge finely wrought golden Buddha images cascading forward in pairs of diminishing stature. Somewhere in the middle of this galaxy of blessedness beamed Most Reverend Fuji, and above him the tumbling swirls of calligraphy proclaiming the sacred mantra: "Na Myo Ho Renge Kyo." But we'd been through that one. Here it was silent. The four Indian workers sat reverentially behind us as we did our evening puja and some meditation. Then they lay down on the floor, so we unrolled our mats, and with our heads pointing toward the shrine, passed the night in periods of sleep interrupted by the snoring of one of them.

The morning brought a clear sky and a further opportunity to marvel at the workmanship of the temple and its idyllic setting. Things here would be as they should be—still and clear. The only uncertainty was the nun. The chaukidar was used to relating to her as his boss, so he was hesitant: maybe we could stay, maybe not. Maybe there would be some food. Meanwhile he made some rotis and shared them with us. That made him relax. It seemed best for me rather than Nick to approach her. The chaukidar would go with me, introduce me, and explain the situation first. I never was good at blind dates.

When the nun arrived, immaculately robed, she immediately took up her position beside the giant drum. It was all precise. She seemed elderly but upright, and my glimpse of her features before she dismissed us testified to a life of determination, duty, and utter control. Physically she seemed composed of a different substance than the bowed, supplicating chaukidar in his grubby workman's clothes. She granted him a couple of seconds of attention, and me, one glance (eyelids flicked up in the motionless head), a negative monosyllable, and a tightening of the lips. So we were out.

Fine. No having to fit into routines, take part in rituals that had no meaning for me, or awkwardly go along with whatever the standards of etiquette were. Well, I never liked formality much anyway. She could keep her immaculate temple, her immaculate robes, and her precision prostrations—the scrub and the dirt were good enough for me.

Out there was Vulture's Peak. We whiled away the afternoon around the temple grounds to avoid being sent down by the police. As the sun lowered, though, we surreptitiously made our way to the crag where the Awakened One had spent many a day and night in meditation. It was still light, but nobody was about. The remnants of a tiny temple still sat on the crag overlooking the valley that the ring of hills enclosed. My heart rose as we drew near—he had been here, his calm gaze had swept over those forested slopes and blessed the wildness. And below, just as I could now, he might have contemplated a pair of great birds slowly wheeling in the currents of air; with the merest flick or inclination of a wing, they would swing out of one air current and glide on another. Here, replete with understanding and compassion, the Master had let his mind move through the realms of form and formlessness in complete equipoise. Here, his heart inclining to ways and expressions that would reach us in our tangle, he had taught the Good Law.

Vulture's Peak lifted us together on a point of balance. We entered the brick rectangle that defined the temple, bowed, offered incense, and let the chanting pour out as it would: "Homage to the Blessed, Noble, and Perfectly Enlightened One!"

The dwelling of an Enlightened One is not a place to sleep. When night dragged our minds down, we retreated a little way to the back of the crag. Nick found a cave, and I took shelter in a ring of rocks, resting in the place of vultures.

Our morning puja back in the temple ruins preceded the dawn. While we sat there, the darkness separated into sky and misty hill masses, paled and coloured into forest wreathed in mist beneath a tender sky, and then allowed the day to begin ... with drumming, drumming approaching from a distance ... a familiar rhythm ... and voices: "...Renge Kyo! Whump whump whump whump whump whump!" Two figures were bounding up Bimbisara's causeway toward the crag— Japanese monks! Striding up the crag were Reverend Nakazoto from Vaishali and the monk from the temple in the town beating handheld drums. It was good to see them—grins and beams all round. They were on their way to Calcutta and stopped off to pay homage to Vulture's Peak. "Ah, Doctor Scott, we are lucky. I was wondering how to cash your cheque, now I meet you here!" Reverend Nakazoto's grin widened— Nick had forgotten to sign the cheque that he had left as a donation to the temple at Vaishali. So there it was. Reverend Nakazoto dug it out of his shoulder bag, and Nick signed it right there, in the Buddha's dwelling place. It was all much too crazy for words.

I watched them go bounding back down the causeway, back to their car, which would take them to Calcutta. Things went so easily for some. For us another restless day had begun; more people would be coming soon. Already a man had approached us trying to sell us incense. We had to go down. But the long forested valley and the line of hills stretching peacefully southwest toward Bodh Gaya told us which way to go from here.

At the bottom of the hill was a jumble of stalls for the tourists. We moved on toward the forest across what had been Old Rajagaha. The jail where the old king had been imprisoned by Ajatasattu was still there. Betrayed, imprisoned, and deprived of food, the old king's only consolation was to gaze at Vulture's Peak through the window of his cell. But death by starvation takes too long; eventually Ajatasattu grew impatient and had his father's feet cut open and the wounds stuffed with salt. It speeded the process up.

It was time to get out of this harsh town.

NICK

As we descended Vulture's Peak, I bought tea and some snacks as our breakfast from the hawkers who were on their way up, their day's wares hanging from poles across their shoulders. Then we crossed back through the stunted forest heading for a forest resthouse, one of the ones I had booked from Patna. We might not have been able to stay at the Japanese temple, but the resthouse should be no problem. The Patna wildlife office had recommended it and assured me the forest officer would be delighted to see us.

It was still early, and birds flitted about the scrub as we made our way. I kept stopping to look at them through my binoculars and then hurrying to catch up Ajahn Sucitto. When I spotted a rufus-backed shrike sitting on a bush, it was such a good-looking bird that I had to point it out to him, offering him my binoculars to take a look. To my surprise he knew all about shrikes. He had owned a bird book as a child and had learned all the names and pictures, and although he had never seen a real shrike then or since, he still remembered it. This was a revelation; Ajahn Sucitto had, up until then, seemed so uninterested, dismissive even, about my enthusiasm for wildlife. I pondered, as we went on, that perhaps I might be able to share it with him after all.

The resthouse was not far, and we arrived within an hour. It was a well-kept bungalow behind the house for the forest officer, with workshops and huts for the workers. It looked a great find, with a veranda and set about with its own small garden. We went next door to the forest officer's house to arrange to stay the night. He was a young chap with good English. He seemed pleased to see us until I mentioned the resthouse, then his face clouded. He told us we could not stay as he had received no booking from the district office. I tried explaining that we had written to the district office, but it did no good; he was adamant. He was also looking increasingly upset by having to turn us away. Then I asked if there was another booking. There was: he was expecting his boss, the district officer.

We met the district officer later. We had hung on in the hope that there would be room for us—after all there were two bedrooms—but when he turned up he had his family with him, and they were all staying the weekend. The institution of the resthouse made a lot of sense when established by the British. Neat bungalows dotted about the district where officials stayed on their horseback tours of duty. Now, they had become a perk. The district office was no more than two hours away by official car, but the visiting official was to be housed and fed at the state's expense in a country bungalow that was probably better than the house he lived in.

So we were out on our ear again. We would have to leave Rajgir two days before we had planned. I hadn't even seen the Bamboo Grove or Jivakambavana, both places where the Buddha gave many teachings, never mind the Jain caves carved into the hillsides, the city walls of old Rajgir that ride along the crest of the farther hills like the Great Wall of China, or the Indasala Cave where the Buddha went to be alone and which was probably the cave I had been to all those years ago. But it seemed we were not supposed to stop in Rajgir. Well, at least we were heading into the forest. We would have more time to enjoy it, and we would be sooner in Bodh Gaya, our next stop, where we were expected by friends for Christmas.

So we left the compound in the early afternoon and set off on a dusty dirt track that was wide enough for a jeep but which appeared little used. The track dropped down to cross a dry riverbed, climbed the other side, and then wound its way through the forest, heading for Jethian. The forest officer had said there was a forest resthouse there where we could stay that night. This must have been the route the Buddha used when travelling from Bodh Gaya to Rajgir. It was the most direct route, and the scriptures mention him stopping in Latthivana, which is today's Jethian, on the way to Rajgir after his enlightenment. It would have been real forest then. Now it was heavily cut, and we were walking through a dense thicket of trees regrowing from their stumps. Not far along the track we came upon a group of women returning to Rajgir with bundles of wood on their heads. As soon as they saw us they dropped their wood and ran off into the forest. They did it without a word and hardly any sound, leaving the wood bundles as the only evidence that we had really seen them. Further on we heard the steady thumping of an axe and then rounded a corner to see a man halfway up the stump of a small tree cutting it even shorter. He immediately jumped down and also ran off, with his axe, into the forest. The disappearing people created an eerie feeling, compounded by the silence of the forest at midday.

An hour's walking later, the forest got taller. There were still no full-size trees, but the cut trees had regrown enough to give a semblance of real woodland. It was then that we came upon a group of six men bending over the carcass of a large animal. These men did not run off but instead looked up to watch us approach. As we did we could see that they had been using axes to prepare poles for carrying the carcass of a water buffalo. Ajahn Sucitto asked in Hindi what they were doing. They replied simply that the water buffalo had died. Looking back now it is obvious that they were poachers and that the water buffalo would have been a stray they had found and killed; one of the animals brought into the forest illegally for grazing.

After we had left the men, the track began to climb. The scrub around us was getting taller, and we could see mature trees on the hillsides above us. We were at last getting into real forest, and I felt elated to be among nature again. I got caught up in an internal debate as to whether I could ask Ajahn Sucitto to stop a bit so that we could walk on later in the day, when wildlife was more likely to be about. Two evenings before, when we had been climbing up to the Japanese stupa, we had come upon a male nilgai, a great blue-black antelope the size of a domestic bull. It had been very exciting, and I was hoping to see more. I was so immersed in this that when I glanced back and thought I saw someone disappearing into the trees, it registered just for a second before I dismissed it.

AJAHN SUCITTO

It was about expectation, surely; that was the heart of the problem. I was expecting India to live up to my projections of a "spiritual place." What that seemed to mean was that it would allow me to stand back from it and feel balanced. And that was a demand that India refused to comply with. The way out, surely, was in letting go: let go of getting a clear picture, let go of wanting things to be my way, especially as I didn't even know what "my way" was. Letting go: although it feels like dying, it gives you the freedom to live without self-importance.

I remember sitting in the garden of the forest resthouse while Nick was engaged in the lengthy parleys with the officials; we were about to wander off through a forest supposedly infested with bandits. At one point even talk of an armed guard arose, but one was not forthcoming. Oh well, I should prepare. There was nothing to prepare. Wait. I had a careful shave, by touch, dipping the razor into my steel mug of cold water and fingering my chin and face. There. Ready to go into the unknown.

We walked for an hour, my outer robe folded and tucked over the top of my bag. The bag was hanging on my left shoulder. Across my chest was slung the water bottle and mug so that they dangled by my right side. It was from behind me on that side that the little chap approached. He caught hold of my mug, and as I turned, asked in Hindi where we were going. There were others with him; they were the men who had been sitting on top of the dead buffalo. "To the next village," I said as he tugged my mug urgently. "What is it? Do you want this thing? It's only a mug...."

Then everything blew up. Nick turned round with a menacing expression on his face; someone was tugging my robe on one side while the first man was hauling frantically at the mug on its strap on the other. Three men charged at Nick who was crouched boxer-style; he wheeled and hit them with his backpack, then ran off with the three of them in hot pursuit. I was being lugged in two directions simultaneously by the strap on my water bottle and on my bag, I could only try to get the stuff off and let them have it, but their pulling on it made that impossible. We were going round in circles, with their excitement spinning into frenzy. I had to stop this. "Wait! Wait! Let me get this stuff off!" Momentarily they stood still. They all had axes and staves. The leader glared at me through twisted features and raised his axe.

Funny how your mind goes clear when the options disappear. Why struggle against the inevitable? The only freedom was to go without fear. I bowed my head and pointed the top of my skull toward him, drew the blade of my hand along it from the crown of my head to the brow. "Hit it right there." Something shifted; he backed off, waving his axe and muttering angrily. I stepped forward and repeated the action. Give it away; let it all go.

Things settled. He lowered his axe. I slipped off the bag and the water bottle and stepped back. The three of them began excitedly picking over the treasure. I imagined that they'd rummage around, find there was nothing there of any value, and run off. Two of them picked up the gear and scurried down the track a way. I felt shaky and sat down. Better keep cool—I started chanting softly. Then Nick ambled along with a smile but without his pack or assailants. "I've hidden the money; Bhante, are you all right?"

His return signalled further frenzy. As his assailants returned, the men charged at him with their sticks and began swinging blows; Nick caught most of them on his arms: "All right, all right! I'll show you where." And the mob had streamed off into the forest by the time that I got to my feet, leaving me with one lad, who sullenly resisted my attempts to strike up a conversation. But he was mellow compared to the older men when they returned—without Nick or the bags. They jumped on me and pulled off the bag that I had around my neck containing the relics and Buddha image; they ripped off the waistband that was threaded through my pouch; they clawed under my sabong and dragged the passport out of another pouch that was hanging around my waist.

Then they were off with the loot tied up in bundles on their heads. The leader turned round and said "Your bags are over there," pointing into the forest. "Fine, OK." I said, in a vaguely warm way. The forest went back to silence as usual ... a sunny day, with the forested slopes on either side.

I took off my shoulder sash and made a belt out of it for my *sabong*. Then I wandered into the scrub from which they had just emerged. "Nick?" Which direction? I just went deeper: "Nick?" and louder: "Ni-ick! Ni-ick!" Maybe they'd killed him! Or at least left him unconscious somewhere in a pool of blood. "NI-CK!! NI-ICK!!" As I probed deeper, the land sloped upward and came to a crest from where I could look over the edge of a ravine to a scrub-filled valley. I scanned back and forth for some sign. Nothing.

NICK

After the robbers had started to pull at Ajahn Sucitto's belongings, three of them turned on me. They came down the track toward me, each with a wooden stave in hand and one of them with an axe. I have never been one for giving in to people easily, even when it was obviously the sensible thing to do, and my reaction this time was typical. I was not going to let three small Indians rob me without some resistance. As they approached I lunged at one of them. He backed quickly away, and then I turned on another who then ran into the forest. I chased him but as soon as I was out of sight, I cut away and took off—I had escaped! I ran on through the forest, crashing through the trees and the spiny shrubs, oblivious to the cuts they were giving me. As I ran I kept thinking that I should hide the valuables before I was found. I was panicking and used the first thing I found—an old rabbit burrow. Into it I stuffed the camera, our money, and my passport. I quickly covered them with earth, then got up and ran on.

The trees suddenly ended at an abrupt drop. I was on the top of a long scree slope that ran down to a dry stream bed—far too steep for me to climb down quickly. I stopped and, bent double and panting heavily, tried to think what to do. There was no sound of them coming after me, and I realised I was probably safe. I had escaped—but I had also left my companion in the hands of six Indian bandits. The sensible thing would have been to stay put, but I was worried about what might happen to him. I was in two minds as I stood there panting. Eventually my heart won over my head, and I decided to go back.

I hid my pack in a hollow and cautiously made my way back to the track. I could hear nothing. As I neared the forest's edge, I spied Ajahn Sucitto sitting with the young lad beside him. Beyond them, down the track, were the others, milling about and looking into the forest. Evidently they lacked the courage to go in after me. As soon as I cautiously emerged, the young lad shouted and they all came running, all shouting and in quite a frenzy. This time I stood there submissively, but they still surrounded me and started hitting me with their sticks. One of them was shouting and gesturing, "WHERE IS THE MONEY? WHERE IS THE BAG?" I tried to say that it was okay and I would take them, but my previous resistance had worked them into too much of a frenzy.

They drove me like some poor water buffalo through the forest to the place where I had hidden the bag. The whole way the blows continued, and even when they had the bag they did not stop. The same man as before shouted at me something I did not understand. He pointed at the hollow where the bag had been. He wanted me to get down there, but by then I was too frightened. I thought they might kill me, and if they did, they would also kill Ajahn Sucitto. So, with my heart in my mouth, I leapt over the cliff and rolled and slid down the scree.

It was a long slope, dotted with thorny shrubs that cut me as I slid past. I ended up against some bushes at the bottom. I pulled myself up and looked back. Two of them were still coming after me, picking their way down the slope. I was badly cut and bruised. I had hurt my leg, and I stumbled as I tried to run off. I realised my only chance was to hide. They would take longer to get down the slope than me, and I reckoned I had just a few minutes. I limped and stumbled out of sight and then crawled under a large dense bush. I lay listening, my heart pounding. At first I heard them coming closer. Then nothing. I was terrified—laying there waiting—in fear of my life. Dampness spread in my crotch. The fear had made me piss myself.

I must have been there for fifteen minutes with nothing happening when I heard Ajahn Sucitto calling my name. I was still frightened and did not come out of cover, first calling back "Have they gone?" Only when Ajahn Sucitto called out "yes" did I emerge. He was standing at the top of the slope, bare-chested with just his sarong on, the rest of his robes had gone. My trousers and shirt were torn, the shirt so badly that it was in shreds, and I was covered in blood. Still, what I felt was a flood of relief that we had both survived.

AJAHN SUCITTO

Letting go was good. It was good being alive; we exchanged stories and chuckled a lot. Destinations, plans, ideas about the purpose of the journey—it was all so ludicrous now, funny to have held on to this stuff for so long. When it comes down to it, nothing really matters—all you can do is die, which you're going to do anyway. It was hilarious.

I suggested we rummage around to search for the bags. Nick checked the hole that he had stashed his camera and the money in. It was empty. After a while, we came across Nick's yellow plastic mug; we saluted it with glee. Then the cylinder of maps, chopped up like salami, its mutilation testifying to the pointless feverishness of the violence. But Nick picked up the mug like it was an antique and tenderly examined the brutalized maps the way a doctor might examine some mangled victim of a car crash. "I think I can salvage these." We even found his binoculars, hanging in a tree where he had thrown them. Well, well...

That was enough for the day. The sun was going down, and we needed to get back to Rajgir before nightfall; back to the Burmese Vihara, where there would be friends. Everything was so light; no bags, no money, no passports. We were trotting along ragged and laughing. But by the time we drew near to human habitation the evening had descended, and dark intense faces peopled the gloom: hawkers and rickshaw drivers looking for customers jeered at us as we hurried by. We had to get to the vihara, quickly. By the time we got there we were racing.

13

Landing Place

AJAHN SUCITTO

According to the Buddhist scriptures, when you pass away from the land of the living, you arise in the darkness before King Yama, the lord of the dead. There you are asked to recall your life, and an assessment becomes clear. Yama's officers haul you off for a sojourn in one of the many hell realms, escort you to one of the abodes of bliss, or usher you straight back into the human arena. I found this difficult to believe until entering the yard of the Rajgir police station on the night of the robbery.

I might as well be dead; after all, I had offered my head to a man with an axe. I felt light and airy, floating in a state like that mentioned by people who have died on an operating table and seen their body far below being worked on by anxious surgeons. Here, in the Rajgir police station, the surgeons were however far from anxious. A few officers wrapped in blankets were slumped in chairs under a tarpaulin roof. Around a gas lantern were a few vacant faces, the eyes gently scanning sheets of paper, an occasional sucking in of cheeks and fidgeting of the body. Reactions and responses hung suspended in the gloom. I was lingering in the assumption that, after some unfathomable cognitive process, our presence would be noticed. It was more like awaiting rebirth than being alive.

The night was cool; at least I had a robe on, and Nick a white wrap. The people at the Burmese Vihara had immediately seen to that. They were shocked and ashamed that such a thing had happened in India to Buddhist pilgrims. Their reactions surprised me. In my mind, the robbery seemed as fair as anything ever is: poor, desperate people see tourists with lots of money; they see Buddhist monks with expensive equipment travelling in air-conditioned buses; they see wealthy Jain pilgrims, and hawkers and sadhus making money out of them—why shouldn't they have a share of the harvest? They owed me no kindness and knew only the law of survival. For them, the human realm was like this.

And as for myself, refuge had become very clear. Something in me on that dusty track handed over my life rather than go into fear. When I looked back on my mindstate at the time, the dominant mood had been to maintain calm and introspection. What had seemed sensible at the time was for the group of robbers to simply go through our belongings, take what they wanted—most was of no monetary worth—and then allow us to continue on our way with the rest. I had felt some irritation at their frenzied mindstates, but I had actually been quite open to them taking our stuff. I had not done anything against Dhamma, so my mind had remained clear. They had left me one robe to wear around my waist, my sandals, and the bandage on my foot; maybe that was enough.

It was incredible how much stuff—water filter, lantern, torch, clock, knife—I had checked over each morning in the predawn gloom to make sure that I hadn't lost it, how much stuff I had struggled over squashing into a bag that I then would sling over my shoulder and lug along for twelve hours each day, cutting into my shoulders at every step. A bag watched carefully whenever we sat down for tea. Sadly, some of the pilgrimage had gone with it: the relics that people had given me and the possibility of offering them to the shrines of the Holy Places, the mala beads and the Buddha rupa with their dimension of noble company. All gone. And the diary too with all the details of where we had been and who we had stayed with, the record that was to be our future offering back to the Sangha. The past—gone; the future—gone; and the present wonderfully free and unformed, unformable. We are going nowhere. I felt no need for direction. Just to rest in the Way It Is. To know that as my heart's intention was worth travelling for a lifetime to discover. I felt dangerously pleased with myself.

The decision to report to the police had come from the vihara. They were anxious and concerned. The manager was insistent that we go with Nick suitably bespattered with blood to make some deeper impression. And certainly our bags were still somewhere in the forest. Maybe some of the items that weren't worth stealing but which were of the greatest significance—film, relics, and diary—might be retrieved. So here we were, looking for reentry into the human world of owning and choosing, a world I did not find very convincing. It seemed better to float for a while.

NICK

In Buddhism much is made of taking refuge in the Buddha and in the wisdom he represents. I had a real physical sense of that refuge, bowing my vulnerable living body to that big stone image in the shrine room of the vihara. I also bowed to Ajahn Sucitto, as I felt that he had done the right thing in the forest, and I wanted to honour that. He kept calm and gave them what they wanted, but I resisted and the robbers got into a frenzy that could have killed us both. I could have left this world with the same mind as that water buffalo they had hounded and killed earlier. It was an important lesson, the kind one rarely gets in a lifetime.

We had lost nearly everything in the robbery. Of the things that had gone it was not the expensive things that mattered to us most. Yet, ironically, it was those—the money, the traveller's cheques, and the camera—that I had tried so hard to save. I had even planned to do that in the event of a robbery, to get away and hide the valuables somewhere. The things we really missed were the irreplaceable ones. Ajahn Sucitto's diary, the names and addresses of all the people we had stayed with, and the sixteen rolls of slide film each with thirty-six pictures. I had been carrying them to Bodh Gaya, where we were to meet Sister Thanissara from Ajahn Sucitto's monastery. I had reckoned that it would be safer to send them back with her than to post them home. We were only three days from Bodh Gaya when we were robbed.

Losing things can be freeing ... providing the mind can put them down. I still clung to the idea that our bags might be out there in the forest. So I set off to the police station with some hope. I imagined constables systematically searching the forest, walking back and forth in line abreast, like they do on the news back home.

Rajgir had a power cut that evening, and the main street was lit by hurricane lamps hanging over the stalls and outside the shops. The police compound was through a dark gap in the wall that ran along one side of the street. Across a wide yard framed by several long buildings, two lamps hung from a tarpaulin strung from one of the buildings, their light bathing a couple of desks and several policemen lounging around them. No one appeared to be doing much except chatting, but they started to busy themselves as we sat down at one of the desks.

The policeman opposite was an officer. His khaki uniform, of shirt and long baggy shorts, was neatly ironed, one silver insignia on each lapel. A leather lanyard ran through one of the lapels and down to his belt, which held a holster with a pistol.

"You have come to report a crime?" This was somewhat obvious as I was covered in blood.

"We have been robbed."

"Then you must fill in the appropriate forms." Rajgir police had sprung into action.

The officer went off for the forms but returned accompanied by another officer. A smaller man, a little older than the first, but much more assertive. "I am the sub-inspector. Your robbery will be dealt with, but first I am insisting that your injuries are seen to."

Across the street at the local hospital, an orderly assiduously cleaned and dressed my cuts with a roll of cotton wool, water, and a very large bottle of iodine. I returned covered in so many large blotches that far more of me was purple than white. The appropriate forms and the sub-inspector were waiting. Everything had to be put down in full, in long-hand, and in duplicate. His questions seemed to take forever. Still little else could be done now; it was the next morning that mattered. Several times I raised this, and each time the sub-inspector would assure me. "We will be visiting the scene of the crime first thing tomorrow." When the forms were finally complete, I asked him what time we would be leaving.

"What time are you wanting to leave?"

"Seven?"

"Certainly! It is seven o'clock we are leaving for the scene of the crime."

It was said with such assurance that we returned to the vihara feeling optimistic. I was certain our bags must be there somewhere, and provided we got there early enough, we might well find them. When I told Venerable Zayanta and the manager our plans for the following day, they were less convinced. The manager seemed particularly sceptical about the idea of the police setting out anywhere at seven in the morning. Later, as he took us up to our room, he offered to come with us despite his misgivings. He was a good man, and it would be useful to have him along.

When we returned the next morning, the police compound was completely empty except for a jeep. After half an hour a sleepy policeman appeared, crossed the yard, climbed into the jeep, and drove it away. Nothing further happened, and by eight I was pacing up and down and getting agitated. I felt that if we did not go soon, someone, probably the robbers, would get our bags. At my signs of agitation the manager, who had been sitting with us looking not in the least surprised by the lack of policemen, announced that he knew where the sub-inspector was staying.

It was a small hotel just down the main street. The sub-inspector was called and came down, still adjusting his dress and obviously having just gotten up.

"You are wanting to go to the scene of the crime?"

"Yes. We were supposed to go at *seven!*"

"An important police incident happened last night, and so I was late to this hotel." The manager had a look of disbelief but I said nothing. At least now we could be on our way.

When we got back to the station, there were actually a couple of policemen sitting outside. The sub-inspector called out loudly to them in Hindi. Where was the jeep? Where was the driver? No one knew. With a sinking heart, I sat down again. After a good while the jeep returned, the sub-inspector came out and did some more shouting, and the driver went off for petrol. Only when the jeep returned again did the sub-inspector order his men to get ready. My agitated mind could not believe it; surely he could have told them to prepare earlier!

I tried to keep calm, but after a further half an hour of waiting I decided to go and look to see what was happening. I went round the back and found the constable's barracks. Inside were half a dozen of them, some still getting dressed, others cleaning their rifles, and one shining the buckle of his belt. Then I noticed, to the side, a figure squatting over a fire with a big pot on it full of rice. They were cooking their meal!

I had had enough! I went back to the sub-inspector and completely lost my cool. I told him that we were supposed to go at seven and it was now nearly ten. What was happening? Where were the constables? If we did not go now then we were going on our own! The result was immediate. He was outside barking out orders in Hindi, and the constables quickly appeared.

Suddenly we were ready, everyone was in the jeep. Ajahn Sucitto and I were in the front, squeezed between the sub-inspector, who was driving, and his number two. In the back sat five policemen and the vihara manager facing each other, the policemen with their rifles upright between their knees. Hanging on the back was the chaukidar who had been cooking the rice. The sub-inspector revved the engine, put the jeep into gear, and it shot forward. Away at last! The jeep lurched and there was a grinding of gears. The sub-inspector did not seem to be much of a driver, but who cared—we were off. He drove out of the compound, turned into the main street, which had the usual assortment of people and animals wandering along it, and set off for the forest. That's when we got the result of all my impatience.

The sub-inspector could hardly drive. We went around the corner far too fast, and with me crunched up against the sub-inspector he couldn't get at the gear stick. He slapped my knee to get it out of the way, and I looked down. When I looked up we were just about to drive into someone. Time seems to stretch out forever when that kind of thing happens. I couldn't believe we were not stopping or swerving, but we didn't. We just got closer and closer and then ploughed into the man from behind. The body and off-white clothes of an Indian peasant crumpled and disappeared from view. There was a sickening softness to the jolting of the jeep. It seemed forever before the jeep finally stopped.

AJAHN SUCITTO

Whump! I had landed. In front of me, a man's body jerked back and then forward and down under the impact from the jeep. The grating and grinding of a body trapped between the jeep and the road skewered into my mind for several long numb moments before we stopped; then we were out of the cab in a scramble. The man casually walking along the main street a few seconds ago had become a moaning bloody heap dragged out from under the back of the jeep. Confused action; I tried to get closer, but the manager caught me with sad knowing eyes, tightened his mouth, and slowly shook his head. "No...better you go." The police clumsily picked the body up and loaded it in the back of the jeep, which turned around and jolted back up the street. Nick and I looked at each other and at the manager, who continued shaking his head. "Police ... not good. What ... do? Go to vihara. Come...." I had landed in India.

My brain, hitherto suspended, was suddenly all action—why hadn't I acted earlier? Standing around in a noncommittal way was an inadequate response to the energy of confusion and irritation at the police station. The young sub-inspector was having a difficult time with his uncooperative officers—perhaps he was new to the post. He had mentioned in a regretful aside that the driver of the jeep was about to retire and no longer obeyed orders. On top of that he had found himself having to cope with two Westerners expecting things to work like they did in England. Caught in the dilemma and bound by duty, finally the mounting tension had snapped him. A demon had rushed in, thrown five armed policemen, the manager, and a boy in the back while compressing the sub-inspector, Nick, myself, and another policeman into the front of the two-seater. A timorous recommendation for caution slowly oozed and coagulated in my brain, but by the time I could read it, it was too late.

Two men walking side by side had appeared through the windscreen with their backs to us—I glanced over to the driver—his attention was off the road, getting Nick's knee out of the way of the gear stick. A cry moved up my throat as my foot stabbed the floor; but it was too late. Now they were bouncing a writhing body off to the hospital in Bihar Sharif. Even if he survived, what about his family? And I felt sorry for the sub-inspector. He shouldn't have been driving; it had been our impatience and agitation that had goaded him into it. And the driver shouldn't have wandered off, and the police force should be run more efficiently, and Nick should be more patient—and I should have said something. But however it should have been, that's how it was.

"Where were you?" nagged the imp that lives in my brain. "You could feel things were going out of balance ... Always hanging back, not wanting to be involved..."

I was left alone for the afternoon. The police officer came and went off with Nick to the scene of the crime. The whole business about getting our bags back seemed increasingly irrelevant. Everything seemed to be caught in the careening of a world that has lost its axis. It didn't matter who and why; the only true action was to get to the point—the mind—and hold it steady. And here, now, there was nobody other than myself to take the responsibility for knowing that.

NICK

I felt very low. I blamed myself for the accident. If I had not finally lost my cool with the sub-inspector, they would not have set off in that frenzied way. As we trudged back to the vihara in silence, Ajahn Sucitto looked in the same state of despair as me. At one point he muttered to himself that it had felt like the same frenzied energy we had seen in the robbers. He was right. And it was the same energy that resulted in the eruptions of awful communal violence that can come from nothing in India. I had now triggered it twice.

At the vihara, the manager told Venerable Zayanta all about the morning's events while we sat there saying hardly anything. There were lots of knowing shakes of the head from the old monk and the manager's wife. An hour later, just as we were about to start the meal, the police returned. I took some chappatis with me and went out to join them. At the edge of the forest we stopped at the forest compound to collect a forest worker, who clambered into the back. Then we set off along the dirt track we had walked the previous day—across the stream and into the forest. Then we stopped. The sub-inspector had spotted the small tree trunk we had seen being cut the day before lying beside the track. The chaukidar and one of the constables were ordered out to manhandle it into the back.

From there it was only fifteen minutes to where we had been robbed. The sub-inspector had me show him the exact spot where they had attacked us. It had happened just a few metres beyond the highest point of the track, where it began to drop toward Jethian. He stood and looked at the spot. I showed him where they had come out of the forest. He looked hard at that too. Then, having also looked up and down the track, he solemnly pronounced with all the gravitas of an old detective movie, "This, then, is the scene of the crime."

He called the other officer and the forest worker over, and they started a conversation in Hindi which involved pointing up and down the track. I interrupted. *"Please,* can we look for our bags. You said we would. They are here somewhere in the forest." The sub-inspector looked vexed at being interrupted, half turned, and barked out something in Hindi over his shoulder. Behind him the police constables got up and ambled into the forest, each setting off in a different direction. I followed them. As I wandered about looking for the bags myself, having given up any idea of a systematic search, I came upon some of the constables. None were searching: one was collecting firewood, two were chopping at a log, and another was standing with the chaukidar at the edge of the cliff looking at the view. I was too depressed by now to do anything about it. I just wandered about on my own, half-heartedly trying to find the bags.

Then I heard the sub-inspector calling, "Mr. Scott, Mr. Scott, where are you?"

I came back out to find him standing there with a look of triumph on his face and my hopes began to rise. "Yes?"

"We have discovered that, in fact, the scene of the crime is not in Rajgir police district but in Atri police district." "This," he continued, pointing at the place we had parked, "is the boundary of Rajgir police district. Therefore your crime is not our responsibility. You must talk to Atri police." And with that he climbed into the jeep. "Now we are returning." I had nothing left. What was the point of anything? I clambered in beside him, and the jeep set off back down the track.

AJAHN SUCITTO

Nick returned, fatigued and exasperated, late in the afternoon. No bags. In some ways it had been the right thing to do, but the mind wasn't right, and that had to be set straight. One man had already been run over through heedlessness. In going or staying, winning or losing, it was clear to me that we had to follow the Dhamma and not the world. First, we needed to settle. There was too much crazy energy around.

"Let's go back to Nalanda and meditate."

So we went. The vihara gave us the few rupees needed to catch a bus, and just after nightfall we arrived back at the gates and the dogs of Wat Thai.

Maechee Ahlee eventually appeared in her long underwear and sweaters—we must have got her out of bed—and gave a hurried welcome as she opened the gates and scampered off into the darkness. It wasn't the time for prolonged conversation. We were let into the accommodation block and told to take whatever we needed. A flask of hot coffee appeared. I sat in meditation until late: the pressure relaxed, the empty, peaceful night absorbed it all.

In the morning, delicately prepared morsels of toast and "Western" food appeared with our hostess, whose eyes widened at our appearance. "Ohh ... what happened to *you*? Are you hurt bad?" Nick sometimes manifests a battered innocence, like a faithful red setter that suffers calamities on account of its exuberance. His tail and ears drooped in sympathy with his numerous cuts and his scruffy shirt and pants, several sizes too small for him, given by a guest at the vihara. His explanation was suitably laconic: "We were robbed, by six men. In Rajgir forest. They had axes and cudgels. I had to throw myself down a ravine to escape...." The words were hardly necessary. Maechee Ahlee sprang into action with some shouting to the temple workers and an injunction to us to look around for whatever we needed, then sprinted in the direction of the kitchen block.

What *did* we need? Back to this realm again. I could use some robes that were my size ... maybe a *small* bag, a bottle for some water. In the bathroom, I found an old toothbrush and cleaned it up; there was a very small hand towel—that would be useful. Something else caught my eye. It was a drawing by the French cartoonist Peynet on the cover of a small notepad. Such blithe innocence. Well, since it had presented itself, along with a pencil and a ballpoint pen, it could come along. It would fit into the palm of my hand ... just to note the names of people who had helped us.

So our world began to find an axis. We were back with positions to work around, places to go, things to carry. I got an upper robe from the stores, picked a handful of Buddha medallions to give to people who might help us. With the water bottle, notepad and pen, small towel, and the used toothbrush, my kit was complete. Maechee had given Nick an old zip-up overnight bag from the stores and a couple of plaid blankets along with his water bottle, and some rupees. Then we had to rush back to Rajgir, this time by bus, to go through some official procedure with the police. Leaving Nalanda should surely have been more elegant, but Maechee Ahlee made nothing of it: having reestablished our pilgrimage supplies, and fed us breakfast and lunch, she bid us farewell a second time.

We had a chance to start again and at least walk as far as Bodh Gaya. And the judgement was, surely, to go back with kindness to the human realm: whatever happened, to connect to it; not to fight, not to complain, not to push.

NICK

The police returned early that afternoon, this time without the sub-inspector. Instead, his second in command came to the door accompanied by his opposite number from Atri, who seemed a much easier character. Ajahn Sucitto was coming with us, as was the manager, and once everyone had been introduced, we all clambered into the jeep,

Ajahn Sucitto in the front, the manager and me in the back, and we set off again for the forest.

Although I now accepted that our bags had probably gone, I still wanted to have one last go at finding them. Then I could forget them and get on to Bodh Gaya. I had also agreed with Ajahn Sucitto that we would offer a five thousand rupee reward. How we would get that much money—one hundred pounds sterling—I left as a problem for later. On the way I got the manager to tell the constables in Hindi that we would give the reward to them if they found our bags. They looked much more interested.

As the back seat was a hard metal bench, it was a bumpy ride. When we arrived I climbed gingerly out. As I did so two of the constables clambered past me, and they were quickly followed by the others. Before I could say or do anything (I had wanted to try to organize the search), they had all disappeared again into the forest. At least this time they were looking. Ajahn Sucitto, the manager, and myself divided up the area between us, and we went into the forest to join them, leaving the two officers having a conversation—presumably about police boundaries. As I walked up and down quartering my bit of the forest, I passed several of the constables. Each was very intent on the task; one of them was even hacking at the branches with a machete. The possibility of a reward had had an amazing effect.

An hour later all we had found were a few more shards of the shredded maps. We had gone over the area thoroughly, and the bags were not there. Back at the jeep the officers had agreed that the scene of the crime was indeed in Atri police district. They had a map with them, and they showed us how it was some ten yards over the boundary. They called the constables, and we all got into the jeep and bounced back along the track to Rajgir.

We would have to walk to Bodh Gaya with only the clothes we stood in and the blankets given to us at Nalanda. If we saved the rupees the maechee had given me, we would have just enough to take the train to

Calcutta. There hopefully we could get the passports, traveller's cheques, and our air tickets replaced. But not the cash. In Patna, because of the trouble I had had previously exchanging traveller's cheques, I had changed half of them to cash. Getting things replaced in Calcutta would involve charges, and with having to pay to live there while we dealt with all that Indian bureaucracy and replaced the essential parts of our gear, it could cost most of any money we recovered. So perhaps our pilgrimage might not get much beyond Bodh Gaya. But I was just glad to be able to start again. To do that, though, we needed a police report to prove that we had been robbed.

The Atri officer said that he would write out his report by copying the report prepared by the Rajgir police. To get it we would now have to go to Atri, twenty miles away. I did ask if we could just have a copy of the Rajgir report, but this was out of the question. Atri was not that far off the new route I had planned, one that avoided the forest, so I told the officer that we would try to be there the following evening. That way the police could put us up that night. This would also solve the problem of where we were to sleep with just a thin blanket. For the first night anyway.

And the man who was run over by the police? We never did find out what happened to him. I did ask. The police said he was at the hospital and being treated. Later, the manager quietly shook his head and told me not to pursue it.

AJAHN SUCITTO

How quickly, how effortlessly, the world arises! The Burmese Vihara, formerly just an unremarkable stopover, was now glowing with Dickensian charm and benevolence. We were the centre of attention; I wrote all their names down on the back page of the notepad—U Zayanta, Dasrat Prasad (formerly "the manager") and his wife Arti (they were from Assam, hence the connection to Buddhism and Burma), then Maechee

Ahlee, and the monk at Vaishali ... and whoever else I could remember on the pilgrimage. Then I wrote in the front the names and attributes of the twenty-eight Buddhas and a brief day-by-day resume of the pilgrimage. After all, as we were now back in the world of relationships and people and time, and I had to keep a record for the Sangha:

"19th Japanese monks and cheque. Forest rest. Robbery > BBV."

"20th BBV Police jeep accident. evening > Nalanda"

But the traces of unknowing hung around our continued walk. Despite my objections, Nick was still determined not to go on the main road to Gaya, so we would be wandering cross-country with no map, just the names of half a dozen villages that Dasrat gave along with his wrap and his warm farewell.

Old patterns arose. Summoned for a snack in Mahadevapur; then flowing across the landscape, the hills to our right, occasionally confronting locals with the mispronounced names of the villages and receiving indefinite responses; somewhere I lost Nick, had to retrace my steps to find him sitting under a tree—"You might have said something." "You were too far ahead for me to call to you." Differences in pace and style, the old irritations. And sometimes it was just a matter of guessing to turn left or right at a crossroads, and laughter because it didn't matter anyway—where was there to get to? Off on the road again. At one time I came out of a reverie to find Nick walking along and talking with a couple of men; they were teachers and invited us to their school for a meal. That opened into a midday interlude in the little schoolroom; the youngsters had finished their exams and were waiting for the results. Some of them ran off to get some food, and we ate in the schoolroom under the beaming gaze of Indira Gandhi and stern warnings about flies spreading disease.

But the patterns had also unwound, and I began to get beyond my ways of thinking. For example I realised that I loved India. I hadn't been able to see that because I'd always assumed that you couldn't love something you were so irritated by. The thinking mind works in such exclusive patterns and then denies that reality doesn't fit them. But when your head gets turned around, you have to accept consciousness dancing like a stream, flowing on even as it appears to be occurring in the same time and place; flowing in contradictory directions according to hidden forces, its surface prickling and wrinkling with every breeze, dimpled by creatures surfacing within it or descending upon it. When the controlling patterns of the will loosen, consciousness is never the same from one moment to the next. It is not even a "thing" at all, just sensitivity trembling according to habits and circumstances.

Meanwhile the mapless, clockless day meandered in the sun, joyful at heart, confused and edgy in the mind—where are we going? The hungry mind hooks onto people and events to assemble some order: A man on a bike stopped and listened to our list of names. "Atri? Atri...? You must go to Tapo, there is an ancient hotspring there where you can bathe and spend the night. It is in that direction." He was a professor at the University of Gaya. "Here is my card. You must stay in my house when you reach Gaya." Then off on his bike. Heading down the road to Tapo, we came to a village. Men intercepted us, blocked our path ... "*Dacoits* ... they will kill you." We tried to laugh it off, but what seemed to be the entire male population of the village gathered and formed a blockade across the road. There was no arguing with that. We turned back, back to the vagaries. Eventually the day decided to rest with the descending sun and dropped us on a road with kilometre stones bearing the word "Atri," one of our projected possible destinations where Nick could tie up some of the police business. How very convenient! Our flagging footsteps livened up.

I was riding on a sense of hope and of wonder that the day had taken care of itself—all we had to do was trust its flow. But the day wasn't through yet. Nearing Atri in the dusk, a little old man squatting beside a tree asked us the familiar "Kaha ja ra hai?" I looked at him; it was strange that someone should be sitting alone in the dusk. Something fishy here. "Nick, that little old guy—something odd...." and in a moment we were both convinced that he was the scout for an ambush party. Almost clutching each other, we hurried up the road toward the scarcely lit village.

NICK

Atri also had a power cut when we got there. The occasional glimmer came from a window, but most of the town was retreating into the gloom of dusk. Someone had explained in Rajgir that Bihar state had become so short of electricity that they were now rationing it. Each district was allocated so many set hours a day when it was on. For the capital city, Patna, this included the evening, the most popular time for electricity consumption. For the more remote districts, like Rajgir and Atri, the electricity times were more inconvenient.

The Atri police station was on top of a slight rise. It was a big square building surrounded by a veranda, and it was lit from inside by hurricane lamps. The light made it look very welcoming as we approached, but inside they knew nothing of our report. When the officer arrived he greeted me warmly, "Ah, Mr. Scott," while ignoring my stranger companion, and explained that the report was not ready yet and that we would have to wait until the morning. I was not surprised; I was getting used to the efficiency of the Bihar police, and anyway it suited us—we could stay the night in the dak bungalow. The officer went off and returned with a shabbily dressed man holding a lamp. "This orderly will take care of you. If there are any problems you are just to tell him." (It was unlikely that he had any English, but it was a nice thought.) "I am also asking what you are eating for your breakfast?" Given the choice I plumped for my favourite, parothas. He said something to the orderly in Hindi, and then we set off following the swinging light through the streets of Atri to the dak bungalow.

In the morning nothing seemed to be happening. The orderly was next door and after a while someone else turned up, but they made no move to do anything with us. Eventually I went out and tried some of my limited Hindi, "Breakfast?" "Food?" "Parotha?" but got no understandable reply. When Ajahn Sucitto tried his Hindi he got nothing better. The day was warming up and we wanted to get under way. We had hoped to get to Gaya that day, as we now had somewhere to stay there. So I produced ten rupees and tried again. "Breakfast?" "Food?" With the slightest movement of his head he took the proffered money and left.

After a while we were taken back to the police station where the police officer came by to tell us that we were to have breakfast at his house. We were waiting again on the bench on the police veranda when the orderly eventually found us an hour later. He had a tray full of steaming savoury pastries that he must have bought in the market. Ajahn Sucitto had to explain that we did not need them now and that he could take them back. Without the slightest flicker of surprise, he turned and carried them away again.

It was nine o'clock by the time we were facing an enormous pile of thick parothas, oozing ghee, in the garden of the police house. The officer's wife had been cooking us breakfast all along. We should have known; the delay was because the duty of feeding us was being taken so seriously. Around the parothas were plates of bean dishes, vegetable curries, chutneys, and curried eggs. Afterward we stopped at the station to get the report, so it was not until eleven that we were on our way again. The parothas lay heavily in our stomachs. We had missed the pleasant part of the day for walking, and if we were to get to Gaya we would have to walk through the midday heat. As we trudged along, wanting only to sit down in the shade and fall asleep, we agreed that next time we were offered breakfast we would turn it down.

AJAHN SUCITTO

A meaningless trudge along a long straight road in the heat. It was late morning, and Gaya was thirty kilometres away, but that didn't mean much either. I felt my will tighten like a bow string and aim south toward Gaya, then the body bend to and follow it. Just go on: the heaviness would pass. I'd occasionally stop and look behind—outlined against the flat landscape and towering over small dark men, a red-bearded giant was stumbling along. What myth had he walked out of, tattered shirt wrapped around his drooping head, tight pants that ended halfway down his shins, clutching an overnight bag? Staggering toward Gaya, this inconceivable, loveable patchwork of humanity. I wait, my heart going out to him. We'll never arrive, but there's no need to stop going on.

14

The Time of Gifts

AJAHN SUCITTO

Christmas Eve. The road was taking us out of the realm of nameless villages to somewhere special—Bodh Gaya, fifteen kilometres south of Gaya, the place where Siddhattha Gotama had his great Awakening. In his time it was a forest grove called Uruvela. He had already mastered the meditation systems of two contemporary teachers and found that although they led to extremely refined states of consciousness, those states didn't last. Having ascended to higher planes, so to speak, a descent to the normal plane of consciousness is inevitable, with no resolution to the fundamental problem of being: that we experience ourselves as semi-, but not completely, separate from experiences. Therefore we can neither ultimately unite with what is pleasant, nor can we be totally divorced from what is unpleasant, nor can we give up the search for happiness in one of these untenable positions:

> *Association with the disliked is dukkha, separation from the liked*
> *is dukkha, not attaining one's wishes is dukkha.*

In an attempt to snuff out the whole pleasure-pain mechanism, Gotama resorted to ferocious austerities in the company of five ascetics at Uruvela. Nearly killing himself in the process, he eventually had to admit that asceticism was not the answer either. In that moment of recognition, he remembered the ease and peacefulness of a time in his childhood when he had been sitting in the shade of a tree watching his father at a ploughing festival. Shaded from the blazing sun, with no particular inclination toward this or that, his mind had by itself settled into a state of calm. Might that gratuitous, unforced calm be the basis for enlightenment?

The world was benevolent on that day in another valuable respect. A local woman called Sujata (Good Birth) made him an offering of milk-rice, which he ate. Although the other ascetics walked off in disgust, he now had both the physical strength and well-being and the mental ease and detachment to collect his highly trained attention and direct it to the roots of the problem of life: the creation of a self that is both alienated from life and besieged by it. Resolving to remain in that very spot until he had discovered an answer, he took up a seated position under one of the common trees of South Asia, *Ficus religiosus,* subsequently to be honoured with the name "Bodhi tree"—the tree of Awakening.

We too had received our share of offerings. The previous night the relentless road had taken us into Gaya, which is one of the largest towns in Bihar. We had the name and address of the professor we had met on the previous day. The streets were suitably incomprehensible. Asking for directions we connected to someone who wanted to get us interested in the huge temple to Vishnu in the city, but we eventually shook him off.

We hired a scooter taxi and gave him the card. The driver pleaded his absolute certainty as to the destination, but we were a long time circulating the backstreets and suburbs of Gaya, stopping here and there to make enquiries. Off we would whirl in another direction until the conviction petered out, and we received the next set of contradictory instructions. Then, surprisingly, just as I had given up, we got out. The name and the address had coincided with a neat house in a quiet and well-lit district connected with the university. Even more surprising, the person at whose home we had arrived bore the same name, title, and address, but wasn't the man we had met yesterday. He did think he knew him, and thought he lived somewhere over the *other* side of town. Never mind—in terms of archetype, this man fitted the bill, spoke excellent English, and warmly invited us to spend the night in his house.

Inside, all was very benevolent. The evening meal was offered and politely refused. "Not even some fruit?" It turned out that, according to their dharma, the hosts could not eat until the guests had eaten. I explained that my dharma as samana was not to eat anything after noon. Nick, more ecumenical with his precepts than I, obligingly took some milk and biscuits. Hindu-Buddhist dharma was satisfied; we could relax. The daughter was told to heat some water so that we could bathe in comfort; the husband and wife ascertained that we could eat breakfast— after dawn. But we emphasized, it must be just a *little* something, and we had to leave just after seven in order to reach Bodh Gaya in time for the meal that would surely be offered us by Nick's friend in the Burmese Vihara. "Katie knows we're coming," said Nick, "She's bound to want to look after us."

After amiable discussions with the professor, we turned in. They of course gave us the front room and all bundled up in some tiny room out the back. I could hear the two women murmuring, and woke up in the darkness to hear them whispering excitedly. The clock said 3:30 A.M., and they were starting to prepare the "little something." It turned up about seven o'clock—a feast of savouries and sweets graciously served on polished metal platters against a background of faces brimming with joy. This sort of stuff just finishes your thinking processes: you open, you rejoice, you chant, you eat.

Our plans pulled us out of the door an hour later, with the thought that a few miles of earnest walking might create the abdominal space needed for the next meal. We didn't get far; a few minutes' walk away, we were stopped by a cry—and the original professor came across the road to beg us enter his house, and stay and eat as we had arranged. We regretfully said we couldn't stay, we had to get to Bodh Gaya, and we had just eaten and were expected for the meal. Negotiations began. Eventually we settled for a very large glass of special creamy tea and some biscuits in his front room; then waddled out some twenty minutes later, with a deadline frenzy pulling us toward our planned destination a few miles south.

Nick was in front, his body bulging out of the small T-shirt, the back seam of his trousers split open; I was behind. With the effect of the food and the heat and the traffic, it was difficult to feel composed. It shouldn't *be* this way; all those sacred relics that I had brought from England to offer to take to the Holy Places had been stolen ... those robbers had left me nothing to offer except some composure, and now I couldn't even make that. Maybe at least we could *look* a bit tidier...

"Nick, maybe you could put your wrap on, just to cover your backside, at least while we're in the villages."

NICK

As so often the case, I was in a contrasting space: enjoying the walk that morning. The day was not that hot, and the small road out of Gaya was lined with big trees casting pools of shade over the road. Bodh Gaya was only ten kilometres away, we had already been fed well, and there was no need to hurry. After all this might be the final lap of the pilgrimage, so why not just relax and enjoy it. The road ran beside the River Phalgu, which at that time of year is a wide expanse of undulating sand, with the river, reduced to the size of a brook, winding through it. Between the road and the bed of the river lay grazing land dotted with trees. Looking between these, and across the open expanse of sand, we could see a line of low hills—another outcrop of bare rocky upland, a familiar feature since we had left the Rajgir hills. These hills ran north-south with the river at their base.

It was all very beautiful, and I felt at ease with the world. We went along at a steady pace with the kilometre posts counting off the distance to Bodh Gaya. The ease and the beauty combined with the steady walking to quiet and centre my mind. We were carrying so little since the robbery that at times it felt like I was floating. As we made our way, we were passing the usual assortment of pedestrians, bicycles, bullock carts, and wandering cows. There were few vehicles—just the occasional three-wheeled taxi carrying pilgrims and tourists between Bodh Gaya and railway station in Gaya.

Eventually we caught sight of the Bodhi Temple up ahead; the top of its intricately carved tower just showing above the trees. The Bodhi Temple, built on the site of the Buddha's enlightenment, is the centre of Bodh Gaya, most of which is Buddhist temples, viharas, and other places for visitors to stay. The Burmese Vihara was beside the road into town, and it was the first building we came to. We turned in at the big gates and asked for Katie.

I had been introduced to Katie the previous summer in England. She was about to leave for India to help with a course in Buddhist studies organized by an American university, and she had invited us to stay with them. We waited at the gate for her while several young Western travellers came and went. Then Katie arrived to collect us. About our age with long light brown hair, an English rose complexion, and a flowing skirt, she was also the first person from home and the first woman we had really met for two months. I was slightly mesmerized as we trooped along behind her. She took us to a modern block of accommodation behind the old vihara, climbing up two flights of outside stairs to come out onto a wide veranda on the roof. There were three rooms up there facing a magnificent view across Bodh Gaya. They were the best rooms in the vihara. They also had the only hot showers in Bodh Gaya and the first we had seen since coming to India. Our room had been Katie's; she had vacated it for us.

We sat on the veranda enjoying the view while we were brought tea—in a teapot, with the milk in a jug as in England. There was some food too: including very English-looking slices of cake. Katie seemed a ministering angel—an English one with a very proper accent. We told her all about the robbery, the police, and our trials of the past two months. She listened attentively and reacted in all the right places. There is nothing quite like the concern of a sympathetic woman.

Katie had encouraged me to get to Bodh Gaya in time for Christmas, and we had just made it. Tomorrow morning, she explained, there would be a big gathering on the veranda in front of our rooms to which we were invited. It happened each year. Most of the Westerners staying long term in Bodh Gaya came for a shared Christmas breakfast.

At some point—I think it must have been later, after we had had our first warm shower and rested—we were taken to meet the monk in charge of the vihara. Venerable Nyaninda was Burmese, probably in his fifties, and was sitting on a chair outside the old building. This, we soon learned, was where he could be found most of the day, smoking a Burmese cheroot and available to talk to anyone who came by. There are a lot of people "coming by" at Bodh Gaya, and as often as not he would be sitting there listening to someone's problems. He was a nice man, quiet but affable, with a laid-back and slightly ironic tone to his Burmese English; he had seen it all from his chair outside the vihara. He told us that we were welcome to stay as long as we wished, that we should join him for the meal each day, and that we were not to pay for anything while we were there.

AJAHN SUCITTO

We had to visit the Maha Bodhi Temple, the shrine at the site of Siddhatha's great Awakening. Of course, I tell myself, Bodh Gaya is just a place on the planet, a scruffy Indian village among a hundred thousand scruffy Indian villages, though marked by its fame with clusters of rickshaw drivers, beggars, and the rest. Transcendence is nothing to do with a place, I tell myself. So the brain holds on, grateful for the ordinariness—the dingy chai stalls, the indeterminate drab buildings—

defending its right to be rational, wary of any feelings of devotion, not wanting to be overawed. Yet, unreasonably, the heart rises to the sense of the occasion, rises so that all that brain reality disappears—and the sacred is born. There was a descent down stone steps ... and a reluctance to look up at the towering temple. We were in a garden of devotion. Stupas blossomed around the temple like heavenly flowers, and in their midst were Tibetan pilgrims—bowing, releasing thousands of prostrations into the world like seeds of a timeless aspiration—pilgrims, devotees processing around the temple in robes and rags and jeans, mumbling mantras, whirling prayer wheels. Silently magnetized onto their footsteps, I was in there somewhere. There it was very peaceful, no frenzy, no press of bodies, no voices; butter lamps and their generations of grease on the forgiving stone, the cascades of wax marking the butts of expired candles; our half-formed prayers, our tattered memories, our gifts accepted as they were.

There was the Bodhi Tree and the Buddha's Great Listening. Underneath the tree sat the stone slab representing the seat of enlightenment. Between it and the overhanging branches, the space attended. The stream of my heart poured out ... this long lifetime journey ... here was the world, the struggle, the burden and the need to put it down. Within me and around me, the whole world was bowing, and had been for so long: Ashoka, the Chinese pilgrims, the Tibetans, the Sri Lankans, the Burmese, the Thais, the Americans. All this stuff born out of eternity, trying to find its origin.

On that night of Awakening, Siddhattha had seen through the picture show of identity. In profound meditation, he had witnessed the long passage of his many births: now being this, now being that—a dozen births, a hundred births—and the road all those beings had travelled on, weeping and laughing, aspiring and forgetting, the self-perpetuating road of kamma. What you do defines you; what you become determines how you see the world and yourself; how that world and self appears determines how you act. To reject the process, to think of getting off the road, is just another road, another becoming, another birth. Knowing there's no person on the road, that is Awakening.

We did some chanting, I remember. Then we went back. Hawkers were trying to sell us postcards and junk. It was almost a relief to get back to the defined grubbiness of Bihar, and then back to the Burmese Vihara and the atmosphere of the West—easy conversation, shared attitudes, hot showers...and Christmas Eve. Katie and Mary; Pat, who had been a bhikkhu in Burma; David; Bill, who translated Tibetan texts; and Robert, the head teacher of the study group staying at the vihara—a strange comfort, that of familiarity.

NICK

Christmas Eve was also the half moon so we sat up till midnight in the vihara. Next morning I got up late to find that things were already happening outside. Ajahn Sucitto was there helping lay the mats and distribute the cushions, and I went out to join him. Then we sat outside our room as the people arriving for the Christmas breakfast were introduced to us. I was surprised to see how many Western residents there were. As well as those running the Buddhist course and a few of the students who had stayed on after it had finished, I remember an Englishman, half Indian by birth, who was involved in a Buddhist aid project working with the local people, a couple of Italians running a cafe for Western visitors, and two Americans studying art at the Tibetan monastery, as well as quite a few others. Most had already heard about our robbery, and it was their main topic of conversation.

Everyone who came brought contributions to the meal. Slowly a sea of dishes gathered, all things we had not seen since England. There were savoury dishes topped with mushrooms or broccoli, fruit flans with whipped cream, chocolate cake covered in melted chocolate, a big platter of cheeses, nuts, fresh dates, and, of course, mince pies, Christmas cake, and Christmas pudding. My attention became increasingly distracted as this sea of food grew. I hardly noticed that everyone also brought presents wrapped in coloured paper, which were put in a big pile on the far side of the food.

Of course I overindulged. But it was a glorious meal and full of laughter and happiness. When we had finished, one of the several children there was given the job of handing out the presents. We had been told that it was the tradition for everyone to bring one present—they had drawn a name from a bag the week before to find out who their present was to be for. A nice tradition in which everyone would get something. We did not mind in the least that it would not include us. However, the first present the little girl picked up had one of our names on it, and then so did the one after next, and then another, and yet another. There were big ones and small ones, each wrapped in different-coloured paper and the little girl tottered back and forth with them making a new pile in front of us. Half of the presents were for us. Everyone's attention turned to the growing pile and to us, but we were initially too stunned to do anything about it. We just let the presents mount up with bemused smiles on our faces. Eventually, when we began to unwrap them, we found that inside were things to replace those lost in the robbery. There was a sleeping bag, water bottles, clothes, two sleeping mats, a bottle of mosquito repellent—anything anyone had in their possession that we might need—even a Swiss army knife for Ajahn Sucitto. Many of the gifts we would never have been able to buy in India. I was in tears by the end.

And that was just the beginning of the generosity we received in Bodh Gaya. Some at the meal had not been part of the arrangements of the night before (Katie had us tell her in detail what we had lost and then gone round telling the others), and they wanted to know what else we needed. Over the next few days various other things arrived, even a new alms bowl for Ajahn Sucitto; and by the time we left Bodh Gaya, nearly everything we had lost had been replaced. We were even offered a water filter like the one I had been carrying unused for Ajahn Sucitto for the past two months, but thankfully he turned it down.

AJAHN SUCITTO

Christmas Day—the time of the great gift. Overwhelmed by all the generosity, I wondered why it had taken us so long to get robbed and provide an opportunity. A distinct lack of faith on our part. The robbery had made us more fragile and open, and hence more capable of living as a samana should. My robes were complete again: Venerable Nyaninda had given me a special Burmese *sanghati* made of hundreds of tiny patches. Now, in the place of the Buddha's enlightenment, how could one not go for alms? It would be a way of giving myself. The road outside the vihara was open and waiting; Bhante loaned me an alms bowl.

I unwound my bandages and let my patched-up feet be naked, with white bands showing where the straps of the sandals had screened them from the sun. My scarred skin was so white in the dust; I was too big, too special, too delicate for the raw gaze of the streets, where gnarled grey-skinned women squatted and begged. I stood with lowered head a few metres away from fruit stalls or chai shops while the seconds beat in my pulse. When I had counted to thirty, I could move on. Sometimes the chink of a sugary snack, or the softer sound of a pastry hitting the bowl would let me off early. Occasionally a Westerner would give me a cake or a banana with a smile. Then there would be coins—fifty paisa pieces. When I got back to the gates of the vihara, I gave the old women beggars the money and some of the food; the rest I would give to the bhikkhus: my brothers in the holy life.

On another day, I wandered on my alms round south through Bodh Gaya, slowly past the market stalls—nothing happening there—and along the dung-strewn road out of the village. Somewhere I came across a settlement in the dust: dry mud-walled shelters crouching on the earth with a few brick houses among them; narrow winding paths with children playing, half naked, hair matted with dirt; and a few old folk squatting. My body felt out of scale, and my bowl was too bright. (I had been given another one, one of those stainless steel bowls they make in Thailand, of better quality than most Bihari villagers' household goods.) But they didn't mind that I was special; they stopped me—the old folk with their friendly inquiries, the children open-mouthed—and they brought rotis and rice. A child came running after me as I was walking away; her face glowing with joy, she heaved a roti over the lip of my bowl.

The road took me gently back to the Maha Bodhi temple. Overwhelmed again, I could only sit in the garden of prostrations with my bowl mothered in my lap. I chanted a blessing and meditated. *They* didn't mind that I was special; in fact they seemed rather to enjoy it. Why was I finding this birth such a crucifixion?

Christmas was always about visiting relatives, reaching out to affirm a connection with small gestures of kinship that get ritualized over the years. So down the road we went, to visit monasteries to pay our respects to the elders of the Sangha in Bodh Gaya. There was Venerable Paññārama at the Mahabodhi Society, which was the Sri Lankan pilgrims' centre. He was busy with people and could only make a little time for us. Then there were the Thai bhikkhus, besieged in the Thai temple, disjointedly polite. Being planted in India, especially Bihar, was difficult for them. Everything was rough, dirty, and exposed—the exact counterpart to what Thais hold dear. But we connected well with Venerable Gnana Jagat, the head of the Maha Bodhi Temple committee. He was Indian, a Brahmin by birth, courteous, solicitous, with just the slightest whistle to his s's. He invited us to share his midmorning snack of chopped fruit and listened intently to our tale. Expressing profound shame that we had been robbed in his country, he decided to extend his patronage to us, offering to take us into the temple, up into the top of the towering shrine itself. I left feeling like a favoured nephew who had just received a shiny copper coin.

More than any of the other places, Wat Thai Bodh Gaya was the embassy of a wealthy occupying power; I was more or less of their tribe, but having "gone native" by living off the land made me a bit odd. The way they looked at me reminded me of how my family had received me when I returned to England from Thailand.

The Buddha described his night of Awakening in different ways. One striking account was his recognition of all the forms of doubt and greed and worry as members of a demon host led by the personification of delusion, Mara. "Mara" also means death, which in this context is more than an event. Mara is the instinct that identifies us with the cycle of birth and decay. Mara's daughters, part of his support team, are Passion, Craving, and Negativity—they are always ready to drag us into some justifiable act of advertence. A meditator is quickly introduced to this host, and generally gets panicked or defensive, or gets into a battle with them—all of which activities to defend the self merely affirm its existence. Therefore one is *something*. And to *be* something, you have to *have* something—a sight, a sound, an idea, an opinion, a future, a belief: an identity. *There* is the source of all the longing and the quarrelling, which sustains the tenacity of the habitual reactions of the mind.

But on that special night, the Buddha didn't react: neither believing nor rejecting Mara, he said, "I know you, Mara," and touched the earth beneath him. "I will not move from this spot until I have seen and understood." At that point of recognition and resolution, the long road of habitual drives came to an end.

That spot has been enshrined ever since. The emperor Ashoka paid his respects and watered the Bodhi Tree. A temple occupied the spot then, and although the original tree died long ago, cuttings from it and its descendants have sheltered the wakened space ever since. The last one was planted in the nineteenth century by the British, who also rebuilt the temple. They were the most recent of the long history of attendants to the temple. As Buddhism waned and was eclipsed in India, pilgrims from Sri Lanka periodically attended to the temple, restored it, and venerated it—for about nine hundred years. Then, when Sri Lanka was going through its colonial stage and Buddhism dwindled, the Burmese took over the responsibility.

Meanwhile local sadhus and swamis had used the temple, and it had circumstantially accrued to them. It was only through the efforts of the Sinhalese Anagarika Dharmapala that a legal campaign had, after fifty years, theoretically restored the custody to the Buddhists. That was in 1949. But this was India; a temple to Shiva still stood by the main entrance of the Maha Bodhi Temple, complete with priests asking for money, and Buddhists were outnumbered by Hindus (including the head priest of the Shiva temple) on the Maha Bodhi Temple Committee.

Venerable Gnana Jagat clucked and shook his head about it—but what was there to do? And such matters should not spoil the vision of the holy place for us. Silence was the order of the day when he led us around the terraces of the sanctuary in the evening, and as we walked into that mandala, India for once checked its squalling. He took us up inside the lofty temple where we could meditate and left us there with a sibilant murmur.

Above the very place of the Buddha's awakening, I looked over the darkness without and within. What was all this to me? A fragile attention was all I had. The Buddha was an indistinct image, and perhaps all the more resonant for that. He was "Tathagata," the "one who has come" into the way things really are, and that defied all images.

When we got tired and decided to leave, we found that someone had locked us inside the temple. India again! We had to beat on the doors to get the night watchman to let us out.

NICK

The next afternoon I also went off on my own, to visit a small stupa that local legend attributes to Sujata, the young woman who gave the ascetic

Gotama milk-rice just prior to his enlightenment. I followed a path worn by the locals across the sands of the river, wading through the two channels of water up to my knees. Beyond the expanse of sand and the line of trees on the far bank, and nearly lost amid the paddy fields, was the slightest of mounds with a small shrine beside it. Having lit and offered incense to the shrine's small Buddha rupa, I then sat there contemplating the mound, the villagers working in the fields around me, and some thoughts of my own on women and how appropriate it was that it was a young woman who broke into the Buddha's fixation on the ascetic path in the story of his enlightenment.

Women are good at doing that, breaking into men's absorptions. They can bring us out into a sensitivity to what is going on around us, which can seem quite delightful. The problem for me was that I tended to confuse the effect with the cause, and fall for the woman. Romance was a cycle I had got to know well. How following it brings both you and the woman into a heightened awareness of the present moment, and how, when it is over, you come down much as one does if one uses drugs to get the same effect, except there is usually an emotional mess one has to deal with as well. I envied the monks their rules of restraint with their very clear lines: lines that cannot be continually adjusted, as I was prone to do with mine.

It was pleasant sitting out in the fields warming myself in the late afternoon sun and musing on the ways of the world. Around Bodh Gaya no one took much heed of me; they were used to Westerners wandering aimlessly about. I remember enjoying being able to do that when I first came to Bodh Gaya in 1973. I spent many afternoons exploring the surrounding area, Indian village life being a novelty then. It was on that visit, and at the Burmese Vihara, that I met my first Theravadan Buddhist monk. He was a big friendly American who had been ordained in Laos, where he had spent several years, until he was forced to leave by the encroaching Vietnam War. I was at the vihara to enquire about the Goenka course that I later did in Rajgir, and I met him in the office. I remember him slapping me on the back and wishing me well on the path.

The next time I came to Bodh Gaya, a year later, it was to do two more Goenka courses, the second a special one that he did once a year. It was his own personal retreat, and he allowed a limited number of his long-term disciples to do it with him. I should not have been there, but having applied from Australia mentioning that I was stopping off at the centre in Burma where Goenka had himself been taught, they assumed I must be such a disciple.

The Burmese Vihara at Bodh Gaya in those days had some fifteen meditation cells in the garden, and that is where we were housed. Goenka was in the main house and we did not see him. The small brick cells looked like garden sheds and lined three sides of the garden. We had to share them, two to each, and because no one knew me, I had to share with the other unknown participant, an English guy ordained as a Tibetan Buddhist monk allowed on the course because of his ordination.

In our little hut were two low benches just long enough to lie down on, and between them a narrow space the width of the door. We spent twenty days together in that hut, me and the English monk, sleeping on the benches at night and sitting on them in meditation during the day. We sat each on our own bench, our backs turned to each other, our faces only a foot from the plain white walls, and we hardly spoke once in the twenty days. I did not even know his name.

The course was intense, and I achieved a level of concentration I had never managed before. I would get so absorbed in the technique of slowly sweeping my attention down my body, feeling every slightest vibration, that in an hour my attention would not have reached my toes. That level of concentration brings with it a refined and blissful sense of peace. I really thought I was getting somewhere—always a bad sign with meditation.

After about two weeks, we had a day of rain. Normally, for our twice-daily breaks, we would stroll about the garden or sit soaking up the sun, always in complete silence. This day the rain was keeping everyone in their huts, but I had two handmade Burmese umbrellas that I was taking home as gifts. One, a plain one, I put out for my companion to use, taking for myself the one painted with colourful Burmese designs. We both walked round the garden, the rain pattering on the umbrellas, while the others looked on. I was rather taken with being the focus of attention and went round three times. At break's end, we returned to the meditation, but just the slight excitement of our little parade had disturbed the balance. The meditation would not go right. I began to panic a little, which made it worse. I tried harder, which made it even worse. The more I tried, the farther I got from being able to do it. The ability to concentrate on those subtle sensations had totally gone. Next day it was the same, and the day after. The more it went on, the more fed up I got. I had fallen from heaven and I could not get back.

The course finished on the night of the full moon with a visit to the Bodhi Temple. Everyone was given candles and incense, and we walked together through the empty streets, still in silence. The temple compound was lit with the flickering light of thousands of butter lamps. Others were already there, sitting quietly under trees or doing prostrations toward the temple. We wandered through the grounds following Goenka and then sat in meditation clustered together under the Bodhi Tree while Goenka did some chanting, his deep melodious voice coming and going in the night air. It was all very uplifting.

As we went back to the vihara, all as high as kites, we were allowed to talk for the first time. We started hesitantly but came through the gates of the vihara producing an excited babble and then clustered together in little groups sharing our experiences of the past three weeks. Myself and the monk ended up sitting up talking in our hut most of the night. That is when I found out that his name was Stephen Batchelor, that he was my age, and that he had also come out to India straight from school. He had ended up in northern India, studying with the Tibetans, where he had eventually become a monk. These courses were his first experience of Theravadan Buddhism.

It was Stephen, now a meditation teacher and writer, who introduced me to Katie when he heard about the pilgrimage. They both lived near Totnes in Devon, a centre for all things alternative, and a place where lots of Buddhists reside. The candidate for the Green Party then, a Buddhist, got the highest vote of any Green candidate in Britain. He too was a teacher and was coming out to Bodh Gaya in a few weeks to teach two retreats, for which Katie was to be one of the organizers. His name was Christopher Titmuss, the Theravadan monk who had been with me on that meditation course in Rajgir the year before I met Stephen. The Buddhist world in the West can be a small one.

Each morning while we were at the vihara we had breakfast with Katie and the others who had been running the Buddhist course. Those breakfasts were very pleasant affairs. We would sit around drinking coffee and munching on toast, marmalade, and other delights that the two of us had not seen for months. The coffee would fuel long conversations about Buddhism, practise, and the world. Our hosts had also become interested in Buddhism in India in the seventies. Now they were here teaching it to another generation.

Now that the course was over, they were packing everything away. They had a library of all manner of books on Buddhism and related subjects which, to our frustration, we only got to see the day it was being put into cases. The locals who had been doing the cooking had to be paid and arrangements made for next year. Then the organizers began to leave, most of them off to do some travelling before returning home. Katie was the first to go. Each year she would spend a week on the beach in Puri, the nearest India gets to a seaside resort, before returning to start organising the Christopher Titmuss retreat. It was sad to see her go. We both felt a lot of gratitude toward her, but she was very English, and somehow, what with us being English too, we never seemed to get the chance to express it.

AJAHN SUCITTO

Our plans: to stay in Bodh Gaya until New Year's Day and then to Calcutta to apply for new passports and visas. Nick would try to get his traveller's cheques and our airline tickets replaced, and so our time as beings who have no nationality, no permission to be here, and no possibility of leaving would come to an end. Time and the road won't be cheated; you've got to move on. And maybe, with the wondrous gift of all our supplies, we might even complete our original plans. All that was certain was that it would now be a "who knows" pilgrimage.

But for now, I didn't feel like going places, limiting my movements to alms-faring and visiting the Maha Bodhi Temple. I didn't go to the enormous Japanese Buddha, or the Tibetan temples, or the archaeological museum. I wanted to spend some time meandering through the village to be with its ordinariness—to get a feeling for the people, and therefore for myself.

There were plenty of pilgrims of all manner and persuasion. Now, in the cold season, Bodh Gaya was particularly attractive to Westerners, especially as Christopher Titmuss made a practise of giving a meditation retreat every January in the Thai temple. It promised to be full, with around one hundred people. This year brought the added interest of Andrew Cohen, self-proclaimed master from America, who reckoned himself enlightened and who would be holding teaching dialogues nearby at the same time.

The Burmese Vihara also regularly housed retreats headed by Venerable Nyaninda in the more sober, deadpan Theravada style. At other times Bhante just hung out. In the evening he would be sitting outside in a chair with a couple of bits of wood smouldering in front of him, occasionally poking at them with a stick. Night and day he would be unflappably responding to the various requests, invitations, queries, and calamities that came up. He wasn't trying to get everything perfect, but he kept his eyes open and saw what he could do. He'd blend the compassion to respond with the equanimity to stay sane.

As far as the residents went, after the local Bihari folk, the most sizeable community was the Tibetan traders. Their simple but clean tea shops were frequented by Westerners in mystically inscribed T-shirts smoking beedees and enjoying the wholesome food. Tibetans are a resourceful folk; they had learned to adapt and to relate to Westerners— who in turn were naturally sympathetically inclined to them as refugees from a holy land. They did a brisk business selling goods on the street. You could never haggle a price; compared with the local people, they were quick-witted and bright. While the Indians seemed to be just about getting by, the Tibetans got the business.

But there was always the sacred power of Tibetan Buddhism. At the end of 1990, out for a stroll, heading for the Bhutanese temple for no special reason, we rounded the corner of the road and were confronted by a loosely defined procession of monks in Tibetan robes. It snaked like a carnival dragon, with a large bare-chested Tibetan man in a wheelchair as its head, coloured gifts on its back, and cymbals and trumpets bristling from its sides. There were Western laypeople in there too. At the gates of the temple, it cheerfully swallowed us up without breaking its stride, swept up the temple steps and disintegrated in the main hall. The mass of blood-red and yellow robes with one saffron misfit, something covered in red hair, and assorted humans swirled and settled before the huge bulging-eyed gaze of Guru Padmasambhava. A silent Buddha was in the centre of the shrine with Avalokiteshvara, the bodhisattva of compassion to his left, but the Guru on his right was the real host of the occasion. He was brandishing a vajra to drive away all forms of delusion. Visually, the place was vibrating with the suffusions of turquoise, the waves of passionate reds, the jewel adornments of citrus yellow, blue, and emerald spheres. Cascades of gorgeously arrayed Buddhas, bodhisattvas,

many-headed manifestations, and fire-wreathed snarling Dharma
protectors—whose side were they on? In a Vajrayana temple such dis-
crimination is foolish: all manifestation is void *and* welcome. How you
use it is what counts.

Things went into action as the monks arranged themselves in rows
and rolled out their grumbling monotones. The chanting was the sea
on which the ailing leader rode like Neptune. He was above us on some
kind of throne, his long grey hair gathered into a topknot on his head,
his face quite serene as his hands turned in circles like the waves. Tea
came round in huge kettles, and sacramental snacks; the monks supped
as they chanted.

The Theravadan—there has to be one wet blanket at every party—
politely declined. I was in one of the rows near the centre of the action;
looking around I could see Nick over at the periphery, happily digging
into the sacred refreshments. Afterward, as we were making our way
back to the vihara, Nick told me what he had gleaned from the laypeople. The elderly sage was Dilgo Khyentse Rinpoche, a very high lama,
senior of a lineage; he was very ill, and the ceremony was about pray-
ing for his health. It was also about bestowing a blessing on the world;
the great mounds of fruit and packages of food and tea were being
offered to ensure a prosperous new year.

We had our own plans: to see the new year in at the Maha Bodhi Temple. It was a full moon, which meant an all-night meditation vigil and
another confrontation with the hosts of Mara. Perhaps all this benevolence would have put the host in a good mood. And tonight we would
also have the added inspiration of being joined by Sister Thanissara from
Amaravati and her companion Nada.

They'd come across me that morning as I was meditating in the
grounds of the temple after my alms round. Funny how with your eyes
closed you can detect someone in front of you. They were regarding
me with the gaze that develops in India—unwavering yet dispassion-
ate. Then they bowed. When you're travelling, you pore over even the

most ordinary letter from home to savour the comfort of the familiar; how much more the appearance and words of old friends from that distant life another identity ago? They both looked crumpled and drawn; I must have appeared rough too—Nick had tightened his belt so far that he had run out of notches and been punching new ones for the past few weeks. My waist band had no holes in it. So I registered the changes in the way Sister Thanissara looked at me. Our words groped toward certainties, information. They had heard something of our recent misfortune, which was the talk, in various embellished forms, of Bodh Gaya. But I seemed to be intact. They were coming to the end of a briefer but wider-ranging pilgrimage that had taken in the Tibetan community in the North around McLeod Ganj and some of the Hindu ashrams in Uttar Pradesh. India had visited them in customary fashion: with raw beauty, human turmoil, and devotion, and bacterial aggression. They had narrowly avoided involvement in riots in Varanasi and, stricken with stomach bugs and slightly delirious, squeezed onto a bus to Kathmandu to get some medicine. Still not fully recovered, they had then journeyed on to Lumbini and Savatthi by bus and train and had just arrived in Bodh Gaya.

Now they were lodging at the Maha Bodhi Society, where they had met up with some Sri Lankan pilgrims from England who were supporters of Amaravati and who were looking after them well. A meal was being offered tomorrow, which we were invited to join. I played my trump and invited them to take a hot shower in our lodgings in the afternoon while Nick and I went off for a walk. Later we could go to the Maha Bodhi Temple for the evening meditation. They could get tidied up and then we'd sit up all night together.

It was a pleasure to have a puja chanting with someone who knew the words and had a feeling for tone, pitch, and devotion; our voices harmonised and rang against the walls of the shrine. After some meditation inside the temple, we went outside. No one else seemed to be around in the temple grounds. The full moon shone down on this abandoned Eden as we wandered along the stone terraces that defined the bower of the Buddha's enlightenment. Seven weeks he had spent here, in this leafy grove, reviewing the processes of consciousness: of suffering, its origin, its cessation, and the path.

I found myself settling beside a pool in the middle of which on a giant lotus leaf sat an image of the Buddha. Light shone on the meditating sage. Around his body were the coils of the giant cobra whose seven heads formed a sheltering canopy over him. Over 2,500 years ago, on such a night, Mucchalinda, the serpent king, had protected the Blessed One from a storm. The others came and joined me. It began to rain and grew cold; we gave the blankets to the women and found some shelter beneath the terrace. Nick had brought some flasks of hot tea and some lumps of jaggery sugar. The rain came down in the darkness, and the pool's stillness broke into trembling fragments of light and dark. There was so much rain in this storm-tossed world, and so much trembling. Only on the Awakened One had it stopped raining, forever. He was here, listening, there was no doubt of that; the problem was that none of the rest of us are. We don't listen deeply enough to get past the storm.

So, moved by compassion, he had decided to teach. He, the Tathagata, is the one who has come into the world for the welfare of beings. And ever since, so much has been said and goes on being said, commented and expounded upon, counteracted, speculated over, proved, and rebuffed. The Theravadins have developed their interpretations; a whole range of Mahayanists had their ways; Pure Land Buddhists were taking refuge in the name of the merciful Buddha who would reward their faith with rebirth in Paradise; bodhisattva aspirants were avowing rebirths for the welfare of all sentient beings; Western empirical sceptics stripped away all the ritual and the devotion and dictated that we should rely only on what we can know for ourselves. Some had even sacked the Buddha from authorship of the teachings altogether. And thousands of years later, after the suttas and the sutras and

the Abhidhamma and the Great Vehicle and the Thunderbolt Vehicle
and Zen and Salvation Buddhism and Western Buddhism and Buddha-
less Buddhism, it is still raining. In all that splash and fragmentation we
forget where Awakening comes into the world:

Now, as before, suffering and the end of suffering is all I teach.

Epilogue

So many people helped us both to make the pilgrimage and then to get this account written. We cannot list them all, not just because of space but because many of the names have now gone with the robbery. However, we sincerely want to thank each person who assisted us in some way. Four people in particular require special mention. They helped us write the original account, looking through various versions of each of the chapters as they got produced over the years, and giving us valuable feedback. They are Ajahn Amaro, Ajahn Thaniya, Sam Ford, and Sue Lunn-Rockliffe. Finally, there is our patient and understanding editor at Wisdom, David Kittelstrom, who helped us get to this final form.

Eventually we did manage to continue the pilgrimage. It became a very different journey. We had little money, fewer possessions, and fewer illusions. We left the Ganges plain to walk through the forested hills to the south. We visited the other Buddhist holy places, and then climbed through the Himalayas to end in a high valley on the Tibetan border. We had many more adventures and met a lot of wildlife, including a tiger. One day we would like to publish the account of the second part. In it we share the lessons we learned from undertaking the whole epic adventure.

On our return Ajahn Sucitto was made the abbot of Chithurst Monastery. Initially Nick would come to stay temporarily to work on this book, but realising how difficult things were for his old companion, he offered to give up his work and join him at Chithurst, working as a volunteer, running the building projects, and sorting out the management of the extensive woodland. Occasionally we also found time to continue to write the account of the pilgrimage. When it was eventually finished, that version was passed around our monasteries and supporters. There was a lot of praise and various attempts to publish it, but nothing happened. It was too long and the structure too unusual for commercial publishers to take the risk. It was also more than just a Buddhist book of teachings and so unsuitable for free distribution. We came to accept that it would probably never be published.

Then several years later Wisdom offered to publish this first half. Somehow it seems right that it now comes out as both of us are leaving Chithurst. After ten years of working together, one taking responsibility for the people in the monastery, the other the practical, the work here is complete, and Ajahn Sucitto leaves to take a well-earned break from being an abbot and Nick moves on. Perhaps we should have known it would work out this way. The book was how we came to both be at Chithurst, and somehow its publication had to wait until we had finished. Perhaps all this book and the pilgrimage ever were, were the means by which we ended up working together to complete the establishment of this monastery so it can benefit others.

Ajahn Sucitto
Nick Scott
Chithurst Monastery, April 2005

Notes

PREFACE

"The mindful exert themselves..." Dhammapada, verse 91. [Dhp 91].

CHAPTER 1: PILGRIM'S WAY

The "four signs" (old age, sickness, death, and the samana) are mentioned by the Buddha as having been witnessed by his (legendary) predecessor, the Buddha Vipassi. See Digha Nikaya, Mahapadana Sutta (sutta 14). [DN ii, 22–29]. There is very little autobiographical or accurate biographical material concerning the Buddha—especially his early life—in the texts that originated during or soon after his lifetime. Much of the personal history of the Buddha seems to have been created a few hundred years after his death, when the patronage of Emperor Ashoka had made "Buddhism" a popular religion. People then needed a person to hang the teachings on.

The Ganges and Indus river systems were receiving and absorbing invasions of outside peoples even before the Aryans. Archaeologists now reckon that not only did a civilized society precede the conquest by the then barbaric Aryans more than 4,000 years ago, but there had also been a previous conquest by the peoples that the Aryans overcame. The statistics on the present-day condition of Bihar state came from Muthiah (1990) and Bhargava (1989). The potted history of the Ganges plain came from Moon (1989) and Spear (1978). The names Fa Hsien and Hsuan Tsiang (and similar spellings used by others) are, according to modern transliteration of Chinese, spelled Fa-xien and Xuanzang.

CHAPTER 2: OVER THE BORDER

The history of the forest tradition in the West is covered by Batchelor (1995) and also by some of the books produced by Amaravati Publications (see Recommended Reading). An account of the pilgrimage from Sussex to Northumberland made by Nick Scott and Ajahn Amaro, written by Ajahn Amaro, was published by Chithurst Monastery in 1985 but is now out of print.

The full Bhikkhu Vinaya was originally translated into English by Horner (1970–86). There is now an excellent guide in English to the Patimokkha (the core of the Vinaya) written by a Western monk (Thanissaro 1994).

CHAPTER 3: LEAVING HOME

"But you should know this Ananda..." Majjhima Nikaya, Acchariya-abbhita Sutta (sutta 123). [MN iii, 124].

The "leaving home" scenario of making off in the middle of the night on first sight of his son is a much later concoction. It must have been a heartrending and inspiring motif at the time: giving up what one holds most dear. Unfortunately the modern age presents many examples of inadequate parenting, and this legendary Buddha gets labelled as irresponsible. Details of the most ancient account are in Majjhima Nikaya, Ariya-pariyesana Sutta (sutta 26). [MN i, 163].

The past history of Lumbini came from Dutt (1962) and Dhammika (1992).

CHAPTER 4: THE OBSERVER

"That end of the world wherein..." Anguttara Nikaya, Fours, chapter 5, "Rohitassa," 45. [AN ii, 48].

CHAPTER 5: LOOKING FOR PURITY

"He who shows no anger..." Sutta Nipata, Vasettha Sutta. [Sn 630, 637, 648–650]. The Buddha's views on the topic of "caste" are numerous and to be found in many of the collection of suttas. These particular lines are a sample from Vasettha Sutta in the Sutta Nipata (trans. Saddhatissa 1985). The Buddha used the term *brahmin* (which apparently used to mean the particular word or mantra whereby an adept obtained influence over the will of a Vedic god) to mean one who is worthy and noble. In this sense see particularly the final chapter of the Dhammapada.

"Then I tell you, bhikkhus, all conditioned processes..." Digha Nikaya, Mahaparinibbana Sutta (sutta 16), 6.7. [DN ii, 156]. The translation of Rilke's poem, "Buddha in Glory," is to be found in Mitchell (1980). Information on the discovery of Kushinagar by Cunningham and Carlyle came from Dhammika (1992). Sangharakshita, the English ex-monk who founded the Western Buddhist Order, gives an account of Kushinagar in 1950 and of Venerable Chadramani, the founder of the Burmese Resthouse and builder of the reconstructed temple and stupa (Sangharakshita 1976). His account of several years wondering around India as a spiritual seeker also includes visits to Sarnath, Lumbini, Calcutta, Butwal, and Tansen, and the comparisons between these places then and at the time of our visit are fascinating, as is his whole account of India at that time.

CHAPTER 6: SPIRITUAL FRIENDSHIP

"Enough, Ananda, do not weep and wail..." Digha Nikaya, Mahaparinibbana Sutta (sutta 16), 5.14. [DN ii, 144]. This sutta is the sixteenth in the Long Discourses (Digha Nikaya). This rambling narrative, very moving in many places, connects many teachings that the Buddha gave in his last days, and is the place where the summary of the Eightfold Path into morality, meditation, and wisdom is presented as the Buddha's last bequest.

In an article in the *Bangkok Post* (17 May 2000), a monk who was previously a doctor, Venerable Mettanando, points out that the symptoms suffered by the Buddha prior to his death and in his previous severe illness fit with a condition suffered by elderly people called mesenteric infarction, where there is an obstruction of the blood vessels to the wall of the intestine. It is a lethal condition, the final stages of which are usually brought on by a particularly large or rich meal. The intestines cannot cope and they rupture. There is internal bleeding, bloody diarrhoea, a lot of pain, and strong thirst, and without modern surgery the person invariably dies within twenty hours.

Molnar and Tapponier (1975) give an account of the collision of India and Asia.

CHAPTER 7: THE KINGDOM OF THE LAW

"Even so have I, bhikkhus, seen an ancient path..." Samyutta Nikaya, chapter 12, "Causes," 65. [SN ii, 105–6].

"An island that you cannot go beyond..." Sutta Nipata (Vuttugatha, Kappa's Question), 1094. [Sn 1094].

"Volition is action (kamma). Having willed, we create kamma through..." Anguttara Nikaya, Sixes, 63. [AN iii, 414].

The Ashokan Inscriptions ("Beloved of the Gods speaks thus:...") come from the translation by Hulzsch (1925). There are three columns in northern Bihar on the old pilgrimage route to Lumbini: Lauriya Nandangarh, Lauriya Areraj, and Rampuria, as well as one at Lumbini. We also saw columns at Sarnath, Bodh Gaya, and the remnants of one at Savatthi. It is likely that all the pilgrimage places associated with the life of the Buddha once had them. One still stands at Kosambi, where the Buddha spent his ninth rains retreat. In one of his inscriptions Ashoka tells us that he had given up royal pleasure trips and instead went on "Dhamma tours," his name for a pilgrimage, to the holy places.

The twenty-eight Buddhas are referred to in the *Buddhavamsa,* a text composed centuries after the life of Gotama. The historical Buddha who appears in the old texts occasionally mentions six preceding Buddhas. It is a tenet of the Theravada teachings that only one Buddha can appear in the world at any time, because a Buddha is someone who reveals a truth that has been lost—so that can only occur when a previous Buddha and his teachings have died away. Mahayana gets over this scarcity by extending the cosmic panorama to include many world systems, each with their own Buddhas.

Mr. Chaudry. This was the name he gave, but as chaudhury means "clerk of works," it is possible he was referring to himself by his occupation.

After crossing the River Gandak we were passing through the Champaran district of Bihar. It was here that Mahatma Ghandi led his first act of civil disobedience in India when supporting the claims of the indigo sharecroppers against the British plantation landlords in 1917. The landlords had been forcing the sharecroppers to buy their land at inflated prices because the indigo market was collapsing due to the invention in Germany of an artificial means of producing indigo (Fischer 1951). It could be that all of the higher land with the modern water pumps we passed through after crossing the border had originally been cleared by the British for indigo.

Chapter 8: Cycles

"They do not brood over the past..." Samyutta Nikaya, Ones, chapter 1, "Reeds," 10. [SN i, 5].

"I shall go well restrained in inhabited areas, this is a training to be done..." From the Bhikkhu Patimokkha. (For translations of this see Nanamoli Thera 1966, Thanissaro 1994).

"Whatever living beings there may be..." Sutta Nipata (Metta Sutta), 147. [Sn 147].

For those who can not decode the diary fragments, *devata* is the word for a Buddhist demigod, generally of a benevolent nature, and is applied to the man who helped us in Bakhra.

Chapter 9: The Deathless Drum

"Ripe I am in years..." Digha Nikaya, Mahaparinibbana Sutta (sutta 16), 3.51. [DN ii, 120].

"Once...when I was at the Sarandada Shrine in Vesali, I taught the Vajjians these seven principles..." Digha Nikaya, Mahaparinibbana Sutta (sutta 16), 1.5. [DN ii, 75].

"...live as lanterns unto yourselves..." Digha Nikaya II, Mahaparinibbana Sutta (sutta 16), 2.26. [DN ii, 100].

"And how does a monk live as a refuge unto himself?..." Digha Nikaya, Mahaparinibbana Sutta (sutta 16), 2.26. [DN ii, 100].

The story of the Dasaharas' drum is in Samyutta Nikaya, chapter 20, "Parables," 7 [SN ii, 266]. The history of Vaishali came from Dutt (1962, 1978) and Dhammika (1992). For a well-written description of the castes in a typical Indian village and how they function see Cohn (1987). The statistics on Bihar came from Bhargava (1989). The Buddha's alms bowl that he left in Vaishali now supposedly resides in a mosque in Kandahar, Afghanistan, where it was taken by Muslim raiders. However it is apparently the size of a garbage can, and hence unlikely to have actually been his bowl.

CHAPTER 10: THE TREASURE HOUSE

"There is nothing but water at the holy bathing places; and I know that they are useless, for I have bathed in them." *Songs of Kabir*, trans. Rabindranath Tagore (1977).

"All conditioned processes are transient, practise with diligence..." Digha Nikaya, Mahaparinibbana Sutta (sutta 16), 6:7. [DN ii, 156].

Information on Sikhs and their religion came from booklets supplied by the Newcastle Sikh Gurdwara and Naipaul (1990).

CHAPTER 11: DARK ANGEL

"Homage to the perfection of wisdom, the lovely, the holy!...here O Sariputta, form is emptiness and the very emptiness is form..." This is from the Heart Sutra, which is a fourth-century c.e. encapsulation of the perfection of wisdom teachings. The prajnaparamita discourses had evolved to such length and complexity by then that their message had to be abbreviated for practical transmission. The Heart Sutra and the Diamond-Cutter Sutra are now the most popular forms, with the Heart Sutra (only twenty-five lines) being frequently chanted in Zen and other Mahayana monasteries. This translation is by Edward Conze (in Conze 1978), an English scholar who devoted his entire working life to translating the Prajnaparamita texts from Sanskrit into English. Incidentally, the one letter that contains the ineffable essence of prajna is "A." For more on this teaching see Hixon (1993).

"...there is no ignorance, nor extinction of ignorance..." Conze's Heart Sutra (Conze 1978)

"...cannot be expounded and learned..." and "Those who are thoroughly devoted to Prajnaparamita will not die suddenly..." Both are from the rendition of the Perfection Of Wisdom in 8,000 lines by Lex Hixon (1993)

"spires which licked the clouds" and "richly adorned towers and fairy-like turrets," etc., Beal (1914).

"an illness of the season" and "late in the day, when the sun was about to set...," etc., Takakusu (1966).

"Ikhtiyar-ud-din-Muhammad, with great vigour and audacity..." This comes from the Muslim historian Minhaju-s-Sirj's Tabaka't-i, who is quoted in several sources, some of which call him Muhammad Bakhtyar, e.g., Dhammika (1992).

Joshi (1967) gives a telling account of the decline of Buddhism during the period of Nalanda's later life, using the accounts of pilgrims to show how increasing wealth was accompanied by moral degeneration and sectarian disputes. For example, I-Tsing: "It is unseemly for a monastery to have such great wealth. Granaries full of rotten corn, many servants, male and female, money and treasures hoarded in the treasury without using them."

To many people's surprise in the West, Theravada Buddhist monks are allowed to eat meat, unless the animal has been specifically killed for them. In fact they are not supposed to refuse anything they are offered. In traditional Buddhist countries the monks will usually eat the same as the local populace, which usually includes some meat. Thais eat a lot of meat, and thus we were given lot of meat to eat when we were staying at the Thai wats in India, such as the one in Nalanda. In the Western monasteries monks accept whatever is offered but encourage regular supporters to bring a vegetarian diet. The vegetarianism of Hindu India appears to date from the time of the flowering of Buddhism there and was probably initiated by Buddhist teachings.

CHAPTER 12: LETTING GO

"Hatred is never cured by hatred..." Dhammapada, verse 5. [Dhp 5].

"As a prince, Lord, I had five wishes..." Vinaya, Mahavagga, chapter 1. [Vin i, 36].

"This is deathlessness: the freedom of the heart through..." Majjhima Nikaya, Ananja-sappaya Sutta (sutta 106). [MN ii, 265].

An account of the teaching of S.N. Goenka is given by Hart (1987).

The story that the First Council was held in the Sattapanni Cave is only from the Sinhalese chronicle and is doubted by some.

CHAPTER 14: THE TIME OF GIFTS

"Association with the disliked is dukkha, separation from the liked is dukkha, not attaining one's wishes is dukkha." From the Buddha's first discourse, Dhammacakkappavattana Sutta, Samyutta Nikaya, chapter 56, The Truths. [SN v, 420].

"Thus you must train yourself..." Anguttara Nikaya, Eights, 63, and several other places. [AN iv, 299].

"Now, as before, suffering and the end of suffering is all I teach." Samyutta Nikaya, chapter 22, "ten elements," 86. [SN iii, 118].

Dhammika (1996) gives a history of Bodh Gaya as derived from the accounts of past pilgrims. Stephen Batchelor, referred to in this chapter, is no longer a monk. Known for books on Buddhist practise as well as an award-winning guide to Tibet, we recommend his book on the spread of Buddhism to the West (Batchelor 1994).

Glossary

Abhidhamma *(Pali)* one of the "three baskets" of the Buddhist Pitaka of the Theravadan canon. Deals with the psychology of the mind and the refined states of experience found through meditation.

ahchaa *(Hindi)* "I understand." Very common expression, equivalent to "okay."

Ajahn *(Thai)* (from the Pali *achariya*, a Buddhist monk's preceptor) "teacher." Often used as a title of the senior monk or monks at a monastery. In the West the forest tradition uses it for all monks and nuns of more than ten years' seniority.

anagarika *(Pali)* "homeless one." A Buddhist following the eight precepts (which includes celibacy) and usually living in a monastery.

anapanasati *(Pali)* "awareness of inhalation and exhalation." Using the breath as a meditation object. A meditation exercise much recommended by the Buddha.

anjali *(Pali)* hands held together as a gesture of respect. Still prevalent in India today.

arahant *(Pali)* an enlightened being, free from all delusion.

baksheesh *(Hindi)* tip to a servant or gift to a beggar. Also slang for a bribe.

beedee *(Hindi)* small cigarette made from tobacco rolled in a leaf.

betel *(Hindi)* nut used in *pan*, a concoction sold for chewing. It is a mild stimulant and gives the mouth a distinctive red stain.

Bhante *(Pali)* "Venerable sir." A term of respect often used when addressing a Buddhist monk or by a monk addressing a more senior monk.

bhikkhu *(Pali)* "Alms mendicant." A Buddhist monk. The Hindi word *baksheesh*, meaning a "tip" or a gift to a beggar, comes from the same root.

bhikkhuni *(Pali)* A Buddhist nun.

Bodhi Tree *(Sanskrit/English)* the tree under which the Buddha attained enlightenment, or any tree of the same species, *Ficus religiosus,* a large spreading fig.

bodhisattva *(Sanskrit)* "awakening being." A person who aspires to be a buddha. An important concept in Mahayana Buddhism, where one aspires to become enlightened for the sake of helping other beings.

Brahmin *(Hindi)* a priest. Within the Indian caste system, the caste of Brahmin is regarded, particularly by brahmins, as being the highest. Many of the caste no longer act as priests, but all wear the traditional length of string over one shoulder and under the other arm and perform a daily personal purification puja with water. The Buddha, in his discourses, also uses the word more generally to refer to a holy person.

Buddha *(Pali/Sanskrit)* "awakened one." A person who has attained Nirvana without receiving instruction. A sammasambuddha also has the optimal capacity to benefit others. A paccekabuddha does not teach.

chai *(Hindi)* tea. Usually made in an open pot with tea dust, milk, sugar, and sometimes spice, then strained into cups.

chalo *(Hindi)* "go." Frequently used as a command.

chappati *(Hindi)* a thin round flatbread made from unleavened flour; in India the generic word for bread, *roti,* is usually used.

chaukidar *(Hindi)* caretaker.

chillum *(Hindi)* a simple smoking pipe that consists of a short cone of clay that is held nestled in two hands with the smoker sucking between the palms. It is usually used to smoke ganja.

chula *(Hindi)* dried rolled rice flakes.

dacoit *(Hindi)* robber, usually those robbers living a fugitive life in the jungle.

dak bungalow *(Hindi)* a resthouse established for government officers to stay in when on tour of the local district. Most small towns in India have one.

dana *(Pali)* "giving." Often used to refer to an offering, particularly food, to Buddhist monastics.

deva or devata *(Pali)* celestial being. Usually resides in a heavenly realm but visits this realm.

dhal *(Hindi)* lentils, or the ubiquitous dish made with lentils, which is usually spicy and hot with chilli, runny, and sometimes slightly oily.

Dhamma/Dharma *(Pali/Sanskrit/Hindi)* We have used *Dhamma* and *Dharma* in the text to mean two different things. The Pali Buddhist term, *dhamma* (which in Sanskrit is *dharma*) means "nature," a thing as it is, or phenomenon. Spelled with a capital it means the Way It Is, the Ultimate Reality, and the Buddha's pointing to that reality (a Buddhist takes refuge in Buddha, Dhamma, and Sangha). The Hindi word *dharma* means duty, particularly religious duty, but also duty to one's family, caste, and society.

dharamsala *(Hindi)* "religious house." In villages this is a hall or meeting place where pilgrims can also stop. In larger Indian towns they are accommodation buildings for pilgrims. The accommodation is always very basic and either free or very cheap.

dhoti *(Hindi)* garment consisting of a long length of cloth that is wrapped in a complicated way around the legs of Indian men.

dukkha *(Pali)* "painful" or "hard to bear." Dis-ease, discontent or suffering, anguish, unsatisfactoriness. Liberation from this is the Buddhist goal.

Fruitee *(Indian English)* mango juice drink that is sold in cartons throughout India.

ganja *(Hindi)* the drug cannabis in leaf form.

garam *(Hindi)* "hot."

ghee *(Hindi)* clarified butter used as a cooking oil.

gurdwara *(Hindi)* Sikh temple.

jaggery *(Hindi)* raw cane sugar.

Jai Ram *(Hindi)* a salutation to Ram that is repeated often by his followers.

kaha ja ra hai? *(Hindi)* "Where are you going?"

kar sevak *(Hindi)* Hindu "holy workers." The storm troopers of the recent Hindu fundamentalist movement against the Muslim mosque said to have been built on the birthplace of Ram in Ayodhya.

khadi *(Hindi)* hand-woven cloth. The movement initiated by Gandhi to promote the hand-produced goods made in Indian villages.

lama *(Tibetan)* a religious teacher, lay or ordained.

lingam *(Hindi)* phallic object of worship in Hinduism, associated with the worship of Shiva.

maechee *(Thai)* nun.

Mahabharata *(Hindi)* the longest Hindu *ithisa,* or epic, several times as long as the Iliad and Odyssey combined.

mahavihara *(Pali)* large vihara. The term used for the large monastic universities that arose in India after the fifth century.

Mahayana *(Sanskrit)* "Great Vehicle." The spiritual path of those who practise Buddhism for the sake of liberating all living beings. The Northern School of Buddhism that arose in India in the first centuries C.E. and subsequently spread to Nepal, Tibet, China, Japan, Korea, and Mongolia.

mala *(Pali/Sanskrit)* "ornament" such as a necklace. Today usually used for a rosary. The clicking movement of mala beads through the hand is a way of counting and supporting the chanting of mantras.

mandala *(Sanskrit)* "disc." A circular symmetrical image used as an object of meditation in Mahayana Buddhism. Also refers to an inscribed area with spiritual significance.

mantra *(Sanskrit)* word or phrase repeated as a concentration object or as a mystical invocation.

Mataji *(Hindi)* mother. The -ji suffix (as with Gandhi-ji and Goenka-ji) denotes respect.

naga *(Pali)* serpents, often hooded. Many were converted by the Buddha, and they are often portrayed as protectors of the Dhamma.

namaste *(Sanskrit/Hindi)* "I salute you." The commonly used word of greeting and parting in India and Nepal.

Naxalites *(Hindi)* a group of anarchists, originally in West Bengal, who retreated to the forests. It is a term now used for any anti-government terrorist, or robber, living in the jungle.

nirvana *(Sanskrit)* *(nibbana* in Pali) cessation of the origins of suffering: delusion and craving.

paisa *(Hindi)* Indian small denomination coinage. There are one hundred paisa to one rupee.

parinirvana *(Sanskrit)* "final extinction." The Buddha on his death is said to have passed into parinirvana.

parotha *(Hindi)* flat bread fried in ghee.

Patimokkha *(Pali)* "a bond." A bhikkhu's 227 rules of conduct, which promote moral virtue, sense restraint, and good conduct.

precepts (five/eight/ten) *(English)* basic codes of conduct recommended by the Buddha for his followers. The five precepts pertain to the ordinary "household" life, while the eight and ten precepts form the foundation of the renunciant life. Nick tried to keep the eight precepts on the walk: to refrain from lying and other harmful speech, stealing, killing, erotic behaviour, and drink and drugs, not to eat after midday, to use no adornments and to avoid shows, and to forgo luxurious beds.

puja *(Pali/Hindi)* act of worship or chanting.

Puranas *(Hindi/Sanskrit)* "ancient texts." Not as ancient as the Vedas, they are a series of tales recounting, and bringing to the fore, the characters of Vishnu, Shiva, Krishna, and others. Probably composed a few centuries after the Buddha. These are the religious texts that the lower castes in India are allowed to hear, and thus represent the core of what Westerners call "Hinduism"—the populist, devotional aspect of Vedic tradition.

puri *(Hindi)* small flatbread fried in deep oil that puffs up to form an inflated disc.

Ramayana *(Hindi)* "The Adventures of Rama." One of the two Hindu *itahisas,* or religious epics.

Refuges *(English)* the three refuges that all Buddhists are encouraged to take and keep. The Buddha, the Dhamma, and the Sangha.

Rinpoche *(Tibetan)* "precious one." A title of respect given to Tibetan lamas of high rank.

roti *(Hindi)* "bread." All breads such as chappati, puri, parotha, and nan.

rupa *(Pali)* "form." A statue of the Buddha.

rupee *(Hindi)* principal Indian unit of money. At the time of the pilgrimage, one British pound was worth about fifty rupees, and the U.S. dollar about thirty rupees.

sabong *(Hindi)* "sarong." A simple wrapped cloth worn like a skirt. This is the name used for the under-robe worn by bhikkhus.

sadhu *(Hindi)* wandering holy man. Formalized by Shankara into orders, bringing the wandering samana ethic into the mainstream. Anyone can become a sadhu, as in becoming one the person renounces caste and takes on a life outside of but supported by secular society. Sadhus live by begging food and money and are usually dressed in ochre robes and often covered in dabs of paint to signify the deity they follow. In Pali *"Sadhu"* is an exclamation meaning "it is well," used by listeners at the end of a Buddhist *desana*.

sal *(Hindi)* dominant tree of the drier soils of northern India and the Himalayan foothills.

samadhi *(Pali/Sanskrit)* "collectedness." Mental calm, a concentrated, equanimous state of mind in which excitement and dullness are overcome.

samana *(Pali)* one who has entered the holy life; a religious. Formerly a loosely defined movement of religious seekers in India on the fringes of or outside of the Vedic mainstream, which they probably predate.

samsara *(Sanskrit)* the frustrating repetitive round of birth and death. The opposite of nirvana.

Sangha *(Pali)* "order." Community of those who follow the Buddha's path. Often, more specifically, those who have committed themselves to a monastic training.

sanghati *(Pali)* the upper robe of a bhikkhu. Today usually not worn but draped over the left shoulder for formal occasions. It is made out of many pieces of cloth sown together.

shikar *(Hindi)* feudal hunting area. In the Ganges Plain these were the only areas of jungle left by the end of the British Raj and the fall of the Indian Rajas. They became state-owned forest or game reserves and got little protection. Many are now nature reserves.

sila *(Pali)* Buddhist morality. The precepts that Buddhists are expected to observe.

sitting cloth *(English)* a rectangular sheet, just big enough to sit on cross-legged, that is made of four patches and comprises a standard part of a bhikkhu's kit.

stupa *(Pali/Sanskrit)* monument, often in the shape of a hemispheric mound, in which is enshrined sacred relics of the Buddha or other revered religious person.

subjee *(Hindi)* cooked vegetables. Along with rice, roti, and dhal, the basic meal throughout northern India.

sutta/sutra *(Pali/Sanskrit)* a Buddhist discourse attributed to Gotama Buddha.

tabla *(Hindi)* hand-played drum.

tantra *(Sanskrit)* "continuum," "weave," or "web." A Buddhist text or practise attributed to Gotama or another buddha that describes an accelerated path to enlightenment by means of mantra, transformative imagination, and yogic exercises.

Terai *(Hindi/Nepali, from Farsi)* "swamp." The undulating swampy lowlands at the base of the Himalayas.

Theravada *(Pali)* "Way of the Elders." The "southern" and oldest still-existing school of Buddhism. Now occurs in Thailand, Burma, Cambodia, and Sri Lanka.

thik *(Hindi)* "yes" or "okay."

uposatha *(Pali)* the Buddhist "Sabbath" or "Observance Day." The uposatha day occurs on the lunar "quarters" of the full and new moons. In the forest tradition these are nights of meditation vigil.

uttarasangha *(Pali)* The principal robe of a bhikkhu.

vihara *(Pali)* "dwelling." Used in early Indian Buddhism as the name for any dwelling. Today it usually means a small monastery.

Vinaya *(Pali)* the monastic discipline, or the scriptural collection of its rules and commentaries.

vipassana *(Pali)* penetrative insight of meditation, as distinguished from *samatha,* the tranquillity of meditation. This is the name also given to a Buddhist meditation movement particularly popular in North America.

wallah *(Hindi)* "worker." Thus rickshaw wallah, chai wallah, etc.

wat *(Thai)* "monastery."

Zen *(Japanese; Chinese:* Chan*)* "meditation." A contemplative form of Buddhism that originated in sixth-century China and spread to Korea and Japan. Now popular in the West.

Bibliography

This covers all books and articles we have drawn on, or refer to in chapter notes, but not all Buddhist scriptural references.

Bailey, D.R.S. *The Satapancasatka [Hundred and Fifty] of Matrceta*. Cambridge: Cambridge University Press, 1951.

Basham, A.L. *The Wonder That Was India*. London: Sidgwick and Jackson, 1954.

Batchelor, Stephen. *The Awakening of the West*. London: Aquarius, 1994.

Beal, Samuel. *Buddhist Records of the Western World*. London: Trübner, 1884 (reprint, Delhi: Motilal Banarsidass, 1981).

————, trans. *The Life of Hiuen Tsang by the Shaman Hwui Li*. London: Kegan Paul, 1914.

Bhargava, V.K. *A Portrait of Population: Bihar Census of India, 1981*. Delhi: Controller of Publications, 1989.

Bose, S.R., and P.P. Gosh. *Agro Economic Survey of Bihar*. Patna: B.K. Enterprise, 1976.

Breiter, Paul. *Venerable Father: A Life with Ajahn Cha*. Bangkok: Buddhadhamma Foundation, 1994.

Chaudhury, P.C. Roy. *Folklore of Bihar*. New Delhi: National Book Trust, 1976.

Cohn, Bernard S. *An Anthropologist among the Historians and Other Essays*. New York and Delhi: Oxford University Press, 1987.

Conze, Edward. *Selected Sayings from the Perfection of Wisdom.* Boulder, Colarado: Prajna Press, 1978.

Dhammika, Shravasti. "Going to Sambodhi." In *Mandala Magazine.* Singapore: Mandala, 1996.

————. *Middle Land Middle Way: A Pilgrim's Guide to the Buddha's India.* Kandy, Sri Lanka: Buddhist Publication Society, 1992.

Dutt, Sukumar. *The Buddha and Five After-Centuries.* London: Luzac, 1957.

————*Buddhist Monks and Monasteries of India.* Dehli: Motilal Banarsidass, 1962.

Elliot, C. *Hinduism and Buddhism: An Historical Sketch.* London: E. Arnold, 1921. (Also, New York: Barnes & Noble, 1954.)

Fischer, Louis. *The Life of Mahatama Gandhi.* London: Jonathan Cape, 1951.

Gupta, S.P. Das, ed. *Atlas of Agricultural Resources of India.* Calcutta: Dept. of Science and Technology, 1980.

Hare, E.M., and F.W. Woodward. *Gradual Sayings (translation of the Anguttaya Nikaya).* London: Pali Text Society, 1932–36.

Hart, William. *The Art of Living: Vipassana Meditation As Taught by S.N. Goenka.* San Francisco: Harper & Row, 1987.

Harvey, Peter. *An Introduction to Buddhism: Teachings, History, and Practices.* New York: Cambridge University Press, 1990.

Hixon, Lex. *Mother of the Buddhas.* Wheaton, Illinois: Quest Books, 1993.

Horner, I.B., trans. *The Book of Discipline.* 6 vols. London: Pali Text Society, 1970–86.

Hultzsch, E. *Inscriptions of Ashoka, vol. I.* Oxford: The Clarendon Press, 1925.

Israel, Samule, and Toby Sinclair. *Indian Wildlife.* Singapore: APA Publications, 1987.

Joshi, Lal. *Studies in the Buddhistic Culture of India during the 7th and 8th Centuries.* Delhi: Motilal Banarsidass, 1967.

Legge, James. *A Record of Buddhist Kingdoms (Translation of Fa Hsien).* New York: Dover, 1965 (reprint of an 1886 book).

Lienhard, Siegfried. "Nepal: The Survival of Indian Buddhism in a Himalayan Kingdom." In Bechert and Gombrich, *World of Buddhism: Buddhist Monks and Nuns in Society and Culture.* New York: Facts on File, 1984 (reprint, London: Thames and Hudson, 1991).

Mitchell, A.G. *Indian Gods and Goddesses.* London: Victoria and Albert Museum, 1982.

Mitchell, Stephen, trans. *The Selected Poetry of Rainer Maria Rilke.* New York: Random House, 1980.

Moon, Sir Penderel. *The British Conquest and Dominion of India.* London: Duckworth, 1989.

Moorhouse, Geoffrey. *India Britannica.* London: Harvill Press, 1983.

Muthiah, S. *An Atlas of India.* Delhi: Oxford University Press, 1990.

———. *A Social and Economic Atlas of India.* Delhi: Oxford University Press, 1987.

Naipaul, V.S. *India: A Million Mutinies Now.* London: William Hienemann, 1990.

Nanamoli, Bhikkhu. *The Life of the Buddha.* Kandy, Sri Lanka: Buddhist Publication Society, 1972.

Nanamoli, Bhikkhu, and Bhikkhu Bodhi, trans. *The Middle Length Discourses: A New Translation of the Majjhima Nikaya.* Boston: Wisdom Publications, 1995.

Prater, S.H. *The Book of Indian Animals.* Bombay Natural History Society, 1980.

Raven-Hart, R. *Where the Buddha Trod: A Buddhist Pilgrimage.* Colombo, 1956.

Russell, Jeremy. *The Eight Places of Buddhist Pilgrimage.* New Delhi: Mahayana Publications, 1981.

Saddhatissa, H. *Sutta Nipata.* London: Curzon Press, 1985.

Sangharakshita. *The Thousand Petalled Lotus: The Indian Journey of an English Buddhist.* Gloucester: Alan Sutton, 1976.

Schumann, H.W. *The Historical Buddha.* London: Arkana, 1989.

Snelling, John. *The Buddhist Handbook: A Complete Guide to Buddhist Teaching, Practice, History, and Schools.* London: Century, 1987.

Spear, P. *A History of India.* London: Penguin, 1978.

Tagore, Rabindrath, trans. *Songs of Kabir.* York Beach, Maine: Samuel Weiser, 1977.

Takakusu, J. *A Record of the Buddhist Religion As Practiced in India and the Malay Archipelago by I Tsing.* Delhi: Munisharam Manoharlal, 1966 (reprint).

Thanissaro Bhikkhu. *The Buddhist Monastic Code.* Valley Centre, California: Metta Forest Monastery, 1994.

Theroux, Paul. *The Great Railway Bazaar: By Train through Asia.* Boston: Houghton Mifflin, 1975.

Thomas, C. "The train now departing..." *The Times Magazine,* London (Nov. 4, 1995).

Tully, Mark. *No Full Stops in India.* London: Penguin, 1992.

Walshe, Maurice, trans. *Thus Have I Heard: The Long Discourses of The Buddha.* London: Wisdom Publications, 1987. Now available as *The Long Discourses of the Buddha: A Translation of the Digha Nikaya.* Boston: Wisdom Publications, 1995.

Warder, A.K. *Indian Buddhism.* Delhi: Motilal Banarsidass, 1970.

Watson, B. *The Great Indian Mutiny.* London: Praeger, 1991.

Winternitz, Maurice. *History of Indian Literature, vol. I.* Calcutta: The University of Calcutta, 1927.

Woodcock, Martin, and Hermann Heinzel. *Collins Handguide to the Birds of the Indian Sub-Continent.* London: Collins, 1980.

Woodward, F.W., and C. Rhys Davids. *Kindred Sayings (Translation of the Samyuta Nikaya).* London: Pali Text Society, 1951.

Recommended Reading

BUDDHIST PILGRIMAGE

Middle Land Middle Way: A Pilgrim's Guide to the Buddha's India. Shravasti Dhammika. Kandy, Sri Lanka: Buddhist Publication Society, 1991. If this excellent and concise pocket book had been available to us for our pilgrimage, we would have seen and understood much more of the Buddhist holy sites and probably had far fewer adventures. Thoroughly recommended for anyone going on pilgrimage. It is distributed in the U.K. by Lavis Marketing, 73 Lime Walk, Headington, Oxford, 0X3 7AD. In the U.S., BPS books can be purchased from Pariyatti Book Service at www.pariyatti.com.

BUDDHIST TEACHINGS

In the Buddha's Words: An Anthology of Discourses from the Pali Canon. Edited by Bhikkhu Bodhi. Boston: Wisdom Publications, 2005. A thoughtful and representative selection from the Pali Nikayas, arranged in thematic chapters with helpful introductions.

What the Buddha Taught. Walpala Rahula. New York: Grove, 1974.

The Heart of Buddhist Meditation. Nyanaponika Thera. London: Rider, 1983.

TEACHINGS FROM THE THERAVADAN FOREST TRADITION

The Mind and the Way: Buddhist Reflections on Life. Ajahn Sumedho. Boston: Wisdom Publications, 1995 (published in England by Rider).

Food for the Heart: The Collected Teachings of Ajahn Chah. Boston: Wisdom Publications, 2002.

Venerable Father: A Life with Ajahn Chah. Paul Breiter. Buddhadhamma Foundation, Tesabahl Songkroh Rd., Lad Yao, Chatuchak, Bangkok 10900, Thailand. 1994. A very funny but moving account of five years spent with Ajahn Chah and the visit he made to the U.S.

Amaravati Publications publishes teachings by monks in the forest tradition, including Ajahn Chah and Ajahn Sumedho. The books have been sponsored for free distribution. For a current publication list write, enclosing a stamped self-addressed envelope, to Amaravati Publications, Amaravati Buddhist Monastery, Great Gaddesden, Hemel Hempstead, Herts, HP1 3BZ, England.

BUDDHIST HISTORY

The Buddha and Five After-Centuries. Sukumar Dutt. London: Luzac, 1957 (reprint available from Motilal Banarsidass, Delhi).

The Awakening of The West. Stephen Batchelor. London: Aquarius. 1994 (published in the U.S. by Parallax). As well as being an excellent account of Europe's historical encounters with Buddhism, this book is also a good introduction to the different forms of Buddhism now established in the West.

INDIAN WILDLIFE

Collins Handguide to the Birds of the Indian Sub-Continent. Martin Woodcock and Hermann Heinzel. London: Collins, 1980. Small, very light, and covering most of the birds likely to be seen on a trip to India.

Index

About the Authors

 AJAHN SUCITTO was born in London in 1949. After going to university in 1971 to study English Literature he travelled to the East, becoming a bhikkhu in Thailand in 1976. Since 1978 he has been based in Britain as a disciple of Ajahn Sumedho. In 1992 he became the abbot of Cittivaveka, Chithurst Buddhist Monastery. He teaches retreats in Europe and North America, and several books of his teachings have been published for free distribution.

 DR. NICK SCOTT was born in 1952. On leaving school he went to India in 1972, where he became interested in Buddhist meditation. He returned to England three years later to complete a degree and then a doctorate in Plant Ecology. He has worked most of his life in nature conservation, as a nature reserve warden, project manager, and then consultant. He now also teaches meditation retreats.

About Wisdom

Wisdom Publications, a nonprofit publisher, is dedicated to making available authentic Buddhist works for the benefit of all. We publish translations of the sutras and tantras, commentaries and teachings of past and contemporary Buddhist masters, and original works by the world's leading Buddhist scholars. We publish our titles with the appreciation of Buddhism as a living philosophy and with the special commitment to preserve and transmit important works from all the major Buddhist traditions.

To learn more about Wisdom, or to browse books online, visit our website at wisdompubs.org. You may request a copy of our mail-order catalog online or by writing to this address:

Wisdom Publications
199 Elm Street
Somerville, Massachusetts 02144 USA
Telephone: (617) 776-7416
Fax: (617) 776-7841
Email: info@wisdompubs.org
www.wisdompubs.org

THE WISDOM TRUST

As a nonprofit publisher, Wisdom is dedicated to the publication of fine Dharma books for the benefit of all sentient beings and dependent upon the kindness and generosity of sponsors in order to do so. If you would like to make a donation to Wisdom, please do so through our Somerville office. If you would like to sponsor the publication of a book, please write or email us at the address above.

Thank you.

Wisdom is a nonprofit, charitable 501(c)(3) organization affiliated with the Foundation for the Preservation of the Mahayana Tradition (FPMT).

In the Buddha's Words

*An Anthology of Discourses
from the Pali Canon*
Edited and introduced by Bhikkhu Bodhi
Foreword by the Dalai Lama
512 pages, ISBN 0-86171-491-1, $18.95

In the Buddha's Words allows even readers unacquainted with Buddhism to grasp the significance of the Buddha's contributions to our world heritage. Taken as a whole, these texts bear eloquent testimony to the breadth and intelligence of the Buddha's teachings, and point the way to an ancient yet ever-vital path. Students and seekers alike will find this systematic presentation indispensable.

"A remarkable book. A gift to the world."—*Buddhadharma, The Practitioner's Quarterly*

Food for the Heart

The Collected Teachings of Ajahn Chah
Foreword by Jack Kornfield
Introduction by Ajahn Amaro
416 pages, ISBN 0-86171-323-0, $18.95

"This collection brings together for the first time the dhamma talks of Thailand's best-known meditation teacher and forest monastic, talks previously available only in rare or limited editions. It presents Ajahn Chah's teachings on meditation, liberation from suffering, calming the mind, enlightenment, and the 'living dhamma.'"—*Tricycle*

"*Food for the Heart* will stand the test of time with the world's great classics of spiritual literature."—John Daishin Buksbazen, author of *Zen Meditation in Plain English*